Workshop on Type Theory and Natural Language Semantics

(TTNLS 2014)

Held at the 14th Conference of the European Chapter of the Association for Computational Linguistics

Gothenburg, Sweden
27 April 2014

Editors:

R. Cooper
S. Dobnik
S. Lappin
S. Larsson

ISBN: 978-1-63266-409-9

Printed from e-media with permission by:

Curran Associates, Inc.
57 Morehouse Lane
Red Hook, NY 12571

Some format issues inherent in the e-media version may also appear in this print version.

Printed by Curran Associates, Inc. (2014)

For permission requests, please contact the Association for Computational Linguistics at the address below.

Association for Computational Linguistics
209 N. Eighth Street
Stroudsburg, Pennsylvania 18360

Phone: 1-570-476-8006
Fax: 1-570-476-0860

acl@aclweb.org

Additional copies of this publication are available from:

Curran Associates, Inc.
57 Morehouse Lane
Red Hook, NY 12571 USA
Phone: 845-758-0400
Fax: 845-758-2634
Email: curran@proceedings.com
Web: www.proceedings.com

EACL 2014

14th Conference of the European Chapter of the Association for Computational Linguistics

Proceedings of the Workshop on Type Theory and Natural Language Semantics (TTNLS)

April 27, 2014
Gothenburg, Sweden

Workshop Organisation

Organising Committee:

Robin Cooper (University of Gothenburg)
Simon Dobnik (University of Gothenburg)
Shalom Lappin (King's College London)
Staffan Larsson (University of Gothenburg)

Programme Committee:

Krasimir Angelov (University of Gothenburg and Chalmers University of Technology)
Patrick Blackburn (University of Roskilde)
Stergios Chatzikyriakidis (Royal Holloway, University of London)
Stephen Clark (University of Cambridge)
Philippe de Groote (Inria Nancy - Grand Est)
Jan van Eijck (University of Amsterdam)
Raquel Fernández (University of Amsterdam)
Tim Fernando (Trinity College, Dublin)
Chris Fox (University of Essex)
Jonathan Ginzburg (Université Paris-Diderot (Paris 7))
Zhaohui Luo (Royal Holloway, University of London)
Uwe Mönnich (University of Tübingen)
Bruno Mery (LaBRI, Université Bordeaux 1)
Glyn Morrill (Universitat Politècnica de Catalunya, Barcelona)
Larry Moss (Indiana University)
Reinhard Muskens (Tilburg University)
Bengt Nordström (University of Gothenburg and Chalmers University of Technology)
Valeria de Paiva (Nuance Communications, Inc., Sunnyvale California)
Carl Pollard (The Ohio State University)
Ian Pratt-Hartmann (University of Manchester)
Stephen Pulman (University of Oxford)
Matt Purver (Queen Mary, University of London)
Aarne Ranta (University of Gothenburg and Chalmers University of Technology)
Christian Retoré (LaBRI, Université Bordeaux 1)
Scott Martin (Nuance Communications, Inc., Sunnyvale California)
Ray Turner (University of Essex)

Invited speaker:

Aarne Ranta (University of Gothenburg and Chalmers University of Technology)

Table of Contents

Conference Program

Sunday, 27 April 2014

8:15	Registration
8:45	Opening remarks by Robin Cooper
	(9:00 - 10:30) Session 1
9:00	*Types and Records for Predication* Aarne Ranta
10:00	*System with Generalized Quantifiers on Dependent Types for Anaphora* Justyna Grudzinska and Marek Zawadowski
10:30	Coffee break
	(11:00 - 12:30) Session 2
11:00	*Monads as a Solution for Generalized Opacity* Gianluca Giorgolo and Ash Asudeh
11:30	*The Phenogrammar of Coordination* Chris Worth
12:00	*Natural Language Reasoning Using Proof-Assistant Technology: Rich Typing and Beyond* Stergios Chatzikyriakidis and Zhaohui Luo
12:30	Lunch
	(14:00 - 15:30) Session 3
14:00	*A Type-Driven Tensor-Based Semantics for CCG* Jean Maillard, Stephen Clark and Edward Grefenstette
14:30	*From Natural Language to RDF Graphs with Pregroups* Antonin Delpeuch and Anne Preller
15:00	*Incremental semantic scales by strings* Tim Fernando
15:30	Coffee break

Sunday, 27 April 2014 (continued)

(16:00 - 17:30) Session 4

16:00 *A Probabilistic Rich Type Theory for Semantic Interpretation*
Robin Cooper, Simon Dobnik, Shalom Lappin and Staffan Larsson

16:30 *Probabilistic Type Theory for Incremental Dialogue Processing*
Julian Hough and Matthew Purver

17:00 *Propositions, Questions, and Adjectives: a rich type theoretic approach*
Jonathan Ginzburg, Robin Cooper and Tim Fernando

17:30 Concluding remarks

Types and Records for Predication

Aarne Ranta
Department of Computer Science and Engineering, University of Gothenburg
aarne@chalmers.se

Abstract

This paper studies the use of records and dependent types in GF (Grammatical Framework) to build a grammar for predication with an unlimited number of subcategories, also covering extraction and coordination. The grammar is implemented for Chinese, English, Finnish, and Swedish, sharing the maximum of code to identify similarities and differences between the languages. Equipped with a probabilistic model and a large lexicon, the grammar has also been tested in wide-coverage machine translation. The first evaluations show improvements in parsing speed, coverage, and robustness in comparison to earlier GF grammars. The study confirms that dependent types, records, and functors are useful in both engineering and theoretical perspectives.

1 Introduction

Predication is the basic level of syntax. In logic, it means building atomic formulas by predicates. In linguistics, it means building sentences by verbs. Categorial grammars (Bar-Hillel, 1953; Lambek, 1958) adapt logical predication to natural language. Thus for instance transitive verbs are categorized as $(n\backslash s/n)$, which is the logical type $n \rightarrow n \rightarrow s$ with the information that one argument comes before the verb and the other one after. But most approaches to syntax and semantics, including (Montague, 1974), introduce predicate categories as primitives rather than as function types. Thus transitive verbs are a category of its own, related to logic via a semantic rule. This gives more expressive power, as it permits predicates with different syntactic properties and variable word order (e.g. inversion in questions). A drawback is that a grammar may need a large number of categories and rules. In GPSG (Gazdar et al., 1985), and later in HPSG (Pollard and Sag, 1994), this is solved by introducing a feature called **subcat** for verbs. Verbs taking different arguments differ in the subcat feature but share otherwise the characteristic of being verbs.

In this paper, we will study the syntax and semantics of predication in GF, Grammatical Framework (Ranta, 2011). We will generalize both over subcategories (as in GPSG and HPSG), and over languages (as customary in GF). We use **dependent types** to control the application of verbs to legitimate arguments, and **records** to control the placement of arguments in sentences. The record structure is inspired by the **topological model** of syntax in (Diderichsen, 1962).

The approach is designed to apply to all languages in the GF Resource Grammar Library (RGL, (Ranta, 2009)), factoring out their typological differences in a modular way. We have tested the grammar with four languages from three families: Chinese, English, Finnish, and Swedish. As the implementation reuses old RGL code for all parts but predication, it can be ported to new languages with just a few pages of new GF code. We have also tested it in wide coverage tasks, with a probabilistic tree model and a lexicon of 60,000 lemmas.

We will start with an introduction to the abstraction mechanisms of GF and conclude with a summary of some recent research. Section 2 places GF on the map of grammar formalisms. Section 3 works out an example showing how abstract syntax can be shared between languages. Section 4 shows how parts of concrete syntax can be shared as well. Section 5 gives the full picture of predication with dependent types and records, also addressing extraction, coordination, and semantics. Section 6 gives preliminary evaluation. Section 7 concludes.

2 GF: an executive summary

GF belongs to a subfamily of categorial grammars inspired by (Curry, 1961). These grammars make a distinction between **tectogrammar**, which specifies the syntactic **structures** (tree-like representations), and **phenogrammar**, which relates these structures to linear representations, such as sequences of characters, words, or phonemes. Other formalisms in this family include ACG (de Groote, 2001) and Lambda grammars (Muskens, 2001).

GF inherits its name from LF, **Logical Frameworks**, which are type theories used for defining logics (Harper et al., 1993). GF builds on the LF called ALF, Another Logical Framework (Magnusson, 1994), which implements Martin-Löf's **higher-level type theory** (first introduced in the preface of (Martin-Löf, 1984); see Chapter 8 of (Ranta, 1994) for more details). Before GF was introduced as an independent formalism in 1998, GF-like applications were built as plug-ins to ALF (Ranta, 1997). The idea was that the LF defines the tectogrammar, and the plug-in defines the phenogrammar. The intended application was natural language interfaces to formal proof systems, in the style of (Coscoy et al., 1995).

GF was born via two additions to the natural language interface idea. The first one was **multilinguality**: one and the same tectogrammar can be given multiple phenogrammars. The second addition was **parsing**: the phenogrammar, which was initially just **linearization** (generating strings from type theoretical formulas), was reversed to rules that parse natural language into type theory. The result was a method for **translation**, which combines parsing the source language with linearization into the target language. This idea was indeed suggested in (Curry, 1961), and applied before GF in the Rosetta project (Landsbergen, 1982), which used Montague's **analysis trees** as tectogrammar.

GF can be seen as a formalization and generalization of Montague grammar. Formalization, because it introduces a formal notation for the linearization rules that in Montague's work were expressed informally. Generalization, because of multilinguality and also because the type system for analysis trees has dependent types.

Following the terminology of programming language theory, the tectogrammar is in GF called the **abstract syntax** whereas the phenogrammar is called the **concrete syntax**. As in compilers and logical frameworks, the abstract syntax encodes the structure relevant for **semantics**, whereas the concrete syntax defines "syntactic sugar".

The resulting system turned out to be equivalent to **parallel multiple context-free grammars** (Seki et al., 1991) and therefore parsable in polynomial time (Ljunglöf, 2004). Comprehensive grammars have been written for 29 languages, and later work has optimized GF parsing and also added probabilistic disambiguation and robustness, resulting in state-of-the-art performance in wide-coverage deep parsing (Angelov, 2011; Angelov and Ljunglöf, 2014).

3 Example: subject-verb-object sentences

Let us start with an important special case of predication: the subject-verb-object structure. The simplest possible rule is

```
fun PredTV : NP -> TV -> NP -> S
```

that is, a **function** that takes a subject NP, a transitive verb TV, and an object NP, and returns a sentence S. This function builds abstract syntax trees. Concrete syntax defines **linearization rules**, which convert trees into strings. The above rule can give rise to different word orders, such as SVO (as in English), SOV (as in Hindi), and VSO (as in Arabic):

```
lin PredTV s v o = s ++ v ++ o
lin PredTV s v o = s ++ o ++ v
lin PredTV s v o = v ++ s ++ o
```

where ++ means concatenation.

The above rule builds a sentence in one step. A more flexible approach is to do it in two steps: **complementation**, forming a VP (verb phrase) from the verb and the object, and **predication** proper that provides the subject. The abstract syntax is

```
fun Compl : TV -> NP -> VP
fun Pred  : NP -> VP -> S
```

These functions are easy to linearize for the SVO and SOV orders:

```
lin Compl v o = v ++ o     -- SVO
lin Compl v o = o ++ v     -- SOV
lin Pred s vp = s ++ vp    -- both
```

where -- marks a comment. However, the VSO order cannot be obtained in this way, because the two parts of the VP are separated by the subject. The solution is to generalize linearization from strings to **records**. Complementation can then return a record that has the verb and the object as separate **fields**. Then we can also generate VSO:

```
lin Compl v o = {verb = v ; obj = o}
lin Pred s vp = vp.verb ++ s ++ vp.obj
```

The dot (`.`) means **projection**, picking the value of a field in a record.

Records enable the abstract syntax to abstract away not only from word order, but also from whether a language uses **discontinuous constituents**. VP in VSO languages is one example. Once we enable discontinuous constituents, they turn out useful almost everywhere, as they enable us to delay the decision about linear order. It can then be varied even inside a single language, if it depends on syntactic context (as e.g. in German; cf. (Müller, 2004) for a survey).

The next thing to abstract away from is **inflection** and **agreement**. Given the lexicon

```
fun We, She : NP
fun Love : TV
```

we can build the abstract syntax tree

```
Pred We (Compl Love She)
```

to represent *we love her*. If we swap the subject and the object, we get

```
Pred She (Compl Love We)
```

for *she loves us*. Now, these two sentences are built from the same abstract syntax objects, but no single word is shared between them! This is because the noun phrases **inflect** for **case** and the verb **agrees** to the subject.

In contrast to English, Chinese just reorders the words:

women ai ta - "we love her"

ta ai women - "she loves us"

Thus the above rules for SVO languages work as they are for Chinese. But in English, we must include case and agreement as **features** in the concrete syntax. Thus the linearization of an NP is a record that includes a **table** producing the case forms, and agreement as an **inherent feature**:

```
lin She = {
  s = table {
    Nom => "she" ;
    Acc => "her"
    } ;
  a = {n = Sg ; p = P3} ;
  }
```

The agreement feature (field `a`) is itself a record, with a number and a gender. In other languages, case and agreement can of course have different sets of values.

Verbs likewise include tables that inflect them for different agreement features:

```
lin Love = {
  s = table {
     {n = Sg ; p = P3} => "loves" ;
     _ => "love"
    }
  }
```

We can now define English linearization:

```
lin Compl v o =
  {s = table {a => v.s ! a ++ o.s ! Acc}}
lin Pred s vp =
  {s = s.s ! Nom ++ vp.s ! np.a}
```

using the same type of records for VP as for TV, and a one-string record for S. The `Compl` rule passes the agreement feature to the verb of the VP, and selects the Acc form of the object (with `!` denoting **selection** from a table). The `Pred` rule selects the `Nom` form of the subject, and attaches to this the VP form selected for `np.a`, i.e. the agreement feature of the subject.

4 Generalized concrete syntax

To see the full power of GF, we now take a look at its type and module system. Figure 1 shows a complete set of grammar modules implementing transitive verb predication for Finnish and Chinese with a maximum of shared code.

The first module in Figure 1 is the abstract syntax `Pred`, where the `fun` rules are preceded by a set of `cat` rules defining the **categories** of the grammar, i.e. the basic types. `Pred` defines five categories: S, Cl, NP, VP, and TV. S is the top-level category of sentences, whereas Cl (**clause**) is the intermediate category of predications, which can be used as sentences in many ways—here, as declaratives and as questions.

The concrete syntax has corresponding `lincat` rules, which equip each category with a **linearization type**, i.e. the type of the values returned when linearizing trees of that category. The module `PredFunctor` in Figure 1 contains four such rules. In `lincat NP`, the type `Case => Str` is the type of tables that produce a string as a function of a case, and `Agr` is the type of agreement features.

When a GF grammar is compiled, each `lin` rule is type checked with respect to the `lincat`s of the categories involved, to guarantee that, for every

$$\text{fun } f : C_1 \to \cdots \to C_n \to C$$

we have

$$\text{lin } f : C_1^* \to \cdots \to C_n^* \to C^*$$

```
abstract Pred = {
  cat S ; Cl ; NP ; VP ; TV ;
  fun Compl : TV -> NP -> VP ;  fun Pred : TV -> NP -> Cl ;
  fun Decl : Cl -> S ; fun Quest : Cl -> S ;
  }
incomplete concrete PredFunctor of Pred = open PredInterface in {
  lincat S = {s : Str} ;   lincat Cl = {subj,verb,obj : Str} ;
  lincat NP = {s : Case => Str ; a : Agr} ;
  lincat VP = {verb : Agr => Str ; obj : Str} ;  lincat TV = {s : Agr => Str} ;
  lin Compl tv np = {verb = tv.s ; obj = np.s ! objCase} ;
  lin Pred np vp = {subj = np.s !subjCase ; verb = vp.verb ! np.a ; obj = vp.obj} ;
  lin Decl cl = {s = decl cl.subj cl.verb cl.obj} ;
  lin Quest cl = {s = quest cl.subj cl.verb cl.obj} ;
  }
interface PredInterface = {
  oper Case, Agr : PType ;
  oper subjCase, objCase : Case ;
  oper decl, quest : Str -> Str -> Str -> Str ;
  }
instance PredInstanceFin of PredInterface = {         concrete PredFin of Pred =
  oper Case = -- Nom | Acc | ... ;                        PredFunctor with
  oper Agr = {n : Number ; p : Person} ;                    (PredInterface =
  oper subjCase = Nom ; objCase = Acc ;                        PredInstanceFin) ;
  oper decl s v o = s ++ v ++ o ;
  oper quest s v o = v ++ "&+ ko" ++ s ++ o ;
  }
instance PredInstanceChi of PredInterface = {         concrete PredChi of Pred =
  oper Case, Agr = {} ;                                   PredFunctor with
  oper subjCase, objCase = <> ;                             (PredInterface =
  oper decl s v o = s ++ v ++ o ;                              PredInstanceChi) ;
  oper quest s v o = s ++ v ++ o ++ "ma" ;
  }
```

Figure 1: Functorized grammar for transitive verb predication.

where A^* is the linearization type of A. Thus linearization is a **homomorphism**. It is actually an instance of denotational semantics, where the `lincats` are the **domains of possible denotations**.

Much of the strength of GF comes from using different linearization types for different languages. Thus English needs case and agreement, Finnish needs many more cases (in the full grammar), Chinese needs mostly only strings, and so on. However, it is both useful and illuminating to unify the types. The way to do this is by the use of **functors**, also known as a **parametrized modules**.

`PredFunctor` in Figure 1 is an example; functors are marked with the keyword `incomplete`. A functor depends on an `interface`, which declares a set of parameters (`PredInterface` in Figure 1). A concrete module is produced by giving an `instance` to the interface (`PredInstanceFin` and `PredInstanceChi`).

The rules in `PredFunctor` in Figure 1 are designed to work for both languages, by varying the definitions of the constants in `PredInterface`. And more languages can be added to use it. Consider for example the definition of NP. The experience from the RGL shows that, if a language has case and agreement, its NPs inflect for case and have inherent agreement. The limiting case of Chinese can be treated by using the unit type ({} i.e. the record type with no fields) for both features. This would not be so elegant for Chinese alone, but makes sense in the code sharing context.

Discontinuity now appears as another useful generalization. With the `lincat` definition in `PredFunctor`, we can share the `Compl` rule in all of the languages discussed so far. In clauses (Cl), we continue on similar lines: we keep the subject, the verb, and the object on separate fields. Notice that `verb` in `Cl` is a plain string, since the value of Agr gets fixed when the subject is added.

The final sentence word order is created as the last step, when converting `Cl` into `S`. As `Cl` is discontinuous, it can be linearized in different orders. In Figure 1, this is used in Finnish for generating the SVO order in declaratives and VSO on questions (with an intervening question particle *ko* glued to the verb). It also supports the other word orders of Finnish (Karttunen and Kay, 1985).

By using an abstract syntax in combination with unordered records, parameters, and functors for the concrete syntax, we follow a kind of a "principles and parameters" approach to language variation (Chomsky, 1981). The actual parameter set for the whole RGL is of course larger than the one shown here.

Mathematically, it is possible to treat *all* differences in concrete syntax by parameters, simply by declaring a new parameter for every `lincat` and `lin` rule! But this is both vacuous as a theory and an unnecessary detour in practice. It is more illuminating to keep the functor simple and the set of parameters small. If the functor does not work for a new language, it usually makes more sense to **override** it than to grow the parameter list, and GF provides a mechanism for this. Opposite to "principles and parameters", this is "a model in which language-particular rules take over the work of parameter settings" (Newmeyer, 2004). A combination of the two models enables language comparison by measuring the amount of overrides.

5 The full predication system

So far we have only dealt with one kind of verbs, TV. But we need more: intransitive, ditransitive, sentence-complement, etc. The general verb category is a dependent type, which varies over argument type lists:

```
cat V (x : Args)
```

The list `x : Args` corresponds to the subcat feature in GPSG and HPSG. Verb phrases and clauses have the same dependencies. Syntactically, a phrase depending on `x : Args` has "holes" for every argument in the list `x`. Semantically, it is a function over the denotations of its arguments (see Section 5.3 below).

5.1 The code

Figure 2 shows the essentials of the resulting grammar, and we will now explain this code. The full code is available at the GF web site.

1. **Argument lists and dependent categories**. The argument of a verb can be an adjectival phrase (AP, *become old*), a clause (Cl, *say that we go*), a common noun (CN, *become a president*), a noun phrase (NP, *love her*), a question (QCl, *wonder who goes*), or a verb phrase (VP, *want to go*). The definition allows an arbitrary list of arguments. For example, NP+QCl is used in verbs such as *ask* (someone whether something).

What about PP (prepositional phrase) complements? The best approach in a multilingual setting is to treat them as NP complements with designated cases. Thus in Figure 2.5, the linearization type of VP has fields of type `complCase`. This covers cases and prepositions, often in combination. For instance, the German verb *lieben* ("love") takes a plain accusative argument, *folgen* ("love") a plain dative, and *warten* ("wait") the preposition *auf* with the accusative. From the abstract syntax point of view, all of them are NP-complement verbs. Cases and prepositions, and thereby transitivity, are defined in concrete syntax.

The category `Cl`, clause, is the discontinuous structure of sentences before word order is determined. Its instance `Cl (c np O)` corresponds to the **slash categories** `S/NP` and `S/PP` in GPSG. Similarly, `VP (c np O)` corresponds to `VP/NP` and `VP/PP`, `Adv (c np O)` to `Adv/NP` (prepositions), and so on.

2. **Initial formation of verb phases**. A VP is formed from a V by fixing its tense and polarity. In the resulting VP, the `verb` depends only on the agreement features of the expected subject. The complement case comes from the verb's lexical entry, but the other fields—such as the objects—are left empty. This makes the VP usable in both complementation and slash operations (where the subject is added before some complement).

VPs can also be formed from adverbials, adjectival phrases, and common nouns, by adding a copula. Thus *was in* results from applying `UseAdv` to the preposition (i.e. `Adv/NP`) *in*, and expands to a VP with `ComplNP` (*was in France*) and to a slash clause with `PredVP` (*she was in*).

3. **Complementation, VP slash formation, reflexivization**. The `Compl` functions in Figure 2.3 provide each verb phrase with its "first" complement. The `Slash` functions provide the "last" complement, leaving a "gap" in the middle. For instance, `SlashCl` provides the slash clause used in the question *whom did you tell that we sleep*. The `Refl` rules fill argument places with reflexive pronouns.

4. **NP-VP predication, slash termination, and adverbial modification**. `PredVP` is the basic NP-VP predication rule. With `x = c np O`, it becomes the rule that combines NP with VP/NP to form S/NP. `SlashTerm` is the GPSG "slash termi-

1. **Argument lists and some dependent categories**

```
cat Arg ; Args                    -- arguments and argument lists
fun ap, cl, cn, np, qcl, vp : Arg -- AP, Cl, CN, NP, QCl, VP argument
fun O : Args                      -- no arguments
fun c : Arg -> Args -> Args       -- one more argument

cat V   (x : Args)                -- verb in the lexicon
cat VP  (x : Args)                -- verb phrase
cat Cl  (x : Args)                -- clause
cat AP  (x : Args)                -- adjectival phrase
cat CN  (x : Args)                -- common noun phrase
cat Adv (x : Args)                -- adverbial phrase
```

2. **Initial formation of verb phases**

```
fun UseV   : (x : Args) -> Temp -> Pol -> V x   -> VP x  -- loved (X)
fun UseAP  : (x : Args) -> Temp -> Pol -> AP x  -> VP x  -- was married to (X)
fun UseCN  : (x : Args) -> Temp -> Pol -> CN x  -> VP x  -- was a son of (X)
fun UseAdv : (x : Args) -> Temp -> Pol -> Adv x -> VP x  -- was in (X)
```

3. **Complementation, VP slash formation, reflexivization**

```
fun ComplNP : (x : Args) -> VP (c np x)        -> NP   -> VP x        -- love her
fun ComplCl : (x : Args) -> VP (c cl x)        -> Cl x -> VP x        -- say that we go
fun SlashNP : (x : Args) -> VP (c np (c np x)) -> NP   -> VP (c np x) -- show (X) to him
fun SlashCl : (x : Args) -> VP (c np (c cl x)) -> Cl x -> VP (c np x) -- tell (X) that..
fun ReflVP  : (x : Args) -> VP (c np x)                -> VP x        -- love herself
fun ReflVP2 : (x : Args) -> VP (c np (c np x))         -> VP (c np x) -- show (X) to herself
```

4. **NP-VP predication, slash termination, and adverbial modification**

```
fun PredVP    : (x : Args) -> NP          -> VP x  -> Cl x          -- she loves (X)
fun SlashTerm : (x : Args) -> Cl (c np x) -> NP    -> Cl x          -- she loves + X
```

5. **The functorial linearization type of VP**

```
lincat VP = {
  verb   : Agr => Str * Str * Str ;    -- finite: would,have,gone
  inf    : VVType => Str ;             -- infinitive: (not) (to) go
  imp    : ImpType => Str ;            -- imperative: go
  c1     : ComplCase ;                 -- case of first complement
  c2     : ComplCase ;                 -- case of  second complement
  vvtype : VVType ;                    -- type of VP complement
  adj    : Agr => Str ;                -- adjective complement
  obj1   : Agr => Str ;                -- first complement
  obj2   : Agr => Str ;                -- second complement
  objagr : {a : Agr ; objCtr : Bool} ; -- agreement used in object control
  adv1   : Str ;                       -- pre-verb adverb
  adv2   : Str ;                       -- post-verb adverb
  ext    : Str ;                       -- extraposed element e.g. that-clause
  }
```

6. **Some functorial linearization rules**

```
lin ComplNP  x vp np = vp ** {obj1 = \\a => appComplCase vp.c1 np}
lin ComplCl  x vp cl = vp ** {ext  = that_Compl ++ declSubordCl cl}
lin SlashNP2 x vp np = vp ** {obj2 = \\a => appComplCase vp.c2 np}
lin SlashCl  x vp cl = vp ** {ext  = that_Compl ++ declSubordCl cl}
```

7. **Some interface parameters**

```
oper Agr, ComplCase : PType               -- agreement, complement case
oper appComplCase : ComplCase -> NP -> Str  -- apply complement case to NP
oper declSubordCl : Cl -> Str               -- subordinate question word order
```

Figure 2: Dependent types, records, and parameters for predication.

nation" rule.

5. **The functorial linearization type of VP**. This record type contains the string-valued fields that can appear in different orders, as well as the inherent features that are needed when complements are added. The corresponding record for `Cl` has similar fields with constant strings, plus a subject field.

6. **Some functorial linearization rules**. The verb-phrase expanding rules typically work with **record updates**, where the old VP is left unchanged except for a few fields that get new values. GF uses the symbol `**` for record updates. Notice that `ComplCl` and `SlashCl` have exactly the same linearization rules; the difference comes from the argument list x in the abstract syntax.

7. **Some interface parameters**. The code in Figure 2.5 and 2.6 is shared by different languages, but it depends on an interface that declares parameters, some of which are shown here.

5.2 More constructions

Extraction. The formation of questions and relatives is straighforward. Sentential (yes/no) questions, formed by `QuestCl` in Figure 3.1, don't in many languages need any changes in the clause, but just a different ordering in final linearization. Wh questions typically put one interrogative (IP) in the focus, which may be in the beginning of the sentence even though the corresponding argument place in declaratives is later. The `focus` field in `QCl` is used for this purpose. It carries a Boolean feature saying whether the field is occupied. If its value is True, the next IP is put into the "normal" argument place, as in *who loves whom*.

Coordination. The VP conjunction rules in Figure 3.2 take care of both intransitive VPs (*she walks and runs*) and of verb phrases with arguments (*she loves and hates us*). Similarly, Cl conjuction covers both complete sentences and slash clauses (*she loves and we hate him*). Some VP coordination instances may be ungrammatical, in particular with inverted word orders. Thus *she is tired and wants to sleep* works as a declarative, but the question is not so good: *?is she tired and wants to sleep*. Preventing this would need a much more complex rules. Since the goal of our grammar is not to define grammaticality (as in formal language theory), but to analyse and translate existing texts, we opted for a simple system in this case (but did not need to do so elsewhere).

5.3 Semantics

The abstract syntax has straightforward denotational semantics: each type in the `Args` list of a category adds an argument to the type of denotations. For instance, the basic VP denotation type is `Ent -> Prop`, and the type for an arbitrary subcategory of `VP x` is

```
(x : Args) -> Den x (Ent -> Prop)
```

where `Den` is a type family defined recursively over `Args`,

```
Den : Args -> Type -> Type
Den O t = t
Den (c np xs) t = Ent  -> Den xs t
Den (c cl xs) t = Prop -> Den xs t
```

and so on for all values of `Arg`. The second argument t varies over the basic denotation types of VP, AP, Adv, and CN.

Montague-style semantics is readily available for all rules operating on these categories. As a logical framework, GF has the expressive power needed for defining semantics (Ranta, 2004). The types can moreover be extended to express **selectional restrictions**, where verb arguments are restricted to **domains of individuals**. Here is a type system that adds a domain argument to NP and VP:

```
cat NP (d : Dom)
cat VP (d : Dom)(x : Args)
fun PredVP : (d : Dom) -> (x : Args)
                  -> NP d -> VP d x -> Cl x
```

The predication rule checks that the NP and the VP have the same domain.

6 Evaluation

Coverage. The dependent type system for verbs, verb phrases, and clauses is a generalization of the old Resource Grammar Library (Ranta, 2009), which has a set of hard-wired verb subcategories and a handful of slash categories. While it covers "all usual cases", many logically possible ones are missing. Some such cases even appear in the Penn treebank (Marcus et al., 1993), requiring extra rules in the GF interpretation of the treebank (Angelov, 2011). An example is a function of type

```
V (c np (c vp O)) ->
              VPC (c np O) -> VP (c np O)
```

which is used 12 times, for example in *This is designed to get the wagons in a circle and defend the smoking franchise*. It has been easy to write conversion rules showing that the old coverage is preserved. But it remains future work to see what new cases are covered by the increased generality.

1. **Extraction**.

```
cat QCl (x : Args)                                            -- question clause
cat IP                                                        -- interrogative phrase
fun QuestCl    : (x : Args)       -> Cl x           -> QCl x  -- does she love him
fun QuestVP    : (x : Args) -> IP -> VP x           -> QCl x  -- who loves him
fun QuestSlash : (x : Args) -> IP -> QCl (c np x) -> QCl x    -- whom does she love

lincat QCl = Cl ** {focus : {s : Str ; isOcc : Bool}}         -- focal IP, whether occupied
```

2. **Coordination**.

```
cat VPC (x : Args)                                              -- VP conjunction
cat ClC (x : Args)                                              -- Clause conjunction
fun StartVPC : (x : Args) -> Conj -> VP x -> VP x  -> VPC x   -- love or hate
fun ContVPC  : (x : Args)         -> VP x -> VPC x -> VPC x   -- admire, love or hate
fun UseVPC   : (x : Args) -> VPC x                 -> VP  x   -- [use VPC as VP]
fun StartClC : (x : Args) -> Conj -> Cl x -> Cl x  -> ClC x   -- he sells and I buy
fun ContClC  : (x : Args) -> Cl x -> ClC x         -> ClC x   -- you steal, he sells and I buy
fun UseClC   : (x : Args) -> ClC x                 -> Cl  x   -- [use ClC as Cl]
```

Figure 3: Extraction and coordination.

Multilinguality. How universal are the concrete syntax functor and interface? In the standard RGL, functorization has only been attempted for families of closely related languages, with Romance languages sharing 75% of syntax code and Scandinavian languages 85% (Ranta, 2009). The new predication grammar shares code across all languages. The figure to compare is the percentage of shared code (abstract syntax + functor + interface) of the total code written for a particular language (shared + language-specific). This percentage is 70 for Chinese, 64 for English, 61 for Finnish, and 76 for Swedish, when calculated as lines of code. The total amount of shared code is 760 lines. One example of overrides is negation and questions in English, which are complicated by the need of auxiliaries for some verbs (*go*) but not for others (*be*). This explains why Swedish shares more of the common code than English.

Performance. Dependent types are not integrated in current GF parsers, but checked by post-processing. This implies a loss of speed, because many trees are constructed just to be thrown away. But when we specialized dependent types and rules to nondependent instances needed by the lexicon (using them as **metarules** in the sense of GPSG), parsing became several times faster than with the old grammar. An analysis remains to do, but one hypothesis is that the speed-up is due to fixing tense and polarity earlier than in the old RGL: when starting to build VPs, as opposed to when using clauses in full sentences. Dependent types made it easy to test this refactoring, since they reduced the number of rules that had to be written.

Robustness. Robustness in GF parsing is achieved by introducing **metavariables** ("question marks") when tree nodes cannot be constructed by the grammar (Angelov, 2011). The subtrees under a metavariable node are linearized separately, just like a sequence of **chunks**. In translation, this leads to decrease in quality, because dependencies between chunks are not detected. The early application of tense and polarity is an improvement, as it makes verb chunks contain information that was previously detected only if the parser managed to build a whole sentence.

7 Conclusion

We have shown a GF grammar for predication allowing an unlimited variation of argument lists: an abstract syntax with a concise definition using dependent types, a concrete syntax using a functor and records, and a straightforward denotational semantics. The grammar has been tested with four languages and shown promising results in speed and robustness, also in large-scale processing. A more general conclusion is that dependent types, records, and functors are powerful tools both for computational grammar engineering and for the theoretical study of languages.

Acknowledgements. I am grateful to Krasimir Angelov and Robin Cooper for comments, and to Swedish Research Council for support under grant nr. 2012-5746 (Reliable Multilingual Digital Communication).

References

K. Angelov and P. Ljunglöf. 2014. Fast statistical parsing with parallel multiple context-free grammars. In *Proceedings of EACL-2014, Gothenburg*.

K. Angelov. 2011. *The Mechanics of the Grammatical Framework*. Ph.D. thesis, Chalmers University of Technology.

Y. Bar-Hillel. 1953. A quasi-arithmetical notation for syntactic description. *Language*, 29:27–58.

N. Chomsky. 1981. *Lectures on Government and Binding*. Mouton de Gruyter.

Y. Coscoy, G. Kahn, and L. Thery. 1995. Extracting text from proofs. In M. Dezani-Ciancaglini and G. Plotkin, editors, *Proc. Second Int. Conf. on Typed Lambda Calculi and Applications*, volume 902 of *LNCS*, pages 109–123.

H. B. Curry. 1961. Some logical aspects of grammatical structure. In Roman Jakobson, editor, *Structure of Language and its Mathematical Aspects: Proceedings of the Twelfth Symposium in Applied Mathematics*, pages 56–68. American Mathematical Society.

Ph. de Groote. 2001. Towards Abstract Categorial Grammars. In *Association for Computational Linguistics, 39th Annual Meeting and 10th Conference of the European Chapter, Toulouse, France*, pages 148–155.

P. Diderichsen. 1962. *Elementær dansk grammatik*. Gyldendal, København.

G. Gazdar, E. Klein, G. Pullum, and I. Sag. 1985. *Generalized Phrase Structure Grammar*. Basil Blackwell, Oxford.

R. Harper, F. Honsell, and G. Plotkin. 1993. A Framework for Defining Logics. *JACM*, 40(1):143–184.

L. Karttunen and M. Kay. 1985. Parsing in a free word order language. In D. Dowty, L. Karttunen, and A. Zwicky, editors, *Natural Language Parsing, Psychological, Computational, and Theoretical Perspectives*, pages 279–306. Cambridge University Press.

J. Lambek. 1958. The mathematics of sentence structure. *American Mathematical Monthly*, 65:154–170.

J. Landsbergen. 1982. Machine translation based on logically isomorphic Montague grammars. In *COLING-1982*.

P. Ljunglöf. 2004. *The Expressivity and Complexity of Grammatical Framework*. Ph.D. thesis, Dept. of Computing Science, Chalmers University of Technology and Gothenburg University. `http://www.cs.chalmers.se/~peb/pubs/p04-PhD-thesis.pdf`.

L. Magnusson. 1994. *The Implementation of ALF - a Proof Editor based on Martin-Löf's Monomorphic Type Theory with Explicit Substitution*. Ph.D. thesis, Department of Computing Science, Chalmers University of Technology and University of Göteborg.

M. P. Marcus, B. Santorini, and M. A. Marcinkiewicz. 1993. Building a Large Annotated Corpus of English: The Penn Treebank. *Computational Linguistics*, 19(2):313–330.

P. Martin-Löf. 1984. *Intuitionistic Type Theory*. Bibliopolis, Napoli.

R. Montague. 1974. *Formal Philosophy*. Yale University Press, New Haven. Collected papers edited by Richmond Thomason.

S. Müller. 2004. Continuous or Discontinuous Constituents? A Comparison between Syntactic Analyses for Constituent Order and Their Processing Systems. *Research on Language and Computation*, 2(2):209–257.

R. Muskens. 2001. Lambda Grammars and the Syntax-Semantics Interface. In R. van Rooy and M. Stokhof, editors, *Proceedings of the Thirteenth Amsterdam Colloquium*, pages 150–155, Amsterdam. `http://let.uvt.nl/general/people/rmuskens/pubs/amscoll.pdf`.

F. J. Newmeyer. 2004. Against a parameter-setting approach to language variation. *Linguistic Variation Yearbook*, 4:181–234.

C. Pollard and I. Sag. 1994. *Head-Driven Phrase Structure Grammar*. University of Chicago Press.

A. Ranta. 1994. *Type Theoretical Grammar*. Oxford University Press.

A. Ranta. 1997. Structures grammaticales dans le français mathématique. *Mathématiques, informatique et Sciences Humaines*, 138/139:5–56/5–36.

A. Ranta. 2004. Computational Semantics in Type Theory. *Mathematics and Social Sciences*, 165:31–57.

A. Ranta. 2009. The GF Resource Grammar Library. *Linguistics in Language Technology*, 2. `http://elanguage.net/journals/index.php/lilt/article/viewFile/214/158`.

A. Ranta. 2011. *Grammatical Framework: Programming with Multilingual Grammars*. CSLI Publications, Stanford.

H. Seki, T. Matsumura, M. Fujii, and T. Kasami. 1991. On multiple context-free grammars. *Theoretical Computer Science*, 88:191–229.

System with Generalized Quantifiers on Dependent Types for Anaphora

Justyna Grudzińska
Institute of Philosophy
University of Warsaw
Krakowskie Przedmieście 3, 00-927 Warszawa
j.grudzinska@uw.edu.pl

Marek Zawadowski
Institute of Mathematics
University of Warsaw
Banacha 2, 02-097 Warszawa
zawado@mimuw.edu.pl

Abstract

We propose a system for the interpretation of anaphoric relationships between unbound pronouns and quantifiers. The main technical contribution of our proposal consists in combining generalized quantifiers with dependent types. Empirically, our system allows a uniform treatment of all types of unbound anaphora, including the notoriously difficult cases such as quantificational subordination, cumulative and branching continuations, and donkey anaphora.

1 Introduction

The phenomenon of unbound anaphora refers to instances where anaphoric pronouns occur outside the syntactic scopes (i.e. the c-command domain) of their quantifier antecedents. The main kinds of unbound anaphora are regular anaphora to quantifiers, quantificational subordination, and donkey anaphora, as exemplified by (1) to (3) respectively:

(1) Most kids entered. They looked happy.

(2) Every man loves a woman. They kiss them.

(3) Every farmer who owns a donkey beats it.

Unbound anaphoric pronouns have been dealt with in two main semantic paradigms: dynamic semantic theories (Groenendijk and Stokhof, 1991); (Van den Berg, 1996); (Nouwen, 2003) and the E-type/D-type tradition (Evans, 1977); (Heim, 1990); (Elbourne, 2005). In the dynamic semantic theories pronouns are taken to be (syntactically free, but semantically bound) variables, and context serves as a medium supplying values for the variables. In the E-type/D-type tradition pronouns are treated as quantifiers. Our system combines aspects of both families of theories. As in the E-type/D-type tradition we treat unbound anaphoric pronouns as quantifiers; as in the systems of dynamic semantics context is used as a medium supplying (possibly dependent) types as their potential quantificational domains. Like Dekker's Predicate Logic with Anaphora and more recent multidimensional models (Dekker, 1994); (Dekker, 2008), our system lends itself to the compositional treatment of unbound anaphora, while keeping a classical, static notion of truth. The main novelty of our proposal consists in combining generalized quantifiers (Mostowski, 1957); (Lindström, 1966); (Barwise and Cooper, 1981) with dependent types (Martin-Löf, 1972); (Ranta, 1994).

The paper is organized as follows. In Section 2 we introduce informally the main features of our system. Section 3 sketches the process of English-to-formal language translation. Finally, sections 4 and 5 define the syntax and semantics of the system.

2 Elements of system

2.1 Context, types and dependent types

The variables of our system are always typed. We write $x : X$ to denote that the variable x is of type X and refer to this as a type specification of the variable x. Types, in this paper, are interpreted as sets. We write the interpretation of the type X as $\|X\|$.

Types can depend on variables of other types. Thus, if we already have a type specification $x : X$, then we can also have type $Y(x)$ depending on the variable x and we can declare a variable y of type Y by stating $y : Y(x)$. The fact that Y depends on X is modeled as a projection

$$\pi : \|Y\| \to \|X\|.$$

So that if the variable x of type X is interpreted as an element $a \in \|X\|$, $\|Y\|(a)$ is interpreted as the fiber of π over a (the preimage of $\{a\}$ under π)

$$\|Y\|(a) = \{b \in \|Y\| : \pi(b) = a\}.$$

One standard natural language example of such a dependence of types is that if m is a variable of the type of months M, there is a type $D(m)$ of the days of the month m. Such type dependencies can be nested, i.e., we can have a sequence of type specifications of the (individual) variables:

$$x : X, y : Y(x), z : Z(x, y).$$

Context for us is a partially ordered sequence of type specifications of the (individual) variables and it is interpreted as a parameter set, i.e. as a set of compatible n-tuples of the elements of the sets corresponding to the types involved (compatible wrt all projections).

2.2 Quantifiers, chains of quantifiers

Our system defines quantifiers and predicates polymorphically. A generalized quantifier Q is an association to every set Z a subset of the power set of Z. If we have a predicate P defined in a context Γ, then for any interpretation of the context $\|\Gamma\|$ it is interpreted as a subset of its parameter set. Quantifier phrases, e.g. *every man* or *some woman*, are interpreted as follows: $\|every_{m:man}\| = \{\|man\|\}$ and $\|some_{w:woman}\| = \{X \subseteq \|woman\| : X \neq \emptyset\}$.

The interpretation of quantifier phrases is further extended into the interpretation of chains of quantifiers. Consider an example in (2):

(2) Every man loves a woman. They kiss them.

Multi-quantifier sentences such as the first sentence in (2) are known to be ambiguous with different readings corresponding to how various quantifiers are semantically related in the sentence. To account for the readings available for such multi-quantifier sentences, we raise quantifier phrases to the front of a sentence to form (generalized) quantifier prefixes - chains of quantifiers. Chains of quantifiers are built from quantifier phrases using three chain-constructors: pack-formation rule $(?, \ldots, ?)$, sequential composition $?|?$, and parallel composition $\frac{?}{?}$. The semantical operations that correspond to the chain-constructors (known as cumulation, iteration and branching) capture in a compositional manner cumulative, scope-dependent and branching readings, respectively.

The idea of chain-constructors and the corresponding semantical operations builds on Mostowski's notion of quantifier (Mostowski, 1957) further generalized by Lindström to a so-called polyadic quantifier (Lindström, 1966), see (Bellert and Zawadowski, 1989). To use a familiar example, a multi-quantifier prefix like $\forall_{m:M}|\exists_{w:W}$ is thought of as a single two-place quantifier obtained by an operation on the two single quantifiers, and it has as denotation:

$$\|\forall_{m:M}|\exists_{w:W}\| = \{R \subseteq \|M\| \times \|W\| : \{a \in \|M\| :$$

$$\{b \in \|W\| : \langle a, b\rangle \in R\} \in \|\exists_{w:W}\|\} \in \|\forall_{m:M}\|\}.$$

In this paper we generalize the three chain-constructors and the corresponding semantical operations to (pre-) chains defined on dependent types.

2.3 Dynamic extensions of contexts

In our system language expressions are all defined in context. Thus the first sentence in (2) (on the most natural interpretation where *a woman* depends on *every man*) translates (via the process described in Section 3) into a sentence with a chain of quantifiers in a context:

$$\Gamma \vdash \forall_{m:M}|\exists_{w:W} Love(m, w),$$

and says that the set of pairs, a man and a woman he loves, has the following property: the set of those men that love some woman each is the set of all men. The way to understand the second sentence in (2) (i.e. the anaphoric continuation) is that every man kisses the women he loves rather than those loved by someone else. Thus the first sentence in (2) must deliver some internal relation between the types corresponding to the two quantifier phrases.

In our analysis, the first sentence in (2) extends the context Γ by adding new variable specifications on newly formed types for every quantifier phrase in the chain $Ch = \forall_{m:M}|\exists_{w:W}$ - for the purpose of the formation of such new types we introduce a new type constructor $\mathbb{T}$. That is, the first sentence in (2) (denoted as φ) extends the context by adding:

$$t_{\varphi,\forall_m} : \mathbb{T}_{\varphi,\forall_{m:M}};\ t_{\varphi,\exists_w} : \mathbb{T}_{\varphi,\exists_{w:W}}(t_{\varphi,\forall_m})$$

The interpretations of types (that correspond to quantifier phrases in Ch) from the extended context Γ_φ are defined in a two-step procedure using the inductive clauses through which we define Ch but in the reverse direction.

Step 1. We define fibers of new types by inverse induction.
Basic step.
For the whole chain $Ch = \forall_{m:M}|\exists_{w:W}$ we put:

$$\|\mathbb{T}_{\varphi,\forall_{m:M}|\exists_{w:W}}\| := \|Love\|.$$

Inductive step.

$$\|\mathbb{T}_{\varphi,\forall_{m:M}}\| = \{a \in \|M\| \colon \{b \in \|W\| \colon \langle a,b\rangle \in \|Love\|\} \in \|\exists_{w:W}\|\}$$

and for $a \in \|M\|$

$$\|\mathbb{T}_{\varphi,\exists_{w:W}}\|(a) = \{b \in \|W\| \colon \langle a,b\rangle \in \|Love\|\}$$

Step 2. We build dependent types from fibers.

$$\|\mathbb{T}_{\varphi,\exists_{w:W}}\| = \bigcup\{\{a\} \times \|\mathbb{T}_{\varphi,\exists_{w:W}}\|(a) : a \in \|\mathbb{T}_{\varphi,\forall_{m:M}}\|\}$$

Thus the first sentence in (2) extends the context Γ by adding the type $\mathbb{T}_{\varphi,\forall_{m:M}}$, interpreted as $\|\mathbb{T}_{\varphi,\forall_{m:M}}\|$ (i.e. the set of men who love some women), and the dependent type $\mathbb{T}_{\varphi,\exists_{w:W}}(t_{\varphi,\forall_m})$, interpreted for $a \in \|\mathbb{T}_{\varphi,\forall_{m:M}}\|$ as $\|\mathbb{T}_{\varphi,\exists_{w:W}}\|(a)$ (i.e. the set of women loved by the man a).

Unbound anaphoric pronouns are interpreted with reference to the context created by the foregoing text: they are treated as universal quantifiers and newly formed (possibly dependent) types incrementally added to the context serve as their potential quantificational domains. That is, unbound anaphoric pronouns $they_m$ and $them_w$ in the second sentence of (2) have the ability to pick up and quantify universally over the respective interpretations. The anaphoric continuation in (2) translates into:

$$\Gamma_\varphi \vdash \forall_{t_{\varphi,\forall_m}:\mathbb{T}_{\varphi,\forall_{m:M}}}|\forall_{t_{\varphi,\exists_w}:\mathbb{T}_{\varphi,\exists_{w:W}}(t_{\varphi,\forall_m})} Kiss(t_{\varphi,\forall_m}, t_{\varphi,\exists_w}),$$

where:

$$\|\forall_{t_{\varphi,\forall_m}:\mathbb{T}_{\varphi,\forall_{m:M}}}|\forall_{t_{\varphi,\exists_w}:\mathbb{T}_{\varphi,\exists_{w:W}}(t_{\varphi,\forall_m})}\| = \{R \subseteq \|\mathbb{T}_{\varphi,\exists_{w:W}}\| : \{a \in \|\mathbb{T}_{\varphi,\forall_{m:M}}\| : \{b \in \|\mathbb{T}_{\varphi,\exists_{w:W}}\|(a) : \langle a,b\rangle \in R\} \in \|\forall_{t_{\varphi,\exists_w}:\mathbb{T}_{\varphi,\exists_{w:W}}(t_{\varphi,\forall_m})}\|(a)\} \in \|\forall_{t_{\varphi,\forall_m}:\mathbb{T}_{\varphi,\forall_{m:M}}}\|\},$$

yielding the correct truth conditions: *Every man kisses every woman he loves.*

Our system also handles intra-sentential anaphora, as exemplified in (3):

(3) Every farmer who owns a donkey beats it.

To account for the dynamic contribution of modified common nouns (in this case common nouns modified by relative clauses) we include in our system $*$-sentences (i.e. sentences with dummy quantifier phrases). The modified common noun gets translated into a $*$-sentence (with a dummy-quantifier phrase $f : F$):

$$\Gamma \vdash f : F|\exists_{d:D} Own(f,d)$$

and we extend the context by dropping the specifications of variables: $(f : F, d : D)$ and adding new variable specifications on newly formed types for every (dummy-) quantifier phrase in the chain Ch^*:

$$t_{\varphi,f} : \mathbb{T}_{\varphi,f:F};\ t_{\varphi,\exists_d} : \mathbb{T}_{\varphi,\exists_{d:D}}(t_{\varphi,f}),$$

The interpretations of types (that correspond to the quantifier phrases in the Ch^*) from the extended context Γ_φ are defined in our two-step procedure. Thus the $*$-sentence in (3) extends the context by adding the type $\mathbb{T}_{\varphi,f:F}$ interpreted as $\|\mathbb{T}_{\varphi,f:F}\|$ (i.e. the set of farmers who own some donkeys), and the dependent type $\mathbb{T}_{\varphi,\exists_{d:D}}(t_{\varphi,f})$, interpreted for $a \in \|\mathbb{T}_{\varphi,f:F}\|$ as $\|\mathbb{T}_{\varphi,\exists_{d:D}}\|(a)$ (i.e. the set of donkeys owned by the farmer a). The main clause translates into:

$$\Gamma_\varphi \vdash \forall_{t_{\varphi,f}:\mathbb{T}_{\varphi,f:F}}|\forall_{t_{\varphi,\exists_d}:\mathbb{T}_{\varphi,\exists_{d:D}}(t_{\varphi,f})} Beat(t_{\varphi,f}, t_{\varphi,\exists_d}),$$

yielding the correct truth conditions *Every farmer who owns a donkey beats every donkey he owns.* Importantly, since we quantify over fibers (and not over $\langle farmer, donkey\rangle$ pairs), our solution does not run into the so-called 'proportion problem'.

Dynamic extensions of contexts and their interpretation are also defined for cumulative and branching continuations. Consider a cumulative example in (4):

(4) Last year three scientists wrote (a total of) five articles (between them). They presented them at major conferences.

Interpreted cumulatively, the first sentence in (4) translates into a sentence:

$$\Gamma \vdash (Three_{s:S}, Five_{a:A})\ Write(s,a).$$

The anaphoric continuation in (4) can be interpreted in what Krifka calls a 'correspondence' fashion (Krifka, 1996). For example, Dr. K wrote one article, co-authored two more with Dr. N, who co-authored two more with Dr. S, and the scientists that cooperated in writing one or more articles also cooperated in presenting these (and no other) articles at major conferences. In our system, the first sentence in (4) extends the context by adding the type corresponding to $(Three_{s:S}, Five_{a:A})$:

$$t_{\varphi,(Three_s, Five_a)} : T_{\varphi,(Three_{s:S};\ Five_{a:A})},$$

interpreted as a set of tuples

$$\|T_{\varphi,(Three_{s:S}, Five_{a:A})}\| = \\ = \{\langle c, d\rangle \ : \ c \in \|S\| \ \& \ d \in \|A\| \ \& \ c \textit{ wrote } d\}$$

The anaphoric continuation then quantifies universally over this type (i.e. a set of pairs), yielding the desired truth-conditions *The respective scientists cooperated in presenting at major conferences the respective articles that they cooperated in writing.*

3 English-to-formal language translation

We assume a two-step translation process.

Representation. The syntax of the representation language - for the English fragment considered in this paper - is as follows.
$S \to Prd^n(QP_1, \ldots, QP_n)$;
$MCN \to Prd^n(QP_1, \ldots, \ CN \ , \ldots, QP_n)$;
$MCN \to CN$;
$QP \to Det\ MCN$;
$Det \to every, most, three, \ldots$;
$CN \to man, woman, \ldots$;
$Prd^n \to enter, love, \ldots$;
Common nouns (CNs) are interpreted as types, and common nouns modified by relative clauses (MCNs) - as $*$-sentences determining some (possibly dependent) types.

Disambiguation. Sentences of English, contrary to sentences of our formal language, are often ambiguous. Hence one sentence representation can be associated with more than one sentence in our formal language. The next step thus involves disambiguation. We take quantifier phrases of a given representation, e.g.:

$$P(Q_1X_1, Q_2X_2, Q_3X_3)$$

and organize them into all possible chains of quantifiers in suitable contexts with some restrictions imposed on particular quantifiers concerning the places in prefixes at which they can occur (a detailed elaboration of the disambiguation process is left for another place):

$$\frac{Q_1x_1{:}X_1|Q_2x_2{:}X_2}{Q_3x_3{:}X_3} \ P(x_1, x_2, x_3).$$

4 System - syntax

4.1 Alphabet

The alphabet consists of:
type variables: $X, Y, Z, \ldots$;
type constants: $M, men, women, \ldots$;
type constructors: $\sum, \prod, \mathbb{T}$;
individual variables: $x, y, z, \ldots$;
predicates: $P, P', P_1, \ldots$;
quantifier symbols: $\exists, \forall, five, Q_1, Q_2, \ldots$;
three chain constructors: $?|?$, $\frac{?}{?}$, $(?, \ldots, ?)$.

4.2 Context

A context is a list of type specifications of (individual) variables. If we have a context

$$\Gamma = x_1 : X_1, \ldots, x_n : X_n(\langle x_i\rangle_{i\in J_n})$$

then the judgement

$$\vdash \Gamma : \mathsf{cxt}$$

expresses this fact. Having a context Γ as above, we can declare a type X_{n+1} in that context

$$\Gamma \vdash X_{n+1}(\langle x_i\rangle_{i\in J_{n+1}}) : \mathsf{type}$$

where $J_{n+1} \subseteq \{1, \ldots, n\}$ such that if $i \in J_{n+1}$, then $J_i \subseteq J_{n+1}$, $J_1 = \emptyset$. The type X_{n+1} depends on variables $\langle x_i\rangle_{i\in J_{n+1}}$. Now, we can declare a new variable of the type $X_{n+1}(\langle x_i\rangle_{i\in J_{n+1}})$ in the context Γ

$$\Gamma \vdash x_{n+1} : X_{n+1}(\langle x_i\rangle_{i\in J_{n+1}})$$

and extend the context Γ by adding this variable specification, i.e. we have

$$\vdash \Gamma, x_{n+1} : X_{n+1}(\langle x_i\rangle_{i\in J_{n+1}}) : \mathsf{cxt}$$

Γ' is a *subcontext* of Γ if Γ' is a context and a sublist of Γ. Let Δ be a list of variable specifications from a context Γ, Δ' the least subcontext of Γ containing Δ. We say that Δ is *convex* iff $\Delta' - \Delta$ is again a context.

The variables the types depend on are always explicitly written down in specifications. We can think of a context as (a linearization of) a partially ordered set of declarations such that the declaration of a variable x (of type X) precedes the declaration of the variable y (of type Y) iff the type Y depends on the variable x.

The formation rules for both Σ- and Π-types are as usual.

4.3 Language

Quantifier-free formulas. Here, we need only predicates applied to variables. So we write

$$\Gamma \vdash P(x_1, \ldots, x_n) : \mathsf{qf\text{-}f}$$

to express that P is an n-ary predicate and the specifications of the variables $x_1, \ldots, x_n$ form a subcontext of Γ.

Quantifier phrases. If we have a context $\Gamma, y : Y(\vec{x}), \Delta$ and quantifier symbol Q, then we can form a *quantifier phrase* $Q_{y:Y(\vec{x})}$ in that context. We write

$$\Gamma, y : Y(\vec{x}), \Delta \vdash Q_{y:Y(\vec{x})} : \mathsf{QP}$$

to express this fact. In a quantifier prase $Q_{y:Y(\vec{x})}$: the variable y is the *binding variable* and the variables $\vec{x}$ are *indexing variables.*

Packs of quantifiers. Quantifiers phrases can be grouped together to form a pack of quantifiers. The pack of quantifiers formation rule is as follows.

$$\frac{\Gamma \vdash Q_{i\; y_i:Y_i(\vec{x}_i)} : \mathsf{QP} \quad i = 1, \ldots k}{\Gamma \vdash (Q_{1\; y_1:Y_1(\vec{x}_1)}, \ldots, Q_{k\; y_k:Y_k(\vec{x}_k)}) : \mathsf{pack}}$$

where, with $\vec{y} = y_1, \ldots, y_k$ and $\vec{x} = \bigcup_{i=1}^{k} \vec{x}_i$, we have that $y_i \neq y_j$ for $i \neq j$ and $\vec{y} \cap \vec{x} = \emptyset$. In so constructed pack: the binding variables are $\vec{y}$ and the indexing variables are $\vec{x}$. We can denote such a pack $Pc_{\vec{y}:\vec{Y}(\vec{x})}$ to indicate the variables involved. One-element pack will be denoted and treated as a quantifier phrase. This is why we denote such a pack as $Q_{y:Y(\vec{x})}$ rather than $(Q_{y:Y(\vec{x})})$.

Pre-chains and chains of quantifiers. Chains and pre-chains of quantifiers have binding variables and indexing variables. By $Ch_{\vec{y}:\vec{Y}(\vec{x})}$ we denote a pre-chain with binding variables $\vec{y}$ and indexing variables $\vec{x}$ so that the type of the variable y_i is $Y_i(\vec{x}_i)$ with $\bigcup_i \vec{x}_i = \vec{x}$. Chains of quantifiers are pre-chains in which all indexing variables are bound. Pre-chains of quantifiers arrange quantifier phrases into N-free pre-orders, subject to some binding conditions. Mutually comparable QPs in a pre-chain sit in one pack. Thus the pre-chains are built from packs via two chain-constructors of sequential ?|? and parallel composition $\frac{?}{?}$. The chain formation rules are as follows.

1. *Packs of quantifiers.* Packs of quantifiers are pre-chains of quantifiers with the same binding variable and the same indexing variables, i.e.

$$\frac{\Gamma \vdash Pc_{\vec{y}:\vec{Y}(\vec{x})} : \mathsf{pack}}{\Gamma \vdash Pc_{\vec{y}:\vec{Y}(\vec{x})} : \mathsf{p\text{-}ch}}$$

2. *Sequential composition of pre-chains*

$$\frac{\Gamma \vdash Ch_{1\; \vec{y}_1:\vec{Y}_1(\vec{x}_1)} : \mathsf{p\text{-}ch}, \Gamma \vdash Ch_{2\; \vec{y}_2:\vec{Y}_2(\vec{x}_2)} : \mathsf{p\text{-}ch}}{\Gamma \vdash Ch_{1\; \vec{y}_1:\vec{Y}_1(\vec{x}_1)} | Ch_{2\; \vec{y}_2:\vec{Y}_2(\vec{x}_2)} : \mathsf{p\text{-}ch}}$$

provided $\vec{y}_2 \cap (\vec{y}_1 \cup \vec{x}_1) = \emptyset$; the specifications of the variables $(\vec{x}_1 \cup \vec{x}_2) - (\vec{y}_1 \cup \vec{y}_2)$ form a context, a subcontext of Γ. In so obtained pre-chain: the binding variables are $\vec{y}_1 \cup \vec{y}_2$ and the indexing variables are $\vec{x}_1 \cup \vec{x}_2$.

3. *Parallel composition of pre-chains*

$$\frac{\Gamma \vdash Ch_{1\; \vec{y}_1:\vec{Y}_1(\vec{x}_1)} : \mathsf{p\text{-}ch}, \Gamma \vdash Ch_{2\; \vec{y}_2:\vec{Y}_2(\vec{x}_2)} : \mathsf{p\text{-}ch}}{\Gamma \vdash \dfrac{Ch_{1\; \vec{y}_1:\vec{Y}_1(\vec{x}_1)}}{Ch_{2\; \vec{y}_2:\vec{Y}_2(\vec{x}_2)}} : \mathsf{p\text{-}ch}}$$

provided $\vec{y}_2 \cap (\vec{y}_1 \cup \vec{x}_1) = \emptyset = \vec{y}_1 \cap (\vec{y}_2 \cup \vec{x}_2)$. As above, in so obtained pre-chain: the binding variables are $\vec{y}_1 \cup \vec{y}_2$ and the indexing variables are $\vec{x}_1 \cup \vec{x}_2$.

A pre-chain of quantifiers $Ch_{\vec{y}:\vec{Y}(\vec{x})}$ is a *chain* iff $\vec{x} \subseteq \vec{y}$. The following

$$\Gamma \vdash Ch_{\vec{y}:\vec{Y}(\vec{x})} : \mathsf{chain}$$

expresses the fact that $Ch_{\vec{y}:\vec{Y}(\vec{x})}$ is a chain of quantifiers in the context Γ.

Formulas, sentences and $*$-sentences. The formulas have binding variables, indexing variables and argument variables. We write $\varphi_{\vec{y}:Y(\vec{x})}(\vec{z})$ for a formula with binding variables $\vec{y}$, indexing variables $\vec{x}$ and argument variables $\vec{z}$. We have the following formation rule for formulas

$$\frac{\Gamma \vdash A(\vec{z}) : \mathsf{qf\text{-}f}, \Gamma \vdash Ch_{\vec{y}:\vec{Y}(\vec{x})} : \mathsf{p\text{-}ch}}{\Gamma \vdash Ch_{\vec{y}:\vec{Y}(\vec{x})}\, A(\vec{z}) : \mathsf{formula}}$$

provided $\vec{y}$ is final in $\vec{z}$, i.e. $\vec{y} \subseteq \vec{z}$ and variable specifications of $\vec{z} - \vec{y}$ form a subcontext of Γ. In so constructed formula: the binding variables are $\vec{y}$, the indexing variables are $\vec{x}$, and the argument variables are $\vec{z}$.

A formula $\varphi_{\vec{y}:Y(\vec{x})}(\vec{z})$ is a *sentence* iff $\vec{z} \subseteq \vec{y}$ and $\vec{x} \subseteq \vec{y}$. So a sentence is a formula without free variables, neither individual nor indexing. The following

$$\Gamma \vdash \varphi_{\vec{y}:Y(\vec{x})}(\vec{z}) : \mathsf{sentence}$$

expresses the fact that $\varphi_{\vec{y}:Y(\vec{x})}(\vec{z})$ is a sentence formed in the context Γ.

We shall also consider some special formulas that we call $*$-sentences. A formula $\varphi_{\vec{y}:Y(\vec{x})}(\vec{z})$ is a $*$-*sentence* if $\vec{x} \subseteq \vec{y} \cup \vec{z}$ but the set $\vec{z} - \vec{y}$ is possibly not empty and moreover the type of each variable in $\vec{z}-\vec{y}$ is *constant*, i.e., it does not depend on variables of other types. In such case we consider the $\vec{z}-\vec{y}$ as a set of biding variables of an additional pack called a *dummy pack* that is placed in front of the whole chain Ch. The chain 'extended' by this dummy pack will be denoted by Ch^*. Clearly, if $\vec{z}-\vec{y}$ is empty there is no dummy pack and the chain Ch^* is Ch, i.e. sentences are $*$-sentences without dummy packs. We write

$$\Gamma \vdash \varphi_{\vec{y}:Y(\vec{x})}(\vec{z}) : *\text{-sentence}$$

to express the fact that $\varphi_{\vec{y}:Y(\vec{x})}(\vec{z})$ is a $*$-sentence formed in the context Γ.

Having formed a $*$-sentence φ we can form a new context Γ_φ defined in the next section.

Notation. For semantics we need some notation for the variables in the $*$-sentence. Suppose we have a $*$-sentence

$$\Gamma \vdash Ch_{\vec{y}:Y(\vec{x})}\ P(\vec{z}) : *\text{-sentence}$$

We define: (i) The environment of pre-chain Ch: $Env(Ch) = Env(Ch_{\vec{y}:\vec{Y}(\vec{x})})$ - is the context defining variables $\vec{x}-\vec{y}$; (ii) The binding variables of pre-chain Ch: $Bv(Ch) = Bv(Ch_{\vec{y}:\vec{Y}(\vec{x})})$ - is the convex set of declarations in Γ of the binding variables in $\vec{y}$; (iii) $\mathbf{env}(Ch) = \mathbf{env}(Ch_{\vec{y}:\vec{Y}(\vec{x})})$ - the set of variables in the environment of Ch, i.e. $\vec{x}-\vec{y}$; (iv) $\mathbf{bv}(Ch) = \mathbf{bv}(Ch_{\vec{y}:\vec{Y}(\vec{x})})$ - the set of biding variables $\vec{y}$; (v) The environment of a pre-chain Ch' in a $*$-sentence $\varphi = Ch_{\vec{y}:Y(\vec{x})}\ P(\vec{z})$, denoted $Env_\varphi(Ch')$, is the set of binding variables in all the packs in Ch^* that are $<_\varphi$-smaller than all packs in Ch'. Note $Env(Ch') \subseteq Env_\varphi(Ch')$. If $Ch' = Ch_1|Ch_2$ is a sub-pre-chain of the chain $Ch_{\vec{y}:Y(\vec{x})}$, then $Env_\varphi(Ch_2) = Env_\varphi(Ch_1) \cup Bv(Ch_1)$ and $Env_\varphi(Ch_1) = Env_\varphi(Ch')$.

4.4 Dynamic extensions

Suppose we have constructed a $*$-sentence in a context

$$\Gamma \vdash Ch_{\vec{y}:\vec{Y}(\vec{x})}\ A(\vec{z}) : *\text{-sentence}$$

We write φ for $Ch_{\vec{y}:\vec{Y}(\vec{x})}\ A(\vec{z})$.

We form a context Γ_φ dropping the specifications of variables $\vec{z}$ and adding one type and one variable specification for each pack in $Packs_{Ch^*}$.

Let $\check{\Gamma}$ denote the context Γ with the specifications of the variables $\vec{z}$ deleted. Suppose $\Phi \in Packs_{Ch^*}$ and Γ' is an extension of the context $\check{\Gamma}$ such that one variable specification $t_{\Phi',\varphi} : T_{\Phi',\varphi}$ was already added for each pack $\Phi' \in Packs_{Ch^*}$ such that $\Phi' <_{Ch^*} \Phi$ but not for Φ yet. Then we declare a type

$$\Gamma' \vdash T_{\Phi,\varphi}(\langle t_{\Phi',\varphi}\rangle_{\Phi' \in Packs_{Ch^*}, \Phi' <_{Ch^*} \Phi}) : \text{type}$$

and we extend the context Γ' by a specification of a variable $t_{\Phi,\varphi}$ of that type

$$\Gamma', t_{\Phi,\varphi} : T_{\Phi,\varphi}(\langle t_{\Phi',\varphi}\rangle_{\Phi' \in Packs_{Ch^*}, \Phi' <_{Ch^*} \Phi}) : \text{cxt}$$

The context obtained from $\check{\Gamma}$ by adding the new variables corresponding to all the packs $Packs_{Ch^*}$ as above will be denoted by

$$\Gamma_\varphi = \check{\Gamma} \cup \mathbb{T}(Ch_{\vec{y}:\vec{Y}(\vec{x})}\ A(\vec{z})).$$

At the end we add another context formation rule

$$\frac{\Gamma \vdash Ch_{\vec{y}:\vec{Y}(\vec{x})}\ A(\vec{z}) : *\text{-sentence},}{\Gamma_\varphi : \text{cxt}}$$

Then we can build another formula starting in the context Γ_φ. This process can be iterated. Thus in this system sentence φ in a context Γ is constructed via *specifying sequence of formulas*, with the last formula being the sentence φ. However, for the lack of space we are going to describe here only one step of this process. That is, sentence φ in a context Γ can be constructed via *specifying $*$-sentence ψ* extending the context as follows

$$\Gamma \vdash \psi : *\text{-sentence}$$

$$\Gamma_\psi \vdash \varphi : \text{sentence}$$

For short, we can write

$$\Gamma \vdash \Gamma_\psi \vdash \varphi : \text{sentence}$$

5 System - semantics

5.1 Interpretation of dependent types

The context Γ

$$\vdash x : X(\ldots), \ldots, z : Z(\ldots, x, y, \ldots) : \text{cxt}$$

gives rise to a dependence graph. A *dependence graph* $DG_\Gamma = (T_\Gamma, E_\Gamma)$ for the context Γ has types of Γ as vertices and an edge $\pi_{Y,x} : Y \to X$ for every variable specification $x : X(\ldots)$ in Γ and every type $Y(\ldots, x, \ldots)$ occurring in Γ that depends on x.

The *dependence diagram* for the context Γ is an association $\| - \| : DG_\Gamma \to Set$ to every type X in T_Γ a set $\|X\|$ and every edge $\pi_{Y,x} : Y \to X$ in E_Γ a function $\|\pi_{Y,x}\| : \|Y\| \to \|X\|$, so that whenever we have a triangle of edges in E_Γ, $\pi_{Y,x}$ as before $\pi_{Z,y} : Z \to Y$, $\pi_{Z,x} : Z \to X$ we have $\|\pi_{Z,x}\| = \|\pi_{Y,x}\| \circ \|\pi_{Z,y}\|$.

The interpretation of the context Γ, the *parameter space* $\|\Gamma\|$, is the limit of the dependence diagram $\| - \| : DG_\Gamma \to Set$. More specifically,

$$\|\Gamma\| = \|x : X(\ldots), \ldots, z : Z(\ldots, x, y, \ldots)\| =$$

$$\{\vec{a} : dom(\vec{a}) = \mathbf{var}(\Gamma),\ \vec{a}(z) \in \|Z\|(\vec{a}\lceil \mathbf{env}(Z)),$$

$$\|\pi_{Z,x}\|(\vec{a}(z)) = \vec{a}(x),\ \text{ for } z : Z \text{ in } \Gamma,\ x \in \mathbf{env}Z\}$$

where $\mathbf{var}(\Gamma)$ denotes variables specified in Γ and $\mathbf{env}(Z)$ denotes indexing variables of the type Z.

The interpretation of the Σ- and Π-types are as usual.

5.2 Interpretation of language

Interpretation of predicates and quantifier symbols. Both predicates and quantifiers are interpreted polymorphically.

If we have a predicate P defined in a context Γ:

$$x_1 : X_1, \ldots, x_n : X_n(\langle x_i \rangle_{i \in J_n]}) \vdash P(\vec{x}) : \mathsf{qf\text{-}f}$$

then, for any interpretation of the context $\|\Gamma\|$, it is interpreted as a subset of its parameter set, i.e. $\|P\| \subseteq \|\Gamma\|$.

Quantifier symbol Q is interpreted as quantifier $\|Q\|$ i.e. an association to every[1] set Z a subset $\|Q\|(Z) \subseteq \mathcal{P}(Z)$.

Interpretation of pre-chains and chains of quantifiers. We interpret QP's, packs, pre-chains, and chains in the environment of a sentence Env_φ. This is the only case that is needed. We could interpret the aforementioned syntactic objects in their natural environment Env (i.e. independently of any given sentence) but it would unnecessarily complicate some definitions. Thus having a $(*\text{-})$ sentence $\varphi = Ch_{\vec{y}:Y(\vec{x})}\ P(\vec{z})$ (defined in a context Γ) and a sub-pre-chain (QP, pack) Ch', for $\vec{a} \in \|Env_\varphi(Ch')\|$ we define the meaning of

$$\|Ch'\|(\vec{a})$$

Notation. Let $\varphi = Ch_{\vec{y}:\vec{Y}}\ P(\vec{y})$ be a $*$-sentence built in a context Γ, Ch' a pre-chain used in the construction of the $(*)$-chain Ch. Then $Env_\varphi(Ch')$ is a sub-context of Γ disjoint from the convex set $Bv(Ch')$ and $Env_\varphi(Ch'), Bv(Ch')$ is a sub-context of Γ. For $\vec{a} \in \|Env_\varphi(Ch')\|$ we define $\|Bv(Ch')\|(\vec{a})$ to be the largest set such that

$$\{\vec{a}\} \times \|Bv(Ch')\|(\vec{a}) \subseteq \|Env_\varphi(Ch'), Bv(Ch')\|$$

Interpretation of quantifier phrases. If we have a quantifier phrase

$$\Gamma \vdash Q_{y:Y(\vec{x})} : \mathsf{QP}$$

and $\vec{a} \in \|Env_\varphi(Q_{y:Y(\vec{x})})\|$, then it is interpreted as $\|Q\|(\|Y\|(\vec{a})) \subseteq \mathcal{P}(\|Y\|(\vec{a}_{\lceil \vec{x}}))$.

Interpretation of packs. If we have a pack of quantifiers in the sentence φ

$$Pc = (Q_{1_{y_1:Y_1(\vec{x}_1)}}, \ldots Q_{n_{y_n:Y_n(\vec{x}_n)}})$$

and $\vec{a} \in \|Env_\varphi(Pc)\|$, then its interpretation with the parameter $\vec{a}$ is

$$\|Pc\|(\vec{a}) = \|(Q_{1_{y_1:Y_1(\vec{x}_1)}}, \ldots, Q_{n_{y_n:Y_n(\vec{x}_n)}})\|(\vec{a}) =$$

$$\{A \subseteq \prod_{i=1}^{n} \|Y_i\|(\vec{a}\lceil \vec{x}_i) : \pi_i(A) \in \|Q_i\|(\|Y_i\|(\vec{a}\lceil \vec{x}_i),$$

$$\text{for } i = 1, \ldots, n\}$$

where π_i is the i-th projection from the product.

Interpretation of chain constructors.

1. *Parallel composition.* For a pre-chain of quantifiers in the sentence φ

$$Ch' = \frac{Ch_{1_{\vec{y}_1:\vec{Y}_1(\vec{x}_1)}}}{Ch_{2_{\vec{y}_2:\vec{Y}_2(\vec{x}_2)}}}$$

and $\vec{a} \in \|Env_\varphi(Ch')\|$ we define

$$\|\frac{Ch_{1_{\vec{y}_1:\vec{Y}_1(\vec{x}_1)}}}{Ch_{2_{\vec{y}_2:\vec{Y}_2(\vec{x}_2)}}}\|(\vec{a}) = \{A \times B :$$

$$A \in \|Ch_{1_{\vec{y}_1:\vec{Y}_1(\vec{x}_1)}}\|(\vec{a}\lceil \vec{x}_1) \text{ and}$$

$$B \in \|Ch_{2_{\vec{y}_2:\vec{Y}_2(\vec{x}_2)}}\|(\vec{a}\lceil \vec{x}_2)\}$$

2. *Sequential composition.* For a pre-chain of quantifiers in the sentence φ

$$Ch' = Ch_{1_{\vec{y}_1:\vec{Y}_1(\vec{x}_1)}} | Ch_{2_{\vec{y}_2:\vec{Y}_2(\vec{x}_2)}}$$

and $\vec{a} \in \|Env_\varphi(Ch')\|$ we define

$$\|Ch_{1_{\vec{y}_1:\vec{Y}_1(\vec{x}_1)}} | Ch_{2_{\vec{y}_2:\vec{Y}_2(\vec{x}_2)}}\|(\vec{a}) =$$

$$\{R \subseteq \|Bv(Ch')\|(\vec{a}) : \{\vec{b} \in \|Bv(Ch_1)\|(\vec{a}) :$$

[1]This association can be partial.

$$\{\vec{c} \in \|Bv(Ch_2)\|(\vec{a},\vec{b}) : \langle \vec{b},\vec{c}\rangle \in R\} \in$$

$$\|Ch2_{\vec{y}_2:\vec{Y}_2(\vec{x}_2)}\|(\vec{a},\vec{b})\} \in \|Ch1_{\vec{y}_1:\vec{Y}_1(\vec{x}_1)}\|(\vec{a})\}$$

Validity. A sentence

$$\vec{x} : \vec{X} \vdash Ch_{\vec{y}:\vec{Y}}\ P(\vec{y})$$

is true under the above interpretation iff

$$\|P\|(\|\vec{Y}\|) \in \|Ch_{\vec{y}:\vec{Y}}\|$$

5.3 Interpretation of dynamic extensions

Suppose we obtain a context Γ_φ from Γ by the following rule

$$\frac{\Gamma \vdash Ch_{\vec{y}:\vec{Y}(\vec{x})}\ A(\vec{z}) : *\text{-sentence},}{\Gamma_\varphi : \text{cxt}}$$

where φ is $Ch_{\vec{y}:\vec{Y}(\vec{x})}\ A(\vec{z})$. Then

$$\Gamma_\varphi = \check{\Gamma} \cup \mathbb{T}(Ch_{\vec{y}:\vec{Y}(\vec{x})}\ A(\vec{z})).$$

From dependence diagram $\| - \|^\Gamma : DG_\Gamma \to Set$ we shall define another dependence diagram

$$\| - \| = \| - \|^{\Gamma_\varphi} : DG_{\Gamma_\varphi} \to Set$$

Thus, for $\Phi \in Pack_{Ch^*}$ we need to define $\|\mathbb{T}_{\Phi,\varphi}\|^{\Gamma_\varphi}$ and for $\Phi' <_{Ch^*} \Phi$ we need to define

$$\|\pi_{\mathbb{T}_{\Phi,\varphi},t_{\Phi'}}\| : \|\mathbb{T}_{\Phi,\varphi}\| \longrightarrow \|\mathbb{T}_{\Phi',\varphi}\|$$

This will be done in two steps:

Step 1. (Fibers of new types defined by inverse induction.)

We shall define for the sub-prechains Ch' of Ch^* and $\vec{a} \in \|Env_\varphi(Ch')\|$ a set

$$\|\mathbb{T}_{\varphi,Ch'}\|(\vec{a}) \subseteq \|Bv(Ch')\|(\vec{a})$$

This is done using the inductive clauses through which we have defined Ch^* but in the reverse direction.

The *basic case* is when $Ch' = Ch^*$. We put

$$\|\mathbb{T}_{\varphi,Ch}\|(\emptyset) = \|P\|$$

The *inductive step.* Now assume that the set $\|\mathbb{T}_{\varphi,Ch'}\|(\vec{a})$ is defined for $\vec{a} \in \|Env_\varphi(Ch')\|$.

Parallel decomposition. If we have

$$Ch' = \frac{Ch1_{\vec{y}_1:\vec{Y}_1(\vec{x}_1)}}{Ch2_{\vec{y}_2:\vec{Y}_2(\vec{x}_2)}}$$

then we define sets

$$\|\mathbb{T}_{\varphi,Ch_i}\|(\vec{a}) \in \|Ch_i\|(\vec{a})$$

for $i = 1,2$ so that

$$\|\mathbb{T}_{\varphi,Ch'}\|(\vec{a}) = \|\mathbb{T}_{\varphi,Ch_1}\|(\vec{a}) \times \|\mathbb{T}_{\varphi,Ch_2}\|(\vec{a})$$

if such sets exist, and these sets ($\|\mathbb{T}_{\varphi,Ch_i}\|(\vec{a})$) are undefined otherwise.

Sequential decomposition. If we have

$$Ch' = Ch1_{\vec{y}_1:\vec{Y}_1(\vec{x}_1)}|Ch2_{\vec{y}_2:\vec{Y}_2(\vec{x}_2)}$$

then we put

$$\|\mathbb{T}_{\varphi,Ch_1}\|(\vec{a}) = \{\vec{b} \in \|Bv(Ch_1)\|(\vec{a}) :$$

$$\{\vec{c} \in \|Bv(Ch_2)\|(\vec{a},\vec{b}) : \langle \vec{b},\vec{c}\rangle \in \|\mathbb{T}_{\varphi,Ch'}\|(\vec{a})\}$$

$$\in \|Ch_2\|(\vec{a},\vec{b})\}$$

For $\vec{b} \in \|Bv(Ch_1)\|$ we put

$$\|\mathbb{T}_{\varphi,Ch_2}\|(\vec{a},\vec{b}) = \{\vec{c} \in \|Bv(Ch_2)\|(\vec{a},\vec{b}) :$$

$$\langle \vec{b},\vec{c}\rangle \in \|\mathbb{T}_{\varphi,Ch'}\|(\vec{a})\}$$

Step 2. (Building dependent types from fibers.)

If Φ is a pack in Ch^*, $\vec{a} \in \|Env_\varphi(\Phi)\|$ then we put

$$\|\mathbb{T}_{\varphi,\Phi}\| = \bigcup\{\{\vec{a}\} \times \|\mathbb{T}_{\phi,\Phi}\|(\vec{a}) : \vec{a} \in \|Env_\varphi(\Phi)\|,$$

$$\forall_{\Phi' <_{Ch^*}\Phi},\ (\vec{a}\lceil \mathbf{env}_\varphi(\Phi')) \in \|\mathbb{T}_{\varphi,\Phi'}\|\}$$

It remains to define the projections between dependent types. If $\Phi' <_\varphi \Phi$ we define

$$\pi_{\mathbb{T}_{\varphi,\Phi},t_{\varphi,\Phi'}} : \|\mathbb{T}_{\varphi,\Phi}\| \longrightarrow \|\mathbb{T}_{\varphi,\Phi'}\|$$

so that $\vec{a} \mapsto \vec{a}\lceil(\mathbf{env}_\varphi(\Phi') \cup \mathbf{bv}\Phi')$.

6 Conclusion

It was our intention in this paper to show that adopting a typed approach to generalized quantification allows a uniform treatment of a wide array of anaphoric data involving natural language quantification.

Acknowledgments

The work of Justyna Grudzińska was funded by the National Science Center on the basis of decision DEC-2012/07/B/HS1/00301. The authors would like to thank the anonymous reviewers for valuable comments on an earlier version of this paper.

References

Barwise, Jon and Robin Cooper. 1981. Generalized Quantifiers and Natural Language. *Linguistics and Philosophy* 4: 159-219.

Bellert, Irena and Marek Zawadowski. 1989. Formalization of the feature system in terms of pre-orders. In Irena Bellert *Feature System for Quantification Structures in Natural Language*. Foris Dordrecht. 155-172.

Dekker, Paul. 1994. Predicate logic with anaphora. In Lynn Santelmann and Mandy Harvey (eds.), *Proceedings SALT IX*. Ithaca, NY: DMLL Publications, Cornell University. 79-95.

Dekker, Paul. 2008. A multi-dimensional treatment of quantification in extraordinary English. *Linguistics and Philosophy* 31: 101-127.

Elworthy, David A. H. 1995. A theory of anaphoric information. *Linguistics and Philosophy* 18: 297-332.

Elbourne, Paul D. 2005. *Situations and Individuals*. Cambridge, MA: MIT Press.

Evans, Gareth 1977. Pronouns, Quantifiers, and Relative Clauses (I). *Canadian Journal of Philosophy* 7: 467-536.

Heim, Irene. 1990. E-type pronouns and donkey anaphora. *Linguistics and Philosophy* 13: 137-78.

Groenendijk, Jeroen and Martin Stokhof. 1991. Dynamic Predicate Logic. *Linguistics and Philosophy* 14: 39-100.

Kamp, Hans and Uwe Reyle. 1993. *From Discourse to Logic*. Kluwer Academic Publishers, Dordrecht.

Krifka, Manfred. 1996. Parametrized sum individuals for plural reference and partitive quantification. *Linguistics and Philosophy* 19: 555-598.

Lindström, Per. 1966. First-order predicate logic with generalized quantifiers. *Theoria* 32: 186-95.

Martin-Löf, Per. 1972. An intuitionstic theory of types. Technical Report, University of Stockholm.

Mostowski, Andrzej. 1957. On a generalization of quantifiers. *Fundamenta Mathematicae* 44: 12-36.

Nouwen, Rick. 2003. *Plural pronominal anaphora in context: dynamic aspects of quantification*. Ph.D. thesis, UiL-OTS, Utrecht, LOT dissertation series, No. 84.

Ranta, Aarne. 1994. *Type-Theoretical Grammar*. Oxford University Press, Oxford.

Van den Berg, Martin H. 1996. *The Internal Structure of Discourse*. Ph.D. thesis, Universiteit van Amsterdam, Amsterdam.

Monads as a Solution for Generalized Opacity

Gianluca Giorgolo
University of Oxford

Ash Asudeh
University of Oxford and Carleton University

{gianluca.giorgolo,ash.asudeh}@ling-phil.ox.ac.uk

Abstract

In this paper we discuss a conservative extension of the simply-typed lambda calculus in order to model a class of expressions that generalize the notion of opaque contexts. Our extension is based on previous work in the semantics of programming languages aimed at providing a mathematical characterization of computations that produce some kind of *side effect* (Moggi, 1989), and is based on the notion of *monads*, a construction in category theory that, intuitively, maps a collection of "simple" values and "simple" functions into a more complex value space, in a canonical way. The main advantages of our approach with respect to traditional analyses of opacity are the fact that we are able to explain in a uniform way a set of different but related phenomena, and that we do so in a principled way that has been shown to also explain other linguistic phenomena (Shan, 2001).

1 Introduction

Opaque contexts have been an active area of research in natural language semantics since Frege's original discussion of the puzzle (Frege, 1892). A sentence like (1) has a non-contradictory interpretation despite the fact that the two referring expressions *Hesperus* and *Phosphorus* refer to the same entity, the planet we know as Venus.

(1) Reza doesn't believe Hesperus is Phosphorus.

The fact that a sentence like (1) includes the modal *believe* has influenced much of the analyses proposed in the literature, and has linked the phenomenon with the notion of modality. In this paper we challenge this view and try to position data like (1) inside a larger framework that also includes other types of expressions.

We decompose examples like (1) along two dimensions: the presence or absence of a modal expression, and the way in which we multiply refer to the same individual. In the case of (1), we have a modal and we use two different co-referring expressions. Examples (2)-(4) complete the landscape of possible combinations:

(2) Dr. Octopus punched Spider-Man but he didn't punch Spider-Man.

(3) Mary Jane loves Peter Parker but she doesn't love Spider-Man.

(4) Reza doesn't believe Jesus is Jesus.

(2) is clearly a contradictory statement, as we predicate of Dr. Octopus that he has the property of having punched Spider-Man and its negation. Notice that in this example there is no modal and the exact same expression is used twice to refer to the object individual. In the case of (3) we still have no modal and we use two different but co-referring expressions to refer to the same individual. However in this case the statement has a non-contradictory reading. Similarly (4) has a non-contradictory reading, which states that, according to the speaker, Reza doesn't believe that the entity he (Reza) calls Jesus is the entity that the speaker calls Jesus (e.g., is not the same individual or does not have the same properties). This case is symmetrical to (3), as here we have a modal expression but the same expression is used twice to refer to the same individual.

If the relevant reading of (4) is difficult to get, consider an alternative kind of scenario, as in (5), in which the subject of the sentence, Kim, suffers from Capgras Syndrome[1] and thinks that Sandy is an impostor. The speaker says:

[1] From Wikipedia: "[Capgras syndrome] is a disorder in which a person holds a delusion that a friend, spouse, par-

(5) Kim doesn't believe Sandy is Sandy

Given the definition of Capgras Syndrome (in fn. 1), there is a clear non-contradictory reading available here, in which the speaker is stating that Kim does not believe that the entity in question, that the speaker and (other non-Capgras-sufferers) would call Sandy, is the entity that she associate with the name Sandy.

We propose an analysis of the non-contradictory cases based on the intuition that the apparently co-referential expressions are in fact interpreted using different interpretation functions, which correspond to different perspectives that are pitted against each other in the sentences. Furthermore, we propose that modal expressions are not the only ones capable of introducing a shift of perspective, but also that verbs that involve some kind of mental attitude of the subject towards the object have the same effect.

Notice that this last observation distinguishes our approach from one where a sentence like (3) is interpreted as simply saying that Mary Jane loves only one *guise* of the entity that corresponds to Peter Parker but not another one. The problem with this interpretation is that if it is indeed the case that different co-referring expressions simply pick out different guises of the same individual, then a sentence like (6) should have a non-contradictory reading, while this seems not to be the case.

(6) Dr. Octopus killed Spider-Man but he didn't kill Peter Parker.

While a guise-based interpretation is compatible with our analysis[2], it is also necessary to correctly model the different behaviour of verbs like *love* with respect to others like *punch* or *kill*. In fact, we need to model the difference between, for example, *kill* and *murder*, since *murder* does involve a mental attitude of intention and the corresponding sentence to (6) is not necessarily contradictory:

(7) Dr. Octopus murdered Spider-Man but he didn't murder Peter Parker.

The implementation of our analysis is based on monads. Monads are a construction in category theory that defines a canonical way to map a set of objects and functions that we may consider as simple into a more complex object and function space. They have been successfully used in the semantics of programming languages to characterise computations that are not "pure". By pure we mean code objects that are totally referentially transparent (i.e. do not depend on external factors and return the same results given the same input independently of their execution context), and also that do not have effects on the "real world". In contrast, monads are used to model computations that for example read from or write to a file, that depend on some random process or whose return value is non-deterministic.

In our case we will use the monad that describe values that are made dependent on some external factor, commonly known in the functional programming literature as the Reader monad.[3] We will represent linguistic expressions that can be assigned potentially different interpretations as functions from interpretation indices to values. Effectively we will construct a different type of lexicon that does not represent only the linguistic knowledge of a single speaker but also her (possibly partial) knowledge of the language of other speakers. So, for example, we will claim that (4) can be assigned a non-contradictory reading because the speaker's lexicon also includes the information regarding Reza's interpretation of the name *Jesus* and therefore makes it possible for the speaker to use the same expression, in combination with a verb such as *believe*, to actually refer to two different entities. In one case we will argue that the name *Jesus* is interpreted using the speaker's interpretation while in the other case it is Reza's interpretation that is used.

Notice that we can apply our analysis to any natural language expression that may have different interpretations. This means that, for example, we can extend our analysis, which is limited to referring expressions here for space reasons, to other cases, such as the standard examples involving ideally synonymous predicates like *groundhog* and *woodchuck* (see, e.g., Fox and Lappin (2005)).

The paper is organised as follows: in section 2 we discuss the technical details of our analysis; in section 3 we discuss our analyses of the motivating examples; section 4 compares our approach with a standard approach to opacity; we conclude in section 5.

ent, or other close family member has been replaced by an identical-looking impostor."

[2]Indeed, one way to understand guises is as different ways in which we interpret a referring term (Heim, 1998).

[3]Shan (2001) was the first to sketch the idea of using the Reader monad to model intensional phenomena.

2 Monads and interpretation functions

To avoid introducing the complexities of the categorical formalism, we introduce monads as they are usually encountered in the computer science literature. A monad is defined as a triple $\langle \Diamond, \eta, \star \rangle$. $\Diamond$ is what we call a functor, in our case a mapping between types and functions. We call the component of $\Diamond$ that maps between types $\Diamond_1$, while the one that maps between functions $\Diamond_2$. In our case $\Diamond_1$ will map each type to a new type that corresponds to the original type with an added interpretation index parameter. Formally, if i is the type of interpretation indices, then $\Diamond_1$ maps any type τ to $i \rightarrow \tau$. In terms of functions, $\Diamond_2$ maps any function $f : \tau \rightarrow \delta$ to a function $f' : (i \rightarrow \tau) \rightarrow i \rightarrow \delta$. $\Diamond_2$ corresponds to function composition:

$$\Diamond_2(f) = \lambda g.\lambda i.f(g(i)) \tag{8}$$

In what follows the component $\Diamond_2$ will not be used so we will use $\Diamond$ as an abbreviation for $\Diamond_1$. This means that we will write $\Diamond\tau$ for the type $i \rightarrow \tau$.

η (pronounced "unit") is a polymorphic function that maps inhabitants of a type τ to inhabitants of its image under $\Diamond$, formally $\eta : \forall\tau.\tau \rightarrow \Diamond\tau$. Using the computational metaphor, η should embed a value in a computation that returns that value without any side-effect. In our case η should simply add a vacuous parameter to the value:

$$\eta(x) = \lambda i.x \tag{9}$$

$\star$ (pronounced "bind") is a polymorphic function of type $\forall\tau.\forall\delta.\Diamond\tau \rightarrow (\tau \rightarrow \Diamond\delta) \rightarrow \Diamond\delta$, and acts as a sort of enhanced functional application.[4] Again using the computational metaphor, $\star$ takes care of combining the side effects of the argument and the function and returns the resulting computation. In the case of the monad we are interested in, $\star$ is defined as in (10).

$$a \star f = \lambda i.f(a(i))(i) \tag{10}$$

Another fundamental property of $\star$ is that, by imposing an order of evaluation, it will provide us with an additional scoping mechanism distinct from standard functional application. This will allow us to correctly capture the multiple readings associated with the expressions under consideration.

We thus add two operators, η and $\star$, to the lambda calculus and the reductions work as expected for (9) and (10). These reductions are implicit in our analyses in section 3.

2.1 Compositional logic

For composing the meanings of linguistic resources we use a logical calculus adapted for the linear case[5] from the one introduced by Benton et al. (1998). The calculus is based on a language with two connectives corresponding to our type constructors: $\multimap$, a binary connective, that corresponds to (linear) functional types, and $\Diamond$, a unary connective, that represents monadic types.

The logical calculus is described by the proof rules in figure 1. The rules come annotated with lambda terms that characterise the Curry-Howard correspondence between proofs and meaning terms. Here we assume a Lexical Functional Grammar-like setup (Dalrymple, 2001), where a syntactic and functional grammar component feeds the semantic component with lexical resources already marked with respect to their predicate-argument relationships. Alternatively we could modify the calculus to a categorial setting, by introducing a structural connective, and using directional versions of the implication connective together with purely structural rules to control the compositional process.

We can prove that the *Cut* rule is admissible, therefore the calculus becomes an effective (although inefficient) way of computing the meaning of a linguistic expression.

A key advantage we gain from the monadic approach is that we are not forced to generalize all lexical entries to the "worst case". With the logical setup we have just described we can in fact freely mix monadic and non monadic resources. For example, in our logic we can combine a pure version of a binary function with arguments that are either pure or monadic, as the following are all

[4] We use for $\star$ the argument order as it is normally used in functional programming. We could swap the arguments and make it look more like standard functional application. Also, we write $\star$ in infix notation.

[5] Linearity is a property that has been argued for in the context of natural language semantics by various researchers (Moortgat (2011), Asudeh (2012), among others).

$$\frac{}{x : A \vdash x : A}\ id \qquad \frac{\Gamma \vdash B \quad B, \Delta \vdash C}{\Gamma, \Delta \vdash C}\ Cut$$

$$\frac{\Gamma, x : A \vdash t : B}{\Gamma \vdash \lambda x.t : A \multimap B} \multimap R \qquad \frac{\Delta \vdash t : A \quad \Gamma, x : B \vdash u : C}{\Gamma, \Delta, y : A \multimap B \vdash u[y(t)/x] : C} \multimap L$$

$$\frac{\Gamma \vdash x : A}{\Gamma \vdash \eta(x) : \Diamond A}\ \Diamond R \qquad \frac{\Gamma, x : A \vdash t : \Diamond B}{\Gamma, y : \Diamond A \vdash y \star \lambda x.t : \Diamond B}\ \Diamond L$$

Figure 1: Sequent calculus for a fragment of multiplicative linear logic enriched with a monadic modality, together with a Curry-Howard correspondence between formulae and meaning terms.

provable theorems in this logic.

$$A \multimap B \multimap C, A, B \vdash \Diamond C \quad (11)$$
$$A \multimap B \multimap C, \Diamond A, B \vdash \Diamond C \quad (12)$$
$$A \multimap B \multimap C, A, \Diamond B \vdash \Diamond C \quad (13)$$
$$A \multimap B \multimap C, \Diamond A, \Diamond B \vdash \Diamond C \quad (14)$$

In contrast, the following is not a theorem in the logic:

$$A \multimap B \multimap C, I \multimap A, I \multimap B \nvdash I \multimap C \quad (15)$$

In general, then, if we were to simply lift the type of the lexical resources whose interpretation may be dependent on a specific point of view, we would be forced to lift all linguistic expressions that may combine with them, thus generalizing to the worst case after all.

The monadic machinery also achieves a higher level of compositionality. In principle we could directly encode our monad using the $\rightarrow$ type constructor, with linear implication, $\multimap$, on the logical side. However this alternative encoding wouldn't have the same deductive properties. Compare the pattern of inferences we have for the monadic type, in (11)–(14), with the equivalent one for the simple type:

$$A \multimap B \multimap C, A, B \vdash C \quad (16)$$
$$A \multimap B \multimap C, I \multimap A, B \vdash I \multimap C \quad (17)$$
$$A \multimap B \multimap C, A, I \multimap B \vdash I \multimap C \quad (18)$$
$$A \multimap B \multimap C, I \multimap A, I \multimap B \vdash I \multimap I \multimap C \quad (19)$$

In the case of the simple type, the final formula we derive depends in some non-trivial way on the entire collection of resources on the left-hand side of the sequent. In contrast in the case of the monadic type, the same type can be derived for all configurations. What is important is that we can predict the final formula without having to consider the entire set of resources available. This shows that the compositionality of our monadic approach cannot be equivalently recapitulated in a simple type theory.

3 Examples

The starting point for the analysis of examples (1)-(4) is the lexicon in table 1. The lexicon represents the linguistic knowledge of the speaker, and at the same time her knowledge about other agents' grammars.

Most lexical entries are standard, since we do not need to change the type and denotation of lexical items that are not involved in the phenomena under discussion. So, for instance, logical operators such as *not* and *but* are interpreted in the standard non-monadic way, as is a verb like *punch* or *kill*. Referring expressions that are possibly contentious, in the sense that they can be interpreted differently by the speaker and other agents, instead have the monadic type $\Diamond e$. This is reflected in their denotation by the fact that their value varies according to an interpretation index. We use a special index σ to refer to the speaker's own perspective, and assume that this is the default index used whenever no other index is specifically introduced. For example, in the case of the name Spider-Man, the speaker is aware of his secret identity and therefore interprets it as another name for the individual Peter Parker, while Mary Jane and Dr. Octopus consider Spider-Man a different entity from Peter Parker.

We assume that sentences are interpreted in a model in which all entities are mental entities, i.e. that there is no direct reference to entities in the world, but only to mental representations. Entities are therefore relativized with respect to the agent that mentally represents them, where non-contentious entities are always relativized according to the speaker. This allows us to represent the

WORD	DENOTATION	TYPE
Reza	$\mathbf{r}_\sigma$	e
Kim	$\mathbf{k}_\sigma$	e
Dr. Octopus	$\mathbf{o}_\sigma$	e
Mary Jane	$\mathbf{mj}_\sigma$	e
Peter Parker	$\mathbf{pp}_\sigma$	e
not	$\lambda p.\neg p$	$t \to t$
but	$\lambda p.\lambda q.p \wedge q$	$t \to t \to t$
is	$\lambda x.\lambda y.x = y$	$e \to e \to t$
punch	$\lambda o.\lambda s.\mathbf{punch}(s)(o)$	$e \to e \to t$
believe	$\lambda c.\lambda s.\lambda i.\mathbf{B}(s)(c(\kappa(s)))$	$\Diamond t \to e \to \Diamond t$
love	$\lambda o.\lambda s.\lambda i.\mathbf{love}(s)(o(\kappa(s)))$	$\Diamond e \to e \to \Diamond t$
Hesperus	$\lambda i.\begin{cases}\mathbf{es}_r & \text{if } i = \mathbf{r},\\ \mathbf{v}_\sigma & \text{if } i = \sigma\end{cases}$	$\Diamond e$
Phosphorus	$\lambda i.\begin{cases}\mathbf{ms}_r & \text{if } i = \mathbf{r},\\ \mathbf{v}_\sigma & \text{if } i = \sigma\end{cases}$	$\Diamond e$
Spider-Man	$\lambda i.\begin{cases}\mathbf{sm}_i & \text{if } i = \mathbf{o} \text{ or } i = \mathbf{mj},\\ \mathbf{pp}_\sigma & \text{if } i = \sigma\end{cases}$	$\Diamond e$
Jesus	$\lambda i.\begin{cases}\mathbf{j}_r & \text{if } i = \mathbf{r},\\ \mathbf{j}_\sigma & \text{if } i = \sigma\end{cases}$	$\Diamond e$
Sandy	$\lambda i.\begin{cases}\mathbf{imp}_k & \text{if } i = \mathbf{k},\\ \mathbf{s}_\sigma & \text{if } i = \sigma\end{cases}$	$\Diamond e$

Table 1: Speaker's lexicon

fact that different agents may have distinct equivalencies between entities. For example, Reza in our model does not equate the evening star and the morning star, but the speaker equates them with each other and with Venus. Therefore, the speaker's lexicon in table 1 represents the fact that the speaker's epistemic model includes what the speaker knows about other agents' models, e.g. that Reza has a distinct denotation (from the speaker) for Hesperus, that Mary Jane has a distinct representation for Spider-Man, that Kim has a distinct representation for Sandy, etc.

The other special lexical entries in our lexicon are those for verbs like *believe* and *love*. The two entries are similar in the sense that they both take an already monadic resource and actively supply a specific interpretation index that corresponds to the subject of the verbs. The function κ maps each entity to the corresponding interpretation index, i.e. $\kappa : e \to i$. For example, in the lexical entries for *believe* and *love*, κ maps the subject to the interpretation index of the subject. Thus, the entry for *believe* uses the subject's point of view as the perspective used to evaluate its entire complement, while *love* changes the interpretation of its object relative to the perspective of its subject. However we will see that the interaction of these lexical entries and the evaluation order imposed by $\star$ will allow us to let the complement of a verb like *believe* and the object of a verb like *love* escape the specific effect of forcing the subject point of view, and instead we will be able to derive readings in which the arguments of the verb are interpreted using the speaker's point of view.

Figure 2 reports the four non-equivalent readings that we derive in our system for example (1), repeated here as (20).[6]

(20) Reza doesn't believe that Hesperus is Phosphorus.

Reading (21) assigns to both Hesperus and Phosphorus the subject interpretation and results, after contextualising the sentence by applying it to the standard σ interpretation index, in the truth conditions in (25), i.e. that Reza does not believe that the evening star is the morning star. This

[6] The logic generates six different readings but the monad we are using here has a commutative behaviour, so four of these readings are pairwise equivalent.

$$[\![\text{believe}]\!] \, ([\![\text{Hesperus}]\!] \star \lambda x. \, [\![\text{Phosphorus}]\!] \star \lambda y.\eta([\![\text{is}]\!] \, (x)(y)))([\![\text{Reza}]\!]) \star \lambda z.\eta([\![\text{not}]\!] \, (z)) \tag{21}$$

$$[\![\text{Hesperus}]\!] \star \lambda x. \, [\![\text{believe}]\!] \, ([\![\text{Phosphorus}]\!] \star \lambda y.\eta([\![\text{is}]\!] \, (x)(y)))([\![\text{Reza}]\!]) \star \lambda z.\eta([\![\text{not}]\!] \, (z)) \tag{22}$$

$$[\![\text{Phosphorus}]\!] \star \lambda x. \, [\![\text{believe}]\!] \, ([\![\text{Hesperus}]\!] \star \lambda y.\eta([\![\text{is}]\!] \, (y)(x)))([\![\text{Reza}]\!]) \star \lambda z.\eta([\![\text{not}]\!] \, (z)) \tag{23}$$

$$[\![\text{Hesperus}]\!] \star \lambda x. \, [\![\text{Phosphorus}]\!] \star \lambda y. \, [\![\text{believe}]\!] \, (\eta([\![\text{is}]\!] \, (x)(y)))([\![\text{Reza}]\!]) \star \lambda z.\eta([\![\text{not}]\!] \, (z)) \tag{24}$$

Figure 2: Non-equivalent readings for *Reza doesn't believe Hesperus is Phosphorus.*

reading would not be contradictory in an epistemic model (such as Reza's model) where the evening star and the morning star are not the same entity.

$$\neg \mathbf{B}(\mathbf{r})(\mathbf{es}_r = \mathbf{ms}_r) \tag{25}$$

In the case of (22) and (23) we get a similar effect although here we mix the epistemic models, and one of the referring expressions is interpreted under the speaker perspective while the other is again interpreted under Reza's perspective. For these two readings we obtain respectively the truth conditions in (26) and (27).

$$\neg \mathbf{B}(\mathbf{r})(\mathbf{v}_\sigma = \mathbf{ms}_r) \tag{26}$$

$$\neg \mathbf{B}(\mathbf{r})(\mathbf{v}_\sigma = \mathbf{es}_r) \tag{27}$$

Finally for (24) we get the contradictory reading that Reza does not believe that Venus is Venus, as both referring expressions are evaluated using the speaker's interpretation index.

$$\neg \mathbf{B}(\mathbf{r})(\mathbf{v}_\sigma = \mathbf{v}_\sigma) \tag{28}$$

The different contexts for the interpretation of referring expressions are completely determined by the order in which we evaluate monadic resources. This means that, just by looking at the linear order of the lambda order, we can check whether a referring expression is evaluated inside the scope of a perspective changing operator such as *believe*, or if it is interpreted using the standard interpretation.

If we consider a case like sentence (2), we ought to get only a contradictory reading as the statement is intuitively contradictory. Our analysis produces a single reading that indeed corresponds to a contradictory interpretation:

$$\begin{aligned}&[\![\text{Spider-Man}]\!] \star \lambda x. \, [\![\text{Spider-Man}]\!] \star \\ &\lambda y.\eta([\![\text{but}]\!] \, ([\![\text{punch}]\!] \, ([\![\text{Dr. Octopus}]\!])(x)) \\ &([\![\text{not}]\!] \, ([\![\text{punch}]\!] \, ([\![\text{Dr. Octopus}]\!])(y))))\end{aligned} \tag{29}$$

The verb *punch* is not a verb that can change the interpretation perspective and therefore the potentially controversial name Spider-Man is interpreted in both instances using the speaker's interpretation index. The result are unsatisfiable truth conditions, as expected:

$$\mathbf{punch}(\mathbf{o}_\sigma)(\mathbf{pp}_\sigma) \wedge \neg \mathbf{punch}(\mathbf{o}_\sigma)(\mathbf{pp}_\sigma) \tag{30}$$

In contrast a verb like *love* is defined in our lexicon as possibly changing the interpretation perspective of its object to that of its subject. Therefore in the case of a sentence like (3), we expect one reading where the potentially contentious name Spider-Man is interpreted according to the subject of *love*, Mary Jane. This is in fact the result we obtain. Figure 3 reports the two readings that our framework generates for (3).

Reading (31), corresponds to the non contradictory interpretation of sentence (3), where Spider-Man is interpreted according to Mary Jane's perspective and therefore is assigned an entity different from Peter Parker:

$$\mathbf{love}(\mathbf{mj}_\sigma)(\mathbf{pp}_\sigma) \wedge \neg \mathbf{love}(\mathbf{mj}_\sigma)(\mathbf{sm}_{mj}) \tag{33}$$

Reading (32) instead generates unsatisfiable truth conditions, as Spider-Man is identified with Peter Parker according to the speaker's interpretation:

$$\mathbf{love}(\mathbf{mj}_\sigma)(\mathbf{pp}_\sigma) \wedge \neg \mathbf{love}(\mathbf{mj}_\sigma)(\mathbf{pp}_\sigma) \tag{34}$$

Our last example, (4), repeated here as (35), is particularly interesting as we are not aware of previous work that discusses this type of sentence. The non-contradictory reading that this sentence has seems to be connected specifically to two different interpretations of the same name, *Jesus*, both under the syntactic scope of the modal *believe*.

(35) Reza doesn't believe Jesus is Jesus.

$$[\![\text{love}]\!]\,(\eta([\![\text{Peter Parker}]\!]))([\![\text{Mary Jane}]\!]) \star \lambda p.\,[\![\text{love}]\!]\,([\![\text{Spider-Man}]\!])([\![\text{Mary Jane}]\!]) \star$$
$$\lambda q.\eta([\![\text{but}]\!]\,(p)([\![\text{not}]\!]\,(q))) \tag{31}$$
$$[\![\text{love}]\!]\,(\eta([\![\text{Peter Parker}]\!]))([\![\text{Mary Jane}]\!]) \star \lambda p.\,[\![\text{Spider-Man}]\!] \star \lambda x.\,[\![\text{love}]\!]\,(\eta(x))([\![\text{Mary Jane}]\!]) \star$$
$$\lambda q.\eta([\![\text{but}]\!]\,(p)([\![\text{not}]\!]\,(q))) \tag{32}$$

Figure 3: Non-equivalent readings for *Mary Jane loves Peter Parker but she doesn't love Spider-Man.*

$$[\![\text{believe}]\!]\,([\![\text{Jesus}]\!] \star \lambda x.\,[\![\text{Jesus}]\!] \star \lambda y.\eta([\![\text{is}]\!]\,(x)(y)))([\![\text{Reza}]\!]) \star \lambda z.\eta([\![\text{not}]\!]\,(z)) \tag{36}$$
$$[\![\text{Jesus}]\!] \star \lambda x.\,[\![\text{Jesus}]\!] \star \lambda y.\,[\![\text{believe}]\!]\,(\eta([\![\text{is}]\!]\,(x)(y)))([\![\text{Reza}]\!]) \star \lambda z.\eta([\![\text{not}]\!]\,(z)) \tag{37}$$
$$[\![\text{Jesus}]\!] \star \lambda x.\,[\![\text{believe}]\!]\,([\![\text{Jesus}]\!] \star \lambda y.\eta([\![\text{is}]\!]\,(x)(y)))([\![\text{Reza}]\!]) \star \lambda z.\eta([\![\text{not}]\!]\,(z)) \tag{38}$$

Figure 4: Non-equivalent readings for *Reza doesn't believe Jesus is Jesus.*

Our system generates three non-equivalent readings, reported here in figure 4.[7]

Reading (36) and (37) corresponds to two contradictory readings of the sentence: in the first case both instances of the name Jesus are interpreted from the subject perspective and therefore attribute to Reza the non-belief in a tautology, similarly in the second case, even though in this case the two names are interpreted from the perspective of the speaker. In contrast the reading in (38) corresponds to the interpretation that assigns two different referents to the two instances of the name Jesus, producing the truth conditions in (39) which are satisfiable in a suitable model.

$$\neg\mathbf{B}(\mathbf{r})(\mathbf{j}_\sigma = \mathbf{j}_r) \tag{39}$$

The analysis of the Capgras example (5), repeated in (40), is equivalent; the non-contradictory reading is shown in (41).

(40) Kim doesn't believe Sandy is Sandy.

$$\neg\mathbf{B}(\mathbf{k})(\mathbf{s}_\sigma = \mathbf{imp}_k) \tag{41}$$

We use $\mathbf{imp}_k$ as the speaker's representation of the "impostor" that Kim thinks has taken the place of Sandy.

More generally, there are again three non-equivalent readings, including the one above, which are just those in figure 4, with $[\![\text{Jesus}]\!]$ replaced by $[\![\text{Sandy}]\!]$ and $[\![\text{Reza}]\!]$ replaced by $[\![\text{Kim}]\!]$.

[7] Again, there are six readings that correspond to different proofs, but given the commutative behaviour of the Reader monad, the fact that equality is commutative, and the fact that we have in this case two identical lexical items, only three of them are non-equivalent readings.

4 Comparison with traditional approaches

In this section we try to sketch how a traditional approach to opaque contexts, such as one based on a *de dicto/de re* ambiguity with respect to a modal operator, would fare in the analysis of (4), our most challenging example.

To try to explain the two readings in the context of a standard possible worlds semantics, we could take (4) to be ambiguous with respect to a *de dicto/de re* reading. In the case of the *de dicto* reading (which corresponds to the non-satisfiable reading) the two names are evaluated under the scope of the doxastic operator *believe*, i.e. they both refer to the same entity that is assigned to the name Jesus in each accessible world. Clearly this is always the case, and so (4) is not satisfiable. In the case of the *de re* reading, we assume that the two names are evaluated at different worlds that assign different referents to the two names. One of these two worlds will be the actual world and the other one of the accesible worlds. The reading is satisfiable if the doxastic modality links the actual world with one in which the name Jesus refers to a different entity. Notice that for this analysis to work we need to make two assumptions: 1. that names behave as quantifiers with the property of escaping modal contexts, 2. that names can be assigned different referents in different worlds, i.e. we have to abandon the standard notion that names are rigid designators (Kripke, 1972). In contrast, in our approach we do not need to abandon the idea of rigid designation for names (within each agent's model).

However, such an approach would present a number of rather serious problems. The first is connected with the assumption that names are scopeless. This is a common hypothesis in natural language semantics and indeed if we model names as generalized quantifiers they can be proven to be scopeless (Zimmermann, 1993). But this is problematic for our example. In fact we would predict that both instances of the name *Jesus* escape the scope of *believe*. The resulting reading would bind the quantified individual to the interpretation of *Jesus* in the actual world. In this way we only capture the non-satisfiable reading. To save the scopal approach we would need to assume that names in fact are sometimes interpreted in the scope of modal operators.

One way to do this would be to set up our semantic derivations so that they allow different scopal relations between quantifiers and other operators. The problem with this solution is that for sentences like (4) we generate twelve different derivations, some of which do not correspond to valid readings of the sentence.

Even assuming that we find a satisfactory solution for these problems, the scopal approach cannot really capture the intuitions behind opacity in all contexts. Consider again (4) and assume that there are two views about Jesus: Jesus as a divine being and Jesus as a human being. Assume that Jesus is a human being in the actual world and that Reza is an atheist, then the only possible reading is the non-satisfiable one, as the referent for Jesus will be the same in the actual world and all accessible Reza-belief-worlds. The problem is that the scopal approach assumes a single modal model, while in this case it seems that there are two doxastic models, Reza's model and the speaker's model, under discussion. In contrast, in our approach the relevant part of Reza's model is embedded inside the speaker's model and interpretation indices indicate which interpretation belongs to Reza and which to the speaker.

Finally an account of modality in terms of scopal properties is necessarily limited to cases in which modal operators are present. While this may be a valid position in the case of typical intensional verbs like *seek* or *want*, it would not be clear how we could extend this approach to cases like 3, as the verb *love* has no clear modal connotation. Thus, the scopal approach would not be sufficiently general.

5 Conclusion

We started by discussing a diverse collection of expressions that share the common property of showing nontrivial referential behaviours. We have proposed a common analysis of all these expressions in terms of a combination of different interpretation contexts. We have claimed that the switch to a different interpretation context is triggered by specific lexical items, such as modal verbs but also verbs that express some kind of mental attitude of the subject of the verb towards its object. The context switch is not obligatory, as witnessed by the multiple readings that the sentences discussed seem to have. We implemented our analysis using monads. The main idea of our formal implementation is that referring expressions that have a potential dependency from an interpretation context can be implemented as functions from interpretation indices to fully interpreted values. Similarly, the linguistic triggers for context switch are implemented in the lexicon as functions that can modify the interpretation context of their arguments. Monads allow us to freely combine these "lifted" meanings with standard ones, avoiding in this way to generalize our lexicon to the worst case. We have also seen how more traditional approaches, while capable of dealing with some of the examples we discuss, are not capable of providing a generalised explanation of the observed phenomena.

Acknowledgements

The authors would like to thank our anonymous reviewers for their comments. This research is supported by a Marie Curie Intra-European Fellowship from the Europoean Commision under contract number 327811 (Giorgolo) and an Early Researcher Award from the Ontario Ministry of Research and Innovation and NSERC Discovery Grant #371969 (Asudeh).

References

Ash Asudeh. 2012. *The Logic of Pronominal Resumption*. Oxford Studies in Theoretical Linguistics. Oxford University Press, New York.

Nick Benton, G. M. Bierman, and Valeria de Paiva. 1998. Computational types from a logical perspective. *Journal of Functional Programming*, 8(2):177–193.

Mary Dalrymple. 2001. *Lexical Functional Grammar*. Academic Press, San Diego, CA.

Chris Fox and Shalom Lappin. 2005. *Foundations of Intensional Semantics*. Blackwell, Oxford.

Gottlob Frege. 1892. Über Sinn und Bedeutung. *Zeitschrift für Philosophie und philosophische Kritik*, 100:25–50.

Gottlob Frege. 1952. On sense and reference. In Peter T. Geach and Max Black, editors, *Translations from the Philosophical Writings of Gottlob Frege*, pages 56–78. Blackwell, Oxford. Translation of Frege (1892).

Irene Heim. 1998. Anaphora and semantic interpretation: A reinterpretation of Reinhart's approach. In Uli Sauerland and Orin Percus, editors, *The Interpretive Tract*, volume 25 of *MIT Working Papers in Linguistics*, pages 205–246. MITWPL, Cambridge, MA.

Saul Kripke. 1972. Naming and necessity. In Donald Davidson and Gilbert Harman, editors, *Semantics of Natural Language*, pages 253–355. Reidel.

Eugenio Moggi. 1989. Computational lambda-calculus and monads. In *LICS*, pages 14–23. IEEE Computer Society.

Michael Moortgat. 2011. Categorial type logics. In Johan van Benthem and Alice ter Meulen, editors, *Handbook of Logic and Language*, pages 95–179. Elsevier, second edition.

Chung-chieh Shan. 2001. Monads for natural language semantics. In Kristina Striegnitz, editor, *Proceedings of the ESSLLI-2001 Student Session*, pages 285–298. 13th European Summer School in Logic, Language and Information.

Thomas Ede Zimmermann. 1993. Scopeless quantifiers and operators. *Journal of Philosophical Logic*, 22(5):545–561, October.

The Phenogrammar of Coordination

Chris Worth
Department of Linguistics
The Ohio State University
worth@ling.osu.edu

Abstract

Linear Categorial Grammar (LinCG) is a sign-based, Curryesque, relational, logical categorial grammar (CG) whose central architecture is based on linear logic. Curryesque grammars separate the abstract combinatorics (tectogrammar) of linguistic expressions from their concrete, audible representations (phenogrammar). Most of these grammars encode linear order in string-based lambda terms, in which there is no obvious way to distinguish right from left. Without some notion of directionality, grammars are unable to differentiate, say, subject and object for purposes of building functorial coordinate structures. We introduce the notion of a phenominator as a way to encode the term structure of a functor separately from its "string support". This technology is then employed to analyze a range of coordination phenomena typically left unaddressed by Linear Logic-based Curryesque frameworks.

1 Overview

Flexibility to the notion of constituency in conjunction with introduction (and composition) rules has allowed categorial grammars to successfully address an entire host of coordination phenomena in a transparent and compositional manner. While "Curryesque" CGs as a rule do not suffer from some of the other difficulties that plague Lambek CGs, many are notably deficient in one area: coordination. Lest we throw the baby out with the bathwater, this is an issue that needs to be addressed. We take the following to be an exemplary subset of the relevant data, and adopt a fragment methodology to show how it may be analyzed.

(1) Tyrion and Joffrey drank.

(2) Joffrey whined and sniveled.

(3) Tyrion slapped and Tywin chastised Joffrey.

The first example is a straightforward instance of noun phrase coordination. The second and third are both instances of what has become known in the categorial grammar literature as "functor coordination", that is, the coordination of linguistic material that is in some way incomplete. The third is particularly noteworthy as being an example of a "right node raising" construction, whereby the argument *Joffrey* serves as the object to both of the higher NP-Verb complexes. We will show that all three examples can be given an uncomplicated account in the Curryesque framework of **Linear Categorial Grammar** (LinCG), and that (2) and (3) have more in common than not.

Section 1 provides an overview of the data and and central issues surrounding an analysis of coordination in Curryesque grammars. Section 2 introduces the reader to the framework of LinCG, and presents the technical innovations at the heart of this paper. Section 3 gives lexical entries and derivations for the examples in section 1, and section 4 discusses our results and suggests some directions for research in the near future, with references following.

1.1 Curryesque grammars and Linear Categorial Grammar

We take as our starting point the **Curryesque** (after Curry (1961)) tradition of categorial grammars, making particular reference to those originating with Oehrle (1994) and continuing with Abstract Categorial Grammar (ACG) of de Groote (2001), Muskens (2010)'s Lambda Grammar (λG), Kubota and Levine's Hybrid Type-Logical Categorial Grammar (Kubota and Levine, 2012) and to a lesser extent the Grammatical Framework of Ranta (2004), and others. These dialects of categorial grammar make a distinction between **Tectogrammar**, or "abstract syntax", and **Phenogrammar**, or "concrete syntax". Tectogrammar is primarily concerned with the structural properties of grammar, among them co-occurrence, case, agreement, tense, and so forth. Phenogrammar is concerned with computing a pre-phonological representation of what will eventually be produced by the speaker, and encompasses word order, morphology, prosody, and the like.

Linear Categorial Grammar (LinCG) is a sign-based, Curryesque, relational, logical categorial grammar whose central architecture is based on linear logic. Abbreviatory overlap has been a regrettably persistent problem, and LinCG is the same in essence as the framework varyingly called Linear Grammar (LG) and Pheno-Tecto-Differentiated Categorial Grammar (PTDCG), and developed in Smith (2010), Mihalicek (2012), Martin (2013), Pollard and Smith (2012), and Pollard (2013). In LinCG, the syntax-phonology and syntax-semantics interfaces amount to noting that the logics for the phenogrammar, the tectogrammar, and the semantics operate in parallel. This stands in contrast to 'syntactocentric' theories of grammar, where syntax is taken to be the fundamental domain within which expressions combine, and then phonology and semantics are 'read off' of the syntactic representation. LinCG is conceptually different in that it has relational, rather than functional, interfaces between the three components of the grammar. Since we do not interpret syntactic types into phenogrammatical or semantic types, this allows us a great deal of freedom within each logic, although in practice we maintain a fairly tight connection between all three components. Grammar rules take the form of derivational rules which generate triples called **signs**, and they bind together the three logics so that they operate concurrently. While the invocation of a grammar rule might simply be, say, point-wise application, the ramifications for the three systems can in principle be different; one can imagine expressions which exhibit type asymmetry in various ways.

By way of example, one might think of 'focus' as an operation which has reflexes in all three aspects of the grammar: it applies pitch accents to the target string(s) in the phenogrammar (the difference between accented and unaccented words being reflected in the phenotype), it creates 'lowering' operators in the tectogrammar (that is, expressions which scope within a continuation), and it 'focuses' a particular meaningful unit in the semantics. A focused expression might share its tectotype $((\mathrm{NP} \multimap \mathrm{S}) \multimap \mathrm{S})$ with, say, a quantified noun phrase, but the two could have different phenotypes, reflecting the accentuation or lack thereof by placing the resulting expression in the domain of prosodic boundary phenomena or not. Nevertheless, the system is constrained by the fact that the tectogrammar is based on linear logic, so if we take some care when writing grammar rules, we should still find resource sensitivity to be at the heart of the framework.

1.2 Why coordination is difficult for Curryesque grammars

Most Curryesque CGs encode linear order in lambda terms, and there is no obvious way to distinguish 'right' from 'left' by examining the types (be they linear or intuitionistic).[1] This is not a problem when we are coordinating strings directly, as de Groote and Maarek (2007) show, but an analysis of the more difficult case of functor coordination remains elusive.[2] Without some notion of directionality, grammars are unable to distinguish between, say, subject and object. This would seem to predict, for example, that $\lambda s.\ s \cdot \textsc{slapped} \cdot \textsc{joffrey}$ and $\lambda s.\ \textsc{tyrion} \cdot \textsc{slapped} \cdot s$ would have the same syntactic category ($\mathrm{NP} \multimap \mathrm{S}$ in the tectogrammar, and $\mathrm{St} \to \mathrm{St}$ in the phenogrammar), and would thus be compatible under coordination, but this is generally not the case. What we need is a way to examine the structure of a lambda term independently of the specific string constants that comprise it. To put it another way, in order to coordinate functors, we need to be able to distinguish between what Oehrle (1995) calls their **string support**, that is, the string constants which make up the body of a particular functional term, and the linearization structure such functors impose on their arguments.

2 Linear Categorial Grammar (LinCG)

Curryesque grammars separate the notion of linear order from the abstract combinatorics of linguis-

[1] A noteworthy exception is Ranta's Grammatical Framework (GF), explored in, e.g. Ranta (2004) and Ranta (2009). GF also makes distinctions between tectogrammar and phenogrammar, though it has a somewhat different conception of each.

[2] A problem explicitly recognized by Kubota (2010) in section 3.2.1.

tic expressions, and as such base their tectogrammars around logics other than bilinear logic; the Grammatical Framework is based on Martin-Löf type theory, and LinCG and its cousins ACG and λG use linear logic. Linear logic is generally described as being "resource-sensitive", owing to the lack of the structural rules of weakening and contraction. Resource sensitivity is an attractive notion, theoretically, since it allows us to describe processes of resource production, consumption, and combination in a manner which is agnostic about precisely how resources are combined. Certain problems which have been historically tricky for Lambek categorial grammars (medial extraction, quantifier scope, etc.) are easily handled by LinCG.

Since a full introduction to the framework is regrettably impossible given current constraints, we refer the interested reader to the references in section 1.1, which contain a more in-depth discussion of the potential richness of the architecture of LinCG. We do not wish to say anything new about the semantics or the tectogrammar of coordination in the current discussion, so we will expend our time fleshing out the phenogrammatical component of the framework, and it is to this topic that we now turn.

2.1 LinCG Phenogrammar

LinCG grammar rules take the form of tripartite inference rules, indicating what operations take place pointwise within each component of the signs in question. There are two main grammar rules, called **application** (App) for combining signs, and **abstraction** (Abs) for creating the potential for combination through hypothetical reasoning. Aside from the lexical entries given as axioms of the theory, it is also possible to obtain typed variables using the rule of **axiom** (Ax), and we make use of this rule in the analysis of right node raising found in section 3.4. While the tectogrammar of LinCG is based on a fragment of linear logic, the phenogrammatical and semantic components are based on higher order logic. Since we are concerned only with the phenogrammatical component here, we have chosen to simplify the exposition by presenting only the phenogrammatical part of the rules of application and abstraction:

$$\frac{}{f : A \vdash f : A}\ \text{Ax}$$

$$\frac{\Gamma \vdash f : A \to B \qquad \Delta \vdash a : A}{\Gamma, \Delta \vdash (f\ a) : B}\ \text{App}$$

$$\frac{\Gamma, x : A \vdash b : B}{\Gamma \vdash \lambda x : A.\ b : A \to B}\ \text{Abs}$$

We additionally stipulate the following familiar axioms governing the conversion and reduction of lambda terms:[3]

$\vdash \lambda x : A.\ b = \lambda y : A.\ [y/x]b$ (α-conversion)
$\vdash (\lambda x.\ b\ a) = [a/x]b$ (β-reduction)

As is common to any number of Curryesque frameworks, we encode the phenogrammatical parts of LinCG signs with typed lambda terms consisting of strings, and functions over strings.[4] We axiomatize our theory of strings in the familiar way:

$\vdash \epsilon : \text{St}$
$\vdash \cdot : \text{St} \to \text{St} \to \text{St}$
$\vdash \forall stu : \text{St}.\ s \cdot (t \cdot u) = (s \cdot t) \cdot u$
$\vdash \forall s : \text{St}.\ \epsilon \cdot s = s = s \cdot \epsilon$

The first axiom asserts that the empty string ϵ is a string. The second axiom asserts that concatenation, written $\cdot$, is a (curried) binary function on strings. The third axiom represents the fact that concatenation is associative, and the fourth, that the empty string is a two-sided identity for concatenation. Because of the associativity of concatenation, we will drop parentheses as a matter of convention.

The phenogrammar of a typical LinCG sign will resemble the following (with one complication to be added shortly):

$$\vdash \lambda s.\ s \cdot \text{SNIVELED} : \text{St} \to \text{St}$$

Since we treat **St** as the only base type, we will generally omit typing judgments in lambda terms when no confusion will result. Furthermore, we use SMALL CAPS to indicate that a particular constant is a string. So, the preceding lexical entry provides us with a function from some string s, to strings, which concatenates the string SNIVELED to the right of s.

2.1.1 Phenominators

The center of our analysis of coordination is the notion of a **phenominator** (short for phenocombinator), a particular variety of typed lambda term. Intuitively, phenominators serve the same purpose for LinCG that bilinear (slash) types do for Lambek categorial grammars. Specifically,

[3]The exact status of the rule of η-conversion with respect to this framework is currently unclear, and since we do not make use of it, we omit its discussion here.

[4]although other structures have been proposed, e.g. the node sets found in Muskens (2001).

they encode the linearization structure of a functor, that is, where arguments may eventually occur with respect to its string support. To put it another way, a phenominator describes the structure a functor "projects", in terms of linear order.

From a technical standpoint, we would like to define a phenominator as a closed monoidal linear lambda term, i.e. a term containing no constants other than concatenation and the empty string. The idea is that phenominators are the terms of the higher order theory of monoids, and they in some ways describe the abstract "shape" of possible string functions. For those accustomed to thinking of "syntax" as being word order, then phenominators can be thought of as a kind of syntactic combinator. In practice, we will make use only of what we call the unary phenominators, the types of which we will refer to using the sort Φ (with φ used by custom as a metavariable over unary phenominators, i.e. terms whose type is in Φ). These are not unary in the strict sense, but they will have as their centerpiece one particular string variable, which will be bound with the highest scope. We will generally abbreviate phenominators by the construction with which they are most commonly associated: **VP** for verb phrases and intransitive verbs, **TV** for transitive verbs, **DTV** for ditransitive verbs, **QNP** for quantified noun phrases, and **RNR** for right node raising constructions. Here are examples of some of the most common phenominators we will make use of and the abbreviations we customarily use for them:

Phenominator	**Abbreviation**
$\lambda s.s$	(omitted)
$\lambda vs.s \cdot v$	VP
$\lambda vst.t \cdot v \cdot s$	TV
$\lambda vstu.u \cdot v \cdot s \cdot t$	DTV
$\lambda vP.(P\ v)$	QNP
$\lambda vs.v \cdot s$	RNR

As indicated previously, the first argument of a phenominator always corresponds to what we refer to (after Oehrle (1995)) as the string support of a particular term. With the first argument dispensed with, we have chosen the argument order of the phenominators out of general concern for what we perceive to be fairly uncontroversial categorial analyses of English grammatical phenomena. That is, transitive verbs take their object arguments first, and then their subject arguments, ditransitives take their first and second object arguments, followed by their subject argument, etc. As long as the arguments in question are immediately adjacent to the string support at each successive application, it is possible to permute them to some extent without losing the general thrust of the analysis. For example, the choice to have transitive verbs take their object arguments first is insignificant.[5] Since strings are implicitly under the image of the identity phenominator $\lambda s.s$, we will consistently omit this subscript.

We will be able to define a function we call `say`, so that it will have the following property:

$$\vdash \forall s : \text{St}.\forall \varphi : \Phi.\texttt{say}\ (\varphi\ s) = s$$

That is, `say` is a left inverse for unary phenominators.

The function `say` is defined recursively via certain objects we call **vacuities**. The idea of a vacuity is that it be in some way an "empty argument" to which a functional term may apply. If we are dealing with functions taking string arguments, it seems obvious that the vacuity on strings should be the empty string ϵ. If we are dealing with second-order functions taking St $\rightarrow$ St arguments, for example, quantified noun phrases like *everyone*, then the vacuity on St $\rightarrow$ St should be the identity function on strings, $\lambda s.s$. Higher vacuities than these become more complicated, and defining all of the higher-order vacuities is not entirely straightforward, as certain types are not guaranteed to have a unique vacuity. Fortunately, we can do it for any higher-function taking as an argument another function under the image of a phenominator – then the vacuity on such a function is just the phenominator applied to the empty string.[6] The central idea is easily understood when one asks what, say, a vacuous transitive verb sounds like. The answer seems to be: by itself, nothing, but it imposes a certain order on its arguments. One practical application of this clause is in analyzing so-called "argument cluster coordination", where this definition will ensure that the argument cluster gets linearized in the correct manner. This analysis is regrettably just outside the scope of the current inquiry, though the notion of the phenomina-

[5]Since we believe it is possible to embed Lambek categorial grammars in LinCG, this fact reflects that the calculus we are dealing with is similar to the **associative** Lambek Calculus.

[6]A reviewer suggests that this concept may be related to the "context passing representation" of Hughes (1995), and the association of a *nil* term with its continuation with respect to contexts is assuredly evocative of the association of the vacuity on a phenominator-indexed type with the continuation of ϵ with respect to a phenominator.

tor can be profitably employed to provide exactly such an analysis by adopting and reinterpreting a categorial account along the lines of the one given in Dowty (1988).

We formally define vacuities as follows:

$$\mathtt{vac}_{\mathrm{St}\to\mathrm{St}} =_{def} \lambda s.s$$
$$\mathtt{vac}_{\tau_\varphi} =_{def} (\varphi\ \epsilon)$$

The reader should note that as a special case of the second clause, we have

$$\mathtt{vac}_{\mathrm{St}} = \mathtt{vac}_{\mathrm{St}_{\lambda s.s}} = (\lambda s.s\ \epsilon) = \epsilon$$

This in turn enables us to define say:

$$\mathtt{say}_{\mathrm{St}} =_{def} \lambda s.s$$
$$\mathtt{say}_{\tau_1\to\tau_2} =_{def} \lambda k : \tau_1 \to \tau_2.\ \mathtt{say}_{\tau_2}(k\ \mathtt{vac}_{\tau_1})$$
$$\mathtt{say}_{(\tau_1\to\tau_2)_\varphi} =_{def} \mathtt{say}_{\tau_1\to\tau_2}$$

For an expedient example, we can apply say to our putative lexical entry from earlier, and verify that it will reduce to the string SNIVELED as desired:

$$\begin{aligned}&\mathtt{say}_{\mathrm{St}\to\mathrm{St}}\ \lambda s.\ s\cdot \text{SNIVELED}\\ &= \lambda k : \mathrm{St} \to \mathrm{St}.\\ &(\mathtt{say}_{\mathrm{St}}(k\ \mathtt{vac}_{\mathrm{St}}))\ \lambda s.\ s\cdot \text{SNIVELED}\\ &= \mathtt{say}_{\mathrm{St}}\ (\lambda s.\ s\cdot \text{SNIVELED}\ \mathtt{vac}_{\mathrm{St}})\\ &= \mathtt{say}_{\mathrm{St}}\ (\lambda s.\ s\cdot \text{SNIVELED}\ \epsilon)\\ &= \mathtt{say}_{\mathrm{St}}\ \epsilon\cdot \text{SNIVELED}\\ &= \mathtt{say}_{\mathrm{St}}\ \text{SNIVELED}\\ &= \lambda s.s\ \text{SNIVELED}\\ &= \text{SNIVELED}\end{aligned}$$

2.1.2 Subtyping by unary phenominators

In order to augment our type theory with the relevant subtypes, we turn to Lambek and Scott (1986), who hold that one way to do subtyping is by defining predicates that amount to the characteristic function of the particular subtype in question, and then ensuring that these predicates meet certain axioms embedding the subtype into the supertype. We will be able to write such predicates using phenominators. A **unary** phenominator is one which has under its image a function whose string support is a single contiguous string. With this idea in place, we are able to assign subtypes to functional types in the following way.

For τ a (functional) type, we write τ_φ (with φ a phenominator) as shorthand for $\tau_{\varphi'}$, where:

$$\varphi' = \lambda f : \tau.\ \exists s : \mathrm{St}.f = (\varphi\ s)$$

Then φ' constitutes a subtyping predicate in the manner of Lambek and Scott (1986). For example, let $\tau = \mathrm{St} \to \mathrm{St}$ and $\varphi = \lambda vs.s{\cdot}v$. Let us consider the following (putative) lexical entry (pheno only):

$$\vdash \lambda s'.\ s'\cdot \text{SNIVELED} : (\mathrm{St} \to \mathrm{St})_{\text{VP}}$$

Then our typing is justified along the following lines:

$$\begin{aligned}\tau_\varphi &::= (\mathrm{St} \to \mathrm{St})_{\text{VP}}\\ &::= (\mathrm{St} \to \mathrm{St})_{\lambda vs.s\cdot v}\\ &::= (\mathrm{St} \to \mathrm{St})_{\lambda f:\mathrm{St}\to\mathrm{St}.\ \exists t:\mathrm{St}.f=(\lambda vs.s\cdot v\ t)}\end{aligned}$$

So applying the subtyping predicate to the term in question, we have

$$\begin{aligned}&(\lambda f : \mathrm{St} \to \mathrm{St}.\ \exists t : \mathrm{St}.\\ &f = (\lambda vs.s\cdot v\ t)\ \lambda s'.\ s'\cdot \text{SNIVELED})\\ &= \exists t : \mathrm{St}.\lambda s'.\ s'\cdot \text{SNIVELED} = (\lambda vs.s\cdot v\ t)\\ &= \exists t : \mathrm{St}.\lambda s'.\ s'\cdot \text{SNIVELED} = \lambda s.\ s\cdot t\\ &= \exists t : \mathrm{St}.\lambda s.\ s\cdot \text{SNIVELED} = \lambda s.\ s\cdot t\end{aligned}$$

which is true with $t = \text{SNIVELED}$, and the term is shown to be well-typed.

3 Analysis

The basic strategy underlying our analysis of coordination is that in order to coordinate two linguistic signs, we need to track two things: their linearization structure, and their string support. If we have access to the linearization structure of each conjunct, then we can check to see that it is the same, and the signs are compatible for coordination. Furthermore, we will be able to maintain this structure independent of the actual string support of the individual signs.

Phenominators simultaneously allow us to check the linearization structure of coordination candidates and to reconstruct the relevant linearization functions after coordination has taken place. The function say addresses the second point. For a given sign, we can apply say to it in order to retrieve its string support. Then, we will be able to directly coordinate the resulting strings by concatenating them with a conjunction in between. Finally, we can apply the phenominator to the resulting string and retrieve the new linearization function, containing the entire coordinate structure as its string support.

3.1 Lexical entries

In LinCG, lexical entries constitute the (nonlogical) axioms of the proof theory. First we consider the simplest elements of our fragment, the phenos for the proper names *Joffrey*, *Tyrion*, and *Tywin*:

(4) a. $\vdash$ JOFFREY : St
b. $\vdash$ TYRION : St
c. $\vdash$ TYWIN : St

Next, we consider the intransitive verbs *drank*, *sniveled* and *whined.* :

(5) a. $\vdash \lambda s.\ s \cdot \text{DRANK} : (\text{St} \rightarrow \text{St})_{\text{VP}}$
b. $\vdash \lambda s.\ s \cdot \text{SNIVELED} : (\text{St} \rightarrow \text{St})_{\text{VP}}$
c. $\vdash \lambda s.\ s \cdot \text{WHINED} : (\text{St} \rightarrow \text{St})_{\text{VP}}$

Each of these is a function from strings to strings, seeking to linearize its 'subject' string argument to the left of the verb. They are under the image of the "verb phrase" phenominator $\lambda vs.s \cdot v$.

The transitive verbs *chastised* and *slapped* seek to linearize their first string argument to the right, resulting in a function under the image of the VP phenominator, and their second argument to the left, resulting in a string.

(6) a. $\vdash \lambda st.\ t \cdot \text{CHASTISED} \cdot s$
$: (\text{St} \rightarrow \text{St} \rightarrow \text{St})_{\text{TV}}$
b. $\vdash \lambda st.\ t \cdot \text{SLAPPED} \cdot s$
$: (\text{St} \rightarrow \text{St} \rightarrow \text{St})_{\text{TV}}$

Technically, this type could be written $(\text{St} \rightarrow (\text{St} \rightarrow \text{St})_{\text{VP}})_{\text{TV}}$, but for the purposes of coordination, the present is sufficient. Each of these entries is under the image of the "transitive verb" phenominator $\lambda vst.t \cdot v \cdot s$.

Finally, we come to the lexical entry schema for *and*:

(7) $\vdash \lambda c_1 : \tau_\varphi.\ \lambda c_2 : \tau_\varphi.$
$\varphi\ ((\mathtt{say}_{\tau_\varphi}\ c_2) \cdot \text{AND} \cdot (\mathtt{say}_{\tau_\varphi}\ c_1))$
$: \tau_\varphi \rightarrow \tau_\varphi \rightarrow \tau_\varphi$

We note first that it takes two arguments of identical types τ, and furthermore that these must be under the image of the same phenominator φ. It then returns an expression of the same subtype.[7] This mechanism bears more detailed examination. First, each conjunct is subjected to the function $\mathtt{say}$, which, given its type, will return the string support of the conjunct. Then, the resulting strings are concatenated to either side of the string AND. Finally, the phenominator of each argument is applied to the resulting string, creating a function identical to the linearization functions of each of the conjuncts, except with the coordinated string in the relevant position.

3.2 String coordination

String coordination is direct and straightforward. Since string-typed terms are under the image of the identity phenominator, and since $\mathtt{say}_{\text{St}}$ is also defined to be the identity on strings, the lexical entry we obtain for *and* simply concatenates each argument string to either side of the string AND. We give the full term reduction here, although this version of *and* can be shown to be equal to the following:

$$\vdash \lambda c_1 c_2 : \text{St}.\ c_2 \cdot \text{AND} \cdot c_1 : \text{St} \rightarrow \text{St} \rightarrow \text{St}$$

Since our terms at times become rather large, we will adopt a convention where proof trees are given with numerical indexes instead of sequents, with the corresponding sequents following below (at times on multiple lines). We will from time to time elide multiple steps of reduction, noting in passing the relevant definitions to consider when reconstructing the proof.

$$\dfrac{6 \qquad \dfrac{\dfrac{1 \quad 2}{3} \quad 4}{5}}{7}$$

1. $\vdash \lambda c_1 : \text{St}.\ \lambda c_2 : \text{St}.$
$\lambda s.s\ ((\mathtt{say}_{\text{St}}\ c_2) \cdot \text{AND} \cdot (\mathtt{say}_{\text{St}}\ c_1))$
$: \text{St} \rightarrow \text{St} \rightarrow \text{St}$
2. $\vdash \text{JOFFREY} : \text{St}$
3. $\vdash \lambda c_2 : \text{St}.$
$\lambda s.s\ ((\mathtt{say}_{\text{St}}\ c_2) \cdot \text{AND} \cdot (\mathtt{say}_{\text{St}}\ \text{JOFFREY}))$
$= \lambda c_2 : \text{St}.$
$\lambda s.s\ ((\mathtt{say}_{\text{St}}\ c_2) \cdot \text{AND} \cdot (\lambda s.s\ \text{JOFFREY}))$
$= \lambda c_2 : \text{St}.\ \lambda s.s\ ((\mathtt{say}_{\text{St}}\ c_2) \cdot \text{AND} \cdot \text{JOFFREY})$
$: \text{St} \rightarrow \text{St}$
4. $\vdash \text{TYRION} : \text{St}$
5. $\vdash \lambda s.s\ ((\mathtt{say}_{\text{St}}\ \text{TYRION}) \cdot \text{AND} \cdot \text{JOFFREY}) :$ St
$= \lambda s.s\ ((\lambda s.s\ \text{TYRION}) \cdot \text{AND} \cdot \text{JOFFREY}) : \text{St}$
$= \lambda s.s\ (\text{TYRION} \cdot \text{AND} \cdot \text{JOFFREY}) : \text{St}$
$= \text{TYRION} \cdot \text{AND} \cdot \text{JOFFREY} : \text{St}$
6. $\vdash \lambda s.\ s \cdot \text{DRANK} : (\text{St} \rightarrow \text{St})_{\text{VP}}$
7. $\vdash \text{TYRION} \cdot \text{AND} \cdot \text{JOFFREY} \cdot \text{DRANK} : \text{St}$

3.3 Functor coordination

Here, in order to understand the term appearing in each conjunct, it is helpful to notice that the following equality holds (with f a function from strings to strings, under the image of the VP phenominator):

$$\begin{aligned} f : (\text{St} \rightarrow \text{St})_{\text{VP}} &\vdash \mathtt{say}_{(\text{St}\rightarrow\text{St})_{\text{VP}}}\ f \\ &= \mathtt{say}_{\text{St}\rightarrow\text{St}}\ f \\ &= \mathtt{say}_{\text{St}}\ (f\ \mathtt{vac}_{\text{St}}) \\ &= \mathtt{say}_{\text{St}}\ (f\ \epsilon) \\ &= \lambda s.s\ (f\ \epsilon) \\ &= (f\ \epsilon) : \text{St} \end{aligned}$$

[7] Since φ occurs within both the body of the term and the subtyping predicate, we note that this effectively takes us into the realm of dependent types. Making the type theory of the phenogrammar precise is an ongoing area of research, and we are aware that constraining the type system is of paramount importance for computational tractability.

This says that to coordinate VPs, we will first need to reduce them to their string support by feeding their linearization functions the empty string. For the sake of brevity, this term reduction will be elided from steps 5 and 8 in the derivations below. Steps 2 and 6 constitute the hypothesizing and subsequent withdrawal of an 'object' string argument t', as do steps 10 and 14 (s'). Formatting restrictions prohibit rule-labeling on the proof trees, so we note that these are each instances of the rules of axiom (Ax) and abstraction (Abs), respectively.

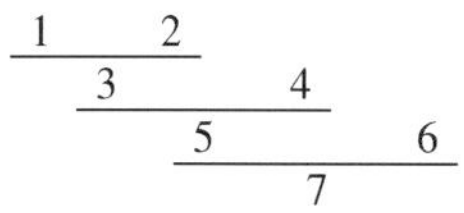

1. $\vdash \lambda c_1 : (\mathrm{St} \to \mathrm{St})_{\mathrm{VP}}.\ \lambda c_2 : (\mathrm{St} \to \mathrm{St})_{\mathrm{VP}}.$
   $\lambda vs.s \cdot v$
   $((\mathtt{say}_{(\mathrm{St}\to\mathrm{St})_{\mathrm{VP}}}\ c_2) \cdot \mathrm{AND} \cdot (\mathtt{say}_{(\mathrm{St}\to\mathrm{St})_{\mathrm{VP}}}\ c_1))$
   $: (\mathrm{St} \to \mathrm{St})_{\mathrm{VP}} \to (\mathrm{St} \to \mathrm{St})_{\mathrm{VP}} \to (\mathrm{St} \to \mathrm{St})_{\mathrm{VP}}$
2. $\vdash \lambda s.\ s \cdot \mathrm{SNIVELED} : (\mathrm{St} \to \mathrm{St})_{\mathrm{VP}}$
3. $\vdash \lambda c_2 : (\mathrm{St} \to \mathrm{St})_{\mathrm{VP}}.\ \lambda vs.s \cdot v$
   $((\mathtt{say}_{(\mathrm{St}\to\mathrm{St})_{\mathrm{VP}}}\ c_2) \cdot \mathrm{AND}$
   $\cdot (\mathtt{say}_{(\mathrm{St}\to\mathrm{St})_{\mathrm{VP}}}\ \lambda s.\ s \cdot \mathrm{SNIVELED}))$
   $\vdots$
   $= \lambda c_2 : (\mathrm{St} \to \mathrm{St})_{\mathrm{VP}}.\ \lambda vs.s \cdot v$
   $((\mathtt{say}_{(\mathrm{St}\to\mathrm{St})_{\mathrm{VP}}}\ c_2) \cdot \mathrm{AND} \cdot \mathrm{SNIVELED})$
   $: (\mathrm{St} \to \mathrm{St})_{\mathrm{VP}} \to (\mathrm{St} \to \mathrm{St})_{\mathrm{VP}}$
4. $\vdash \lambda s.\ s \cdot \mathrm{WHINED} : (\mathrm{St} \to \mathrm{St})_{\mathrm{VP}}$
5. $\vdash \lambda vs.s \cdot v\ ((\mathtt{say}_{(\mathrm{St}\to\mathrm{St})_{\mathrm{VP}}}\ \lambda s.\ s \cdot \mathrm{WHINED})$
   $\cdot \mathrm{AND} \cdot \mathrm{SNIVELED})$
   $\vdots$
   $= (\lambda vs.s \cdot v\ \mathrm{WHINED} \cdot \mathrm{AND} \cdot \mathrm{SNIVELED})$
   $= \lambda s.\ s \cdot \mathrm{WHINED} \cdot \mathrm{AND} \cdot \mathrm{SNIVELED}$
   $: (\mathrm{St} \to \mathrm{St})_{\mathrm{VP}}$
6. $\vdash \mathrm{JOFFREY} : \mathrm{St}$
7. $\vdash \mathrm{JOFFREY} \cdot \mathrm{WHINED} \cdot \mathrm{AND} \cdot \mathrm{SNIVELED} : \mathrm{St}$

3.4 Right node raising

In the end, 'right node raising' constructions prove only to be a special case of functor coordination. The key here is the licensing of the 'rightward-looking' functors, which are under the image of the phenominator $\lambda vs.v \cdot s$. As was the case with the 'leftward-looking' functor coordination example in section 3.3, this analysis is essentially the same as the well-known Lambek categorial grammar analysis originating in Steedman (1985) and continuing in Dowty (1988) and Morrill (1994). The difference is that we encode directionality in the phenominator, rather than in the type. Since our system does not include function composition as a rule, but as a theorem, we will need to make use of hypothetical reasoning in order to permute the order of the string arguments in order to construct expressions with the correct structure.[8]

As was the case with the functor coordination example in section 3.3, applying `say` to the conjuncts passes them the empty string, reducing them to their string support, as shown here:

$$\begin{aligned} f : (\mathrm{St} \to \mathrm{St})_{\mathrm{RNR}} &\vdash \mathtt{say}_{(\mathrm{St}\to\mathrm{St})_{\mathrm{RNR}}}\ f \\ &= \mathtt{say}_{\mathrm{St}\to\mathrm{St}}\ f \\ &= \mathtt{say}_{\mathrm{St}}\ (f\ \mathtt{vac}_{\mathrm{St}}) \\ &= \mathtt{say}_{\mathrm{St}}\ (f\ \epsilon) \\ &= \lambda s.s\ (f\ \epsilon) \\ &= (f\ \epsilon) : \mathrm{St} \end{aligned}$$

As before, this reduction is elided in the proof given below, occurring in steps 8 and 15.

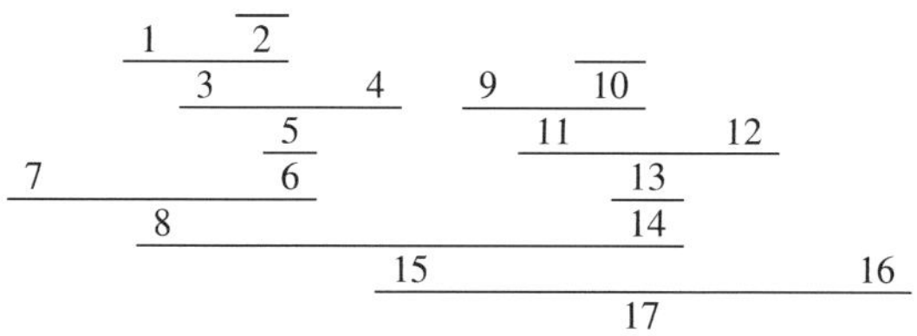

1. $\vdash \lambda st.\ t \cdot \mathrm{CHASTISED} \cdot s : (\mathrm{St} \to \mathrm{St} \to \mathrm{St})_{\mathrm{TV}}$
2. $t' : \mathrm{St} \vdash t' : \mathrm{St}$
3. $t' : \mathrm{St} \vdash \lambda t.\ t \cdot \mathrm{CHASTISED} \cdot t' : (\mathrm{St} \to \mathrm{St})_{\mathrm{VP}}$
4. $\vdash \mathrm{TYWIN} : \mathrm{St}$
5. $t' : \mathrm{St} \vdash \mathrm{TYWIN} \cdot \mathrm{CHASTISED} \cdot t' : \mathrm{St}$
6. $\vdash \lambda t'.\ \mathrm{TYWIN} \cdot \mathrm{CHASTISED} \cdot t' : (\mathrm{St} \to \mathrm{St})_{\mathrm{RNR}}$
7. $\vdash \lambda c_1 : (\mathrm{St} \to \mathrm{St})_{\mathrm{RNR}}.\ \lambda c_2 : (\mathrm{St} \to \mathrm{St})_{\mathrm{RNR}}.$
   $\lambda vs.v \cdot s\ ((\mathtt{say}_{(\mathrm{St}\to\mathrm{St})_{\mathrm{RNR}}}\ c_2)$
   $\cdot \mathrm{AND} \cdot (\mathtt{say}_{(\mathrm{St}\to\mathrm{St})_{\mathrm{RNR}}}\ c_1))$
   $: (\mathrm{St} \to \mathrm{St})_{\mathrm{RNR}} \to (\mathrm{St} \to \mathrm{St})_{\mathrm{RNR}}$
   $\to (\mathrm{St} \to \mathrm{St})_{\mathrm{RNR}}$
8. $\vdash \lambda c_2 : (\mathrm{St} \to \mathrm{St})_{\mathrm{RNR}}.\ \lambda vs.v \cdot s$
   $((\mathtt{say}_{(\mathrm{St}\to\mathrm{St})_{\mathrm{RNR}}}\ c_2) \cdot \mathrm{AND}$
   $\cdot (\mathtt{say}_{(\mathrm{St}\to\mathrm{St})_{\mathrm{RNR}}}\ \lambda t'.\ \mathrm{TYWIN} \cdot \mathrm{CHASTISED} \cdot t'))$
   $\vdots$
   $= \lambda c_2 : (\mathrm{St} \to \mathrm{St})_{\mathrm{RNR}}.\ \lambda vs.v \cdot s$

[8] Regrettably, space constraints prohibit a discussion verifying the typing for the 'right node raised' terms. The reader can verify that the terms are in fact well-typed given the subtyping schema in section 2.1.2. It is possible to write inference rules that speak directly to the introduction and elimination of the relevant functional subtypes, but these are omitted here for the sake of brevity.

$((\texttt{say}_{(\mathrm{St}\to\mathrm{St})_{\mathrm{RNR}}}\ c_2)$
$\cdot\ \textsc{and} \cdot \textsc{tywin} \cdot \textsc{chastised})$
$: (\mathrm{St} \to \mathrm{St})_{\mathrm{RNR}} \to (\mathrm{St} \to \mathrm{St})_{\mathrm{RNR}}$

9. $\vdash \lambda st.\ t \cdot \textsc{slapped} \cdot s : (\mathrm{St} \to \mathrm{St} \to \mathrm{St})_{\mathrm{TV}}$
10. $s' : \mathrm{St} \vdash s' : \mathrm{St}$
11. $s' : \mathrm{St} \vdash \lambda t.\ t \cdot \textsc{slapped} \cdot s' : (\mathrm{St} \to \mathrm{St})_{\mathrm{VP}}$
12. $\vdash \textsc{tyrion} : \mathrm{St}$
13. $s' : \mathrm{St} \vdash \textsc{tyrion} \cdot \textsc{slapped} \cdot s' : \mathrm{St}$
14. $\vdash \lambda s'.\ \textsc{tyrion} \cdot \textsc{slapped} \cdot s' : (\mathrm{St} \to \mathrm{St})_{\mathrm{RNR}}$
15. $\vdash \lambda vs.v \cdot s\ ((\texttt{say}_{(\mathrm{St}\to\mathrm{St})_{\mathrm{RNR}}}$
$\lambda s'.\ \textsc{tyrion} \cdot \textsc{slapped} \cdot s')$
$\cdot\ \textsc{and} \cdot \textsc{tywin} \cdot \textsc{chastised})$
$\vdots$
$= (\lambda vs.v \cdot s\ \textsc{tyrion} \cdot \textsc{slapped}$
$\cdot\ \textsc{and} \cdot \textsc{tywin} \cdot \textsc{chastised})$
$= \lambda s.\ \textsc{tyrion} \cdot \textsc{slapped} \cdot \textsc{and}$
$\cdot\ \textsc{tywin} \cdot \textsc{chastised} \cdot s : (\mathrm{St} \to \mathrm{St})_{\mathrm{RNR}}$
16. $\vdash \textsc{joffrey} : \mathrm{St}$
17. $\vdash \textsc{tyrion} \cdot \textsc{slapped} \cdot \textsc{and}$
$\cdot\ \textsc{tywin} \cdot \textsc{chastised} \cdot \textsc{joffrey} : \mathrm{St}$

4 Discussion

We provide a brief introduction to the framework of Linear Categorial Grammar (LinCG). One of the primary strengths of categorial grammar in general has been its ability to address coordination phenomena. Coordination presents a uniquely particular problem for grammars which distinguish between structural combination (tectogrammar) and the actual linear order of the strings generated by such grammars (part of phenogrammar). Due to the inability to distinguish 'directionality' in string functors within a standard typed lambda calculus, a general analysis of coordination seems difficult.

We have elaborated LinCG's concept of phenogrammar by introducing phenominators, closed monoidal linear lambda terms. We have shown how the recursive function `say` provides a left inverse for unaryphenominators, and we have defined a more general notion of an 'empty category' known as a vacuity, which `say` is defined in terms of. It is then possible to describe subtypes of functional types suitable to make the relevant distinctions. These technologies enable us to give analyses of various coordination phenomena in LinCG, extending the empirical coverage of the framework.

4.1 Future work

It is possible to give an analysis of argument cluster coordination using phenominators, instantiating the lexical entry for *and* with τ as the type $(\mathrm{St} \to \mathrm{St} \to \mathrm{St} \to \mathrm{St})_{\mathrm{DTV}} \to (\mathrm{St} \to \mathrm{St})_{\mathrm{VP}}$ and φ as $\lambda vPs.\ s \cdot (P\epsilon\epsilon\epsilon) \cdot v$, and using hypothetical reasoning. Regrettably, the necessity of brevity prohibits a detailed account here.

Given that phenominators provide access to the structure of functional terms which concatenate strings to the right and left of their string support, it is our belief that any Lambek categorial grammar analysis can be recast in LinCG by an algorithmic translation of directional slash types into phenominator-indexed functional phenotypes, and we are currently in the process of evaluating a potential translation algorithm from directional slash types to phenominators. This should in turn provide us with most of the details necessary to describe a system which emulates the HTLCG of Kubota and Levine (2012), which provides analyses of various gapping phenomena, greatly increasing the overall empirical coverage.

There are a number of coordination phenomena that require modifications to the tectogrammatical component. We would like to be able to analyze unlike category coordinations like *rich and an excellent cook* in the manner of Bayer (1996), as well as Morrill (1996), which would require the addition of some variety of sum types in the tectogrammar. Further muddying the waters is so-called "iterated" or "list" coordination, which requires the ability to generate coordinate structures containing a number of conjuncts with no coordinating conjunction, as in *Thurston, Kim, and Steve*.

It is our intent to extend the use of phenominators to analyze intonation as well, and we expect that they can be fruitfully employed to give accounts of focus, association with focus, contrastive topicalization, "in-situ" topicalization, alternative questions, and any number of other phenomena which are at least partially realized prosodically.

Acknowledgements

I am grateful to Carl Pollard, Bob Levine, Yusuke Kubota, Manjuan Duan, Gerald Penn, the TTNLS 2014 committee, and two anonymous reviewers for their comments. Any errors or misunderstandings rest solely on the shoulders of the author.

References

Samuel Bayer. 1996. The coordination of unlike categories. *Language*, pages 579–616.

Haskell B. Curry. 1961. Some Logical Aspects of Grammatical Structure. In Roman. O. Jakobson, editor, *Structure of Language and its Mathematical Aspects*, pages 56–68. American Mathematical Society.

Philippe de Groote and Sarah Maarek. 2007. Type-theoretic Extensions of Abstract Categorial Grammars. In Reinhard Muskens, editor, *Proceedings of Workshop on New Directions in Type-Theoretic Grammars*.

Philippe de Groote. 2001. Towards Abstract Categorial Grammars. In *Association for Computational Linguistics, 39th Annual Meeting and 10th Conference of the European Chapter, Proceedings of the Conference*, pages 148–155.

David Dowty. 1988. Type raising, functional composition, and non-constituent conjunction. In Richard T. Oehrle, Emmon Bach, and Deirdre Wheeler, editors, *Categorial Grammars and Natural Language Structures*, volume 32 of *Studies in Linguistics and Philosophy*, pages 153–197. Springer Netherlands.

John Hughes. 1995. The design of a pretty-printing library. In *Advanced Functional Programming*, pages 53–96. Springer.

Yusuke Kubota and Robert Levine. 2012. Gapping as like-category coordination. In D. Béchet and A. Dikovsky, editors, *Logical Aspects of Computational Linguistics (LACL) 2012*.

Yusuke Kubota. 2010. *(In)flexibility of Constituency in Japanese in Multi-Modal Categorial Grammar with Structured Phonology*. Ph.D. thesis, The Ohio State University.

J. Lambek and P.J. Scott. 1986. *Introduction to higher order categorical logic*. Cambridge University Press.

Scott Martin. 2013. *The Dynamics of Sense and Implicature*. Ph.D. thesis, The Ohio State University.

Vedrana Mihalicek. 2012. *Serbo-Croatian Word Order: A Logical Approach*. Ph.D. thesis, The Ohio State University.

Glyn V. Morrill. 1994. *Type Logical Grammar*. Kluwer Academic Publishers.

Glyn Morrill. 1996. Grammar and logic*. *Theoria*, 62(3):260–293.

Reinhard Muskens. 2001. Lambda grammars and the syntax-semantics interface. In *Proceedings of the Thirteenth Amsterdam Colloquium*, pages 150–155. Universiteit van Amsterdam.

Reinhard Muskens. 2010. New Directions in Type-Theoretic Grammars. *Journal of Logic, Language and Information*, 19(2):129–136. DOI 10.1007/s10849-009-9114-9.

Richard Oehrle. 1994. Term-Labeled Categorial Type Systems. *Linguistics and Philosophy*, 17:633–678.

Dick Oehrle. 1995. Some 3-dimensional systems of labelled deduction. *Logic Journal of the IGPL*, 3(2-3):429–448.

Carl Pollard and E. Allyn Smith. 2012. A unified analysis of *the same*, phrasal comparatives, and superlatives. In Anca Chereches, editor, *Proceedings of SALT 22*, pages 307–325. eLanguage.

Carl Pollard. 2013. Agnostic Hyperintensional Semantics. *Synthese*. to appear.

Aarne Ranta. 2004. Grammatical Framework: A Type-Theoretical Grammar Formalism. *Journal of Functional Programming*, 14:145–189.

Aarne Ranta. 2009. The GF resource grammar library. *Linguistic Issues in Language Technology*, 2(1).

E. Allyn Smith. 2010. *Correlational Comparison in English*. Ph.D. thesis, The Ohio State University.

Mark Steedman. 1985. Dependency and coördination in the grammar of dutch and english. *Language*, pages 523–568.

Natural Language Reasoning Using proof-assistant technology: Rich Typing and beyond*

Stergios Chatzikyriakidis
Dept of Computer Science,
Royal Holloway, Univ of London
Egham, Surrey TW20 0EX, U.K; Open University of Cyprus
stergios.chatzikyriakidis@cs.rhul.ac.uk

Zhaohui Luo
Dept of Computer Science,
Royal Holloway, Univ of London
Egham, Surrey TW20 0EX, U.K;
zhaohui@cs.rhul.ac.uk

Abstract

In this paper, we study natural language inference based on the formal semantics in modern type theories (MTTs) and their implementations in proof-assistants such as Coq. To this end, the type theory UTT with coercive subtyping is used as the logical language in which natural language semantics is translated to, followed by the implementation of these semantics in the Coq proof-assistant. Valid inferences are treated as theorems to be proven via Coq's proof machinery. We shall emphasise that the rich typing mechanisms in MTTs (much richer than those in the simple type theory as used in the Montagovian setting) provide very useful tools in many respects in formal semantics. This is exemplified via the formalisation of various linguistic examples, including conjoined NPs, comparatives, adjectives as well as various linguistic coercions. The aim of the paper is thus twofold: a) to show that the use of proof-assistant technology has indeed the potential to be developed into a new way of dealing with inference, and b) to exemplify the advantages of having a rich typing system to the study of formal semantics in general and natural language inference in particular.

1 Introduction

Natural Language Inference (NLI), i.e. the task of determining whether an NL hypothesis can be inferred from an NL premise, has been an active research theme in computational semantics in which various approaches have been proposed (see, for example (MacCartney, 2009) and some of the references therein). In this paper, we study NLI based on formal semantics in MTTs with coercive subtyping (Luo, 2012b) and its implementation in the proof assistant Coq (Coq, 2007).

A *Modern Type Theory* (MTT) is a dependent type theory consisting of an internal logic, which follows the propositions-as-types principle. This latter feature along with the availability of powerful type structures make MTTs very useful for formal semantics. The use of MTTs for NL semantics has been proposed with exciting results as regards various issues of NL semantics, ranging from quantification and anaphora to adjectival modification, co-predication, belief and context formalization. (Sundholm, 1989; Ranta, 1994; Boldini, 2000; Cooper, 2005; Fox and Lappin, 2005; Retoré, 2013; Ginzburg and Cooper, forthcoming; Luo, 2011a; Luo, 2012b; Chatzikyriakidis and Luo, 2012; Chatzikyriakidis and Luo, 2013a). Recently, there has been a systematic study of MTT semantics using Luo's UTT with coercive subtyping (type theory with coercive subtyping, henceforth TTCS) (Luo, 2010; Luo, 2011a; Luo, 2012b; Chatzikyriakidis and Luo, 2012; Chatzikyriakidis and Luo, 2013a; Chatzikyriakidis and Luo, 2013b; Chatzikyriakidis and Luo, 2014). This is the version of MTT used in this paper. More specifically, the paper concentrates on one of the key differences between MTTs and simple typed ones, i.e. rich typing. Rich typing will be shown to be a key ingredient for both formal semantics in general and the study of NLI in particular.

A proof assistant is a computer system that assists the users to develop proofs of mathematical theorems. A number of proof assistants implement MTTs. For instance, the proof assistant Coq (Coq, 2007) implements pCIC, the predicative Calculus of Inductive Constructions[1] and sup-

*This work is supported by the research grant F/07-537/AJ of the Leverhulme Trust in the U.K.

[1]pCIC is a type theory that is rather similar to UTT, especially after its universe Set became predicative since Coq 8.0. A main difference is that UTT does not have co-inductive types. The interested reader is directed to Goguen's PhD the-

ports some very useful tactics that can be used to help the users to automate (parts of) their proofs. Proof assistants have been used in various applications in computer science (e.g., program verification) and formalised mathematics (e.g., formalisation of the proof of the 4-colour theorem in Coq).

The above two developments, the use of MTT semantics on the one hand and the implementation of MTTs in proof assistants on the other, has opened a new research avenue: the use of existing proof assistants in dealing with NLI. In this paper, two different goals are to be achieved: a) on a more practical level, to show how proof-assistant technology can be used in order to deal with NLI and b) on a theoretical level, the significance of rich typing for formal semantics and NLI in particular. These two different aspects of the paper will be studied on a par, by concentrating on a number of NLI cases (quite a lot actually) that are adequately dealt with on a theoretical level via rich typing and the implementation of the account making use of rich type structures in Coq on a more practical level. We shall also consider how to employ dependent typing in the coercive subtyping framework to formalise linguistic coercions.

2 Rich typing in MTTs

A Modern Type Theory (MTT) is a variant of a class of type theories in the tradition initiated by the work of Martin-Löf (Martin-Löf, 1975; Martin-Löf, 1984), which have dependent and inductive types, among others. We choose to call them Modern Type Theories in order to distinguish them from Church's simple type theory (Church, 1940) that is commonly employed within the Montagovian tradition in formal semantics.

Among the variants of MTTs, we are going to employ the Unified Theory of dependent Types (UTT) (Luo, 1994) with the addition of the coercive subtyping mechanism (see, for example, (Luo, 1999; Luo et al., 2012) and below). UTT is an impredicative type theory in which a type $Prop$ of all logical propositions exists.[2] This stands as part of the study of linguistic semantics using MTTs rather than simply typed ones. In particular, in this paper we discuss a number of key issues as regards the typing system, which will be shown to allow more fine-grained distinctions and expressivity compared to classical simple typed systems as these are used in mainstream Montagovian semantics.

2.1 Type many-sortedness and CNs as types

In Montague semantics (Montague, 1974), the underlying logic (Church's simple type theory (Church, 1940)) can be seen as 'single-sorted' in the sense that there is only one type e of all entities. The other types such as t of truth values and the function types generated from e and t do not stand for types of entities. In this respect, there are no fine-grained distinctions between the elements of type e and as such all individuals are interpreted using the same type. For example, *John* and *Mary* have the same type in simple type theories, the type e of individuals. An MTT, on the other hand, can be regarded as a 'many-sorted' logical system in that it contains many types and as such one can make fine-grained distinctions between individuals and further use those different types to interpret subclasses of individuals. For example, one can have $John : [\![man]\!]$ and $Mary : [\![woman]\!]$, where $[\![man]\!]$ and $[\![woman]\!]$ are different types.

An important trait of MTT-based semantics is the interpretation of common nouns (CNs) as *types* (Ranta, 1994) rather than sets or predicates (i.e., objects of type $e \to t$) as it is the case within the Montagovian tradition. The CNs *man*, *human*, *table* and *book* are interpreted as types $[\![man]\!]$, $[\![human]\!]$, $[\![table]\!]$ and $[\![book]\!]$, respectively. Then, individuals are interpreted as being of one of the types used to interpret CNs. The interpretation of CNs as Types is also a prerequisite in order for the subtyping mechanism to work. This is because, assuming CNs to be predicates, subtyping would go wrong given contravariance of function types.[3]

2.2 Subtyping

Coercive subtyping (Luo, 1999; Luo et al., 2012) provides an adequate framework to be employed for MTT-based formal semantics (Luo, 2010; Luo, 2012b).[4] It can be seen as an abbreviation mechanism: A is a (proper) subtype of B ($A < B$) if

sis (Goguen, 1994) as regards the meta-theory of UTT.

[2]This is similar to simple type theory where a type t of truth values exists.

[3]See (Chatzikyriakidis and Luo, 2013b) for more information. See also (Luo, 2012a) for further philosophical argumentation on the choosing to represent CNs as types.

[4]It is worth mentioning that subsumptive subtyping, i.e. the traditional notion of subtyping that adopts the subsumption rule (if $A \leq B$, then every object of type A is also of type B), is inadequate for MTTs in the sense that it would destroy some important metatheoretical properties of MTTs (see, for example, §4 of (Luo et al., 2012) for details).

there is a unique implicit coercion c from type A to type B and, if so, an object a of type A can be used in any context $\mathfrak{C}_B[\_]$ that expects an object of type B: $\mathfrak{C}_B[a]$ is legal (well-typed) and equal to $\mathfrak{C}_B[c(a)]$.

As an example, assuming that both $[\![man]\!]$ and $[\![human]\!]$ are base types, one may introduce the following as a basic subtyping relation:

(1) $[\![man]\!] < [\![human]\!]$

In case that $[\![man]\!]$ is defined as a composite Σ-type (see §2.3 below for details), where $male\colon [\![human]\!] \rightarrow Prop$:

(2) $[\![man]\!] = \Sigma h\colon [\![human]\!].\ male(h)$

we have that (1) is the case because the above Σ-type is a subtype of $[\![human]\!]$ via the first projection π_1:

(3) $(\Sigma h\colon [\![human]\!].\ male(h)) <_{\pi_1} [\![human]\!]$

We will see in the next section the importance of the coercive subtyping mechanism when dealing with NLI.

2.3 Dependent typing and universes

One of the basic features of MTTs is the use of Dependent Types. A dependent type is a family of types depending on some values. Here we explain two basic constructors for dependent types, Σ and Π, both highly relevant for the study of linguistic semantics.

The constructor/operator Σ is a generalization of the Cartesian product of two sets that allows the second set to depend on values of the first. For instance, if $[\![human]\!]$ is a type and $male\colon [\![human]\!] \rightarrow Prop$, then the Σ-type $\Sigma h\colon [\![human]\!].\ male(h)$ is intuitively the type of humans who are male.

More formally, if A is a type and B is an A-indexed family of types, then $\Sigma(A, B)$, or sometimes written as $\Sigma x : A.B(x)$, is a type, consisting of pairs (a, b) such that a is of type A and b is of type $B(a)$. When $B(x)$ is a constant type (i.e., always the same type no matter what x is), the Σ-type degenerates into product type $A \times B$ of non-dependent pairs. Σ-types (and product types) are associated projection operations π_1 and π_2 so that $\pi_1(a, b) = a$ and $\pi_2(a, b) = b$, for every (a, b) of type $\Sigma(A, B)$ or $A \times B$.

The linguistic relevance of Σ-types can be directly appreciated once we understand that in its dependent case, Σ-types can be used to interpret linguistic phenomena of central importance, like for example adjectival modification (Ranta, 1994). For example, *handsome man* is interpreted as a Σ-type (4), the type of handsome men (or more precisely, of those men together with proofs that they are handsome):

(4) $\Sigma m\colon [\![man]\!].\ [\![handsome]\!](m)$

where $[\![handsome]\!](m)$ is a family of propositions/types that depends on the man m.[5]

The other basic constructor for dependent types is Π. Π-types can be seen as a generalization of the normal function space where the second type is a family of types that might be dependent on the values of the first. A Π-type degenerates to the function type $A \rightarrow B$ in the non-dependent case. In more detail, when A is a type and P is a predicate over A, $\Pi x : A.P(x)$ is the dependent function type that, in the embedded logic, stands for the universally quantified proposition $\forall x : A.P(x)$. For example, the following sentence (5) is interpreted as (6):

(5) Every man walks.

(6) $\Pi x\colon [\![man]\!].[\![walk]\!](x)$

Type Universes. An advanced feature of MTTs, which will be shown to be very relevant in interpreting NL semantics, is that of universes. Informally, a universe is a collection of (the names of) types put into a type (Martin-Löf, 1984).[6] For example, one may want to collect all the names of the types that interpret common nouns into a universe $\text{CN}\colon Type$. The idea is that for each type A that interprets a common noun, there is a name $\overline{A}$ in CN. For example,

$$\overline{[\![man]\!]}\colon \text{CN} \quad \text{and} \quad T_{\text{CN}}(\overline{[\![man]\!]}) = [\![man]\!].$$

[5]Adjectival modification is a notoriously difficult issue and as such not all cases of adjectives can be captured via using a Σ type analysis. For a proper treatment of adjectival modification within this framework, see (Chatzikyriakidis and Luo, 2013a).

[6]There is quite a long discussion on how these universes should be like. In particular, the debate is largely concentrated on whether a universe should be predicative or impredicative. A strongly impredicative universe U of all types (with $U\colon U$ and Π-types) is shown to be paradoxical (Girard, 1971) and as such logically inconsistent. The theory UTT we use here has only one impredicative universe $Prop$ (representing the world of logical formulas) together with infinitely many predicative universes which as such avoids Girard's paradox (see (Luo, 1994) for more details).

In practice, we do not distinguish a type in CN and its name by omitting the overlines and the operator T_{CN} by simply writing, for instance, $[\![man]\!]: \text{CN}$. Thus, the universe includes the collection of the names that interpret common nouns. For example, in CN, we shall find the following types:

(7) $[\![man]\!], [\![woman]\!], [\![book]\!], ...$

(8) $\Sigma m\colon [\![man]\!].[\![handsome]\!](m)$

(9) $G_R + G_F$

where the Σ-type in (8 is the proposed interpretation of 'handsome man' and the disjoint sum type in (9) is that of 'gun' (the sum of real guns and fake guns – see above).[7] Interesting applications of the use of universes can be proposed like for example, their use in giving the types for quantifiers and VP adverbs as extending over the universe CN (Luo, 2011b) as well as coordination extending over the universe of all linguistic types LType (Chatzikyriakidis and Luo, 2012).

3 NL Inference in Coq

Coq is a dependently typed interactive theorem prover implementing the calculus of Inductive Constructions (pCiC, see (Coq, 2007)). Coq, and in general proof-assistants, provide assistance in the development of formal proofs. The idea is simple: you use Coq in order to see whether statements as regards anything that has been either predefined or user-defined (definitions, parameters, variables) can be proven or not. In the case of NLI, the same idea applies: once the semantics of NL words are defined, then these semantics can be reasoned about by using Coq's proof mechanism. In this sense, valid NLIs can be seen as theorems, or better valid NLIs must be theorems.

A very simple case of semantic entailment, that of example (10), will therefore be formulated as the following theorem in Coq (11):

(10) John walks ⇒ some man walks

(11) Theorem x: John walks → some man walks

Now, depending on the semantics of the individual lexical items one may or may not prove the theorem that needs to be proven in each case. Inferences like the one shown in (11) are easy cases in Coq. Assuming the semantics of *some* which specify that given any A of type CN and a predicate of type $A \rightarrow Prop$, there exists an $x\colon A$ such that $P(x)\colon Prop$, such cases are straightforwardly proven.

[7]The use of disjoint sum types was proposed by (Chatzikyriakidis and Luo, 2013a) in order to deal with privative modification. The interested reader is directed there for details.

3.1 The FraCas test suite

In this section we present how implementing MTT NL semantics in Coq can deal with various cases of NLI inference. For this reason, we use examples from the FraCas test suite. The FraCas Test Suite (Cooper et al., 1996) arose out of the FraCas Consortium, a huge collaboration with the aim to develop a range of resources related to computational semantics. The FraCas test suite is specifically designed to reflect what an adequate theory of NL inference should be able to capture. It comprises NLI examples formulated in the form of a premise (or premises) followed by a question and an answer. For instance,

(12) Either Smith, Jones and Anderson signed the contract.
Did Jones sign the contract? [Yes]

The examples are quite simple in format but are designed to cover a very wide spectrum of semantic phenomena, e.g. generalized quantifiers, conjoined plurals, tense and aspect related phenomena, adjectives and ellipsis, among others. In what follows, we show how the use of a rich type system can deal with NLI adequately (at least for the cases looked at) from both a theoretical and an implementational point of view.

3.2 Rich typing and NLI

3.2.1 Quantifiers

A great deal of the FraCas examples are cases of inference that result from the monotone properties of quantifiers. Examples concerning monotonicity on the first argument are very easily treated in a system encoding an MTT with coercive subtyping, by employing the subtyping relations between CNs. To put this claim in context, let us look at the following example (3.55) from the FraCas test suite:

(13) Some Irish delegates finished the survey on time.
Did any delegate finish the report on time [Yes]

Treating adjectival modification as involving a Σ type where the first projection is always a coercion as in (Luo, 2011a), we get *Irish delegate* to be a subtype of *delegate*, i.e. $[\![Irishdelegate]\!] <$

$[\![delegate]\!]$. This is basically all that Coq needs in order to prove the inference.[8]

Moving on to quantifier cases involving monotonicity on the second argument, we notice that these are more difficult to get since an adjunct (e.g. a PP) is involved in deriving the inference:

(14) Some delegates finished the survey on time.
Did any delegate finish the survey? [Yes]

The type proposed for VP adverbs by Luo (Luo, 2011b) is based on the idea of a type universe of CNs. As already said in the introduction, type universes a universe is a collection of (the names of) types put into a type. In this respect, one can form the universe CN which basically stands for the collection of names interpreting common nouns. The type proposed for VP adverbs makes use of this CN universe and assumes quantification over it (Chatzikyriakidis and Luo, 2013a; Chatzikyriakidis and Luo, 2012):

(15) $\Pi A\colon \mathrm{CN}.\ (A \to Prop) \to (A \to Prop)$

However, in order to derive the inference needed in cases of monotonicity on the second argument cases, this typing alone is not enough. Σ types can be used in order to slightly modify the typing. In order to do this, we first introduce an auxiliary object ADV as follows:

(16) $ADV\colon \Pi A\colon \mathrm{CN}.\Pi v\colon A \to Prop.\Sigma p\colon A \to Prop.\forall x : A.p(x) \supset v(x)$

This reads as follows: for any common noun A and any predicate v over A, $ADV(A, v)$ is a pair (p, m) such that for any $x\colon A$, $p(x)$ implies $v(x)$. Taking the sentence (14) as an example, for the CN *delegate* and predicate $[\![finish]\!]$[9], we define on time to be the first projection of the auxiliary object (16) which is of type (15):

(17) $on\ time = \lambda A : \mathrm{CN}.\lambda v : A \to Prop.\ \pi_1(ONTIME(A, v))$

As a consequence, for instance, any delegate who finished the survey on time ($p(x)$) in (16) did finish the survey ($v(x)$).

[8]For details on the semantics of the other lexical items like e.g. VP adverbs in the sentence, see the following discussion. Also, following Luo (Luo, 2011a) we implement Σ-types as dependent record types in Coq. Again, see (Chatzikyriakidis and Luo, 2013b) for details.

[9]Note that $[\![finish]\!]\colon [\![human]\!] \to Prop < [\![delegate]\!] \to Prop$.

3.2.2 Conjoined NPs

Inference involving conjoined NPs concerns cases like the one shown below:

(18) Smith, Jones and Anderson signed the contract.
Did Jones sign the contract? [Yes]

In (Chatzikyriakidis and Luo, 2012), a polymorphic type for binary coordinators that extends over the constructed universe $LType$, the universe of linguistic types was proposed. This can be extended to n-ary coordinators. For example, the coordinator *and* may take three arguments, as in the premise of (18). In such cases, the type of the coordinator, denoted as and_3 in semantics, is:

(19) $and_3\colon \Pi A\colon LType.A \to A \to A \to A.$

Intuitively, we may write this type as $\Pi A\colon LType.A^3 \to A$. For instance, the semantics of (18) is (20), where c is 'the contract':

(20) $[\![sign]\!](and_3(s, j, a), c)$

In order to consider such coordinators in reasoning, we consider the following auxiliary object (similarly to the auxiliary object ADV) and define and_3 as follows:

(21) $AND_3\colon \Pi A : LType.\ \Pi x, y, z : A.\ \Sigma a : A.\ \forall p : A \to Prop.\ p(a) \supset p(x) \wedge p(y) \wedge p(z).$

(22) $and_3 = \lambda A : LType.\lambda x, y, z : A.\ \pi_1(AND_3(A, x, y, z))$

Having defined the coordinators such as *and* in such a way, we can get the desired inferences. For example, from the semantics (20), we can infer that 'Jones signed the contract', the hypothesis in (18).[10] Coordinators such as *or* can be defined in a similar way.

3.2.3 Comparatives

Inference with comparatives can also be treated by using Σ types. Two ways of doing this will be proposed, one not involving and one involving measures. We shall consider *shorter than* as a typical example. Intuitively, *shorter than* should be

[10]A note about Coq is in order here: building new universes is not an option in Coq (or, put in another way, Coq does not support building of new universes). Instead, we shall use an existing universe in Coq in conducting our examples for coordination.

of type $Human \rightarrow Human \rightarrow Prop$ as in the following example:

(23) Mary is shorter than John.

We assume that there be a predicate $short\colon Human \rightarrow Prop$, expressing that a human is short. Intuitively, if Mary is shorter than John and John is short, then so is Mary. Furthermore, one should be able to take care of the transitive properties of comparatives. Thus, if A is $COMP$ than B and B is $COMP$ than C, then A is also $COMP$ than C. All these can be captured by considering $COMP$ of the following Σ-type and define *shorter than* to be its first projection:

(24) $COMP\colon \Sigma p\colon Human \rightarrow Human \rightarrow Prop.\forall h_1, h_2, h_3 : Human.$
$p(h_1, h_2) \wedge p(h_2, h_3) \supset p(h_1, h_3) \wedge \forall h_1, h_2 : Human.p(h_1, h_2) \supset short(h_2) \supset short(h_1).$

(25) $[\![shorter\_than]\!] = \pi_1(COMP)$

With the above, we can easily show that the inferences like (26) can be obtained as expected.[11]

(26) John is shorter than George.
George is shorter than Stergios.
Is John shorter than Stergios? [Yes]

Given the definition in $COMP$ according to which if two elements stand in a $COMP$ relation (meaning that the first argument is shorter than the second one), and there is also a third element standing in a $COMP$ relation with the second, then by transitivity defined in $COMP$, this third element also stands in a $COMP$ relation with the first, i.e. the third element is shorter than the first.

3.2.4 Factive/Implicative verbs

This section concerns inference cases with various types of verbs that presuppose the truth of their complement like for example factive or implicative verbs. Example (27) is an example of such a verb, while (28) is not:

(27) Smith knew that Itel had won the contract 1991.
Did Itel win the contract in 1991? [Yes]

[11]In giving a full analysis of compratives, one may further consider measures. Such an account is also possible using Σ types, in effect extending the account just proposed for comparatives. The idea is basically to extend the above account using dependent typing over measures. Such an account can be found in (Chatzikyriakidis and Luo, 2013b)

(28) Smith believed that Itel had won the contract 1991.
Did Itel win the contract in 1991? [Don't know]

What we need is to encode that verbs like *know* presuppose their argument's truth while verbs like *believe* do not. For instance, *know* belongs to the former class and its semantics is given as follows:

(29) $KNOW = \Sigma p : Human \rightarrow Prop \rightarrow Prop.\ \forall h : Human \forall P : Prop.\ p(h, P) \supset P$

(30) $[\![know]\!] = \pi_1(KNOW)$

In effect, a similar reasoning to the one used in dealing with VP adverbs is proposed. In effect, an auxiliary object is firstly used, followed by the definition of know as the first projection of the Σ type involved in the auxiliary object. With this, the inference (27) can be obtained as expected. Intensional verbs like *believe* on the other hand do not imply their arguments and inferences like (28) cannot be shown to be valid inferences.

3.2.5 Adjectival inference

As a last example of the use of rich typing in order to deal with NLI, we discuss NLI cases involving adjectives. In (Chatzikyriakidis and Luo, 2013a) we have shown that the use of subtyping, Σ types and universes can give us a correct account of at least intersective and subsective adjectives. Note that the original Σ type analysis proposed by researchers like Ranta (Ranta, 1994) is inadequate to capture the inferential properties of either intersective or subsective adjectives. The FraCas test suite has a rather different classification. One major distinction is between affirmative and non-affirmative adjectives shown below:

(31) Affirmative: Adj(N) $\Rightarrow$ (N)

(32) Non-affirmative: Adj(N) $\nRightarrow$ (N)

Concentrating on affirmative adjectives for the moment, we see that a Σ type analysis is enough in these cases.Cases of affirmative adjectives are handled well with the existing record mechanism already used for adjectives. The following inference as well as similar inferences are correctly captured, given that a CN modified by an intersective adjective is interpreted as a Σ-type which is a subtype of the CN via means of the first projection.

Cases of subsective adjectives are discussed in the section dubbed as *extensional comparison classes* in the FraCas test suite. There, cases of adjectival inference involving adjectives like *small* and *large* are discussed. Cases like these can be handled using a typing which quantifies over a universe. In the case of *large* and *small* this universe is the universe CN:[12]

(33) $\Pi A\colon \text{CN}.\ (A \to Prop)$

With this typing, cases like the one shown below are correctly treated:

(34) All mice are small animals.
Mickey is a large mouse.
Is Mickey a large animal? [No]

Lastly, one should be able to take care of inferences associated with intersective adjectives like the one shown below:

(35) Adj_{inter} man $\Rightarrow$ Adj_{inter} human

A concrete example would be *black man* implying *black human*. Given that coercions according to Luo's MTT propagate via the various type constructors, we have: $\Sigma([\![man]\!], black) < \Sigma([\![human]\!], black)$. [13]

4 Linguistic Coercions in MTTs with Coercive Subtyping

Besides being crucial for MTT-semantics, coercive subtyping (Luo, 1999; Luo et al., 2012) also provides us a framework to interpret various linguistic coercions (Asher and Luo, 2012). Besides explaining the basic mechanisms, we shall also show (in §4.3) that dependent types have interesting applications in dealing with situations with sophisticated coercions in MTT-semantics.

4.1 Basic coercions

The basic coercive subtyping mechanism that coerces $f(a)$ into $f(c(a))$ by inserting the coercion c into a gap between f and a, suffices to represent many linguistic coercions. For example, consider

(36) Julie enjoyed a book.

The MTT-semantics of (36) is (37):

(37) $\exists x\colon [\![book]\!].\ [\![enjoy]\!](j, x)$

where

(38) $[\![enjoy]\!]\colon Human \to Event \to Prop.$

However, the domain type of $[\![enjoy]\!](j)$ is $Event$, which is different from $Book$! Then, how can $[\![enjoy]\!](j, x)$ in (37) be well-typed? The answer is that, in the framework of coercive subtyping and, in particular, under the assumption of the following coercion:

(39) $Book <_{reading} Event$

$[\![enjoy]\!](j, x)$ is coerced into (and, formally, equal to) $[\![enjoy]\!](j, reading(x))$ and hence well-typed. Informally, the sentence (36) is coerced into (40):

(40) Julie enjoyed reading a book.

Note that, in the above, we have considered only one possible coercion (39): from 'enjoy a book' to 'enjoy reading a book'. As we noted in the previous section, however, there are in fact context-dependent 'multiple coercions': e.g., (36) could have meant 'Julie enjoyed writing a book'; there could also be several reading events of that book. Coercive subtyping requires contextual uniqueness of coercions[14], we must restrict the scope/context using *local coercions* (Luo, 2011a).

4.2 Local Coercions

In many situations, it is necessary to limit the scope of a coercion. (36) furnishes an example: with the formal coercion (39), (37) is the correct interpretation of (36). However, there may be several possible coercions and hence (36) may have several meanings: which one to use can only be decided contextually. But note that coherence in coercive subtyping (contextual uniqueness of coercions) is necessary for formal semantics to deal with ambiguity. In such situations, we use local coercions to limit the scope of applicability of coercions. For instance, if (36) is used to mean (40) or 'Julie enjoyed writing a book', we exploit the following two coercions for (36):

(41) **coercion** $Book <_{reading} Event$ **in** (37)

[12]Other more restricted universes will be needed for adjectives like *skilful* given that we may want to avoid constructions like *skilful table*. Universe subtyping can take care of these issues. In effect, one can introduce a subuniverse of CN containing the names of the types $[\![human]\!]$ and its subtypes only. Let us call this universe CN_H, which is a subtype of CN: $\text{CN}_H < \text{CN}$. Now *skillful* extends over this more restricted universe. See (Chatzikyriakidis and Luo, 2013a) for more detalis.

[13]Cases of non-committal and privative adjectives will not be dealt with in this paper for reasons of space. The interested reader is directed to (Chatzikyriakidis and Luo, 2013a) for a treatment of these types of adjectives within the MTT setting discussed in this paper.

[14]This refers to the notion of *coherence*, the requirement that any two coercions between the same two types (in the same context) be the same. See (Luo, 1999; Luo et al., 2012) for its formal definition.

(42) **coercion** $Book <_{writing} Event$ **in** (37)

Note that such interpretations involve different local coercions and can be used in the same context. There is no ambiguity or confusion as to which coercion is to be employed, but we must make clear the scope of each one of the coercions, over what terms they are operative.

Local coercions have a dual notion – coercion contexts, which are contexts (in type theory) which may contain coercion entries of the form $A <_c B$ as well as entries of the usual form $x: A$. Coercion contexts occur left to the $\vdash$-sign. One can move a coercion entry in a coercion context to the right-hand side of the $\vdash$-sign to form a local coercion, while the inversion of this moves the coercion in a local coercion to the left. These constructs are governed by the relevant inference rules, some of which are discussed in, for example, (Luo, 2011a).

4.3 Dependent Types in Coercion Semantics

Sometimes, a simple scoping restriction is not enough. For example, consider

(43) Jill just started *War and Peace*, which Tolstoy finished after many years of hard work. But that won't last because she never gets through long novels.

It is not difficult to see that in (43) the scopes of the reading and writing coercions overlap intertwiningly, and so restrictions on the scopes of coercions will not be sufficient here to ensure uniqueness to eliminate ambiguity.

In many such cases, dependent typing proves to be useful. Indeed, this is the first time in the literature, as far as we know, that dependent types have been shown to be useful directly in the formal semantics of linguistic coercions.

For example, for the above sentences (43), instead of $Event$, we may consider the family of types

$$Evt: Human \rightarrow Type;$$

intuitively, for any $h: Human$, the dependent type $Evt(h)$ is the type of events conducted by h. Now, we can assume that the verbs $start$, $finish$ and $last$ have type $\Pi h: Human.\ (Evt(h) \rightarrow Prop)$ and $read$ and $write$ have type $\Pi h: Human.\ (Book \rightarrow Evt(h))$. Furthermore, we can consider the following parameterised coercions, for any $h: Human$,

$$Book <_{c(h)} Evt(h),$$

where the coercion $c(h)$ is the function from $Book$ to $Evt(h)$ defined as follows: for any $b: Book$,

$$c(h,b) = \begin{cases} write(h,b) & \text{if } h \text{ wrote } b, \\ read(h,b) & \text{otherwise.} \end{cases}$$

where we have simplified the second case by assuming that one would read a book if he/she has not written it. (One may think of other actions to consider more subcases here.) Having the above, we can now interpret (43) as follows (in a simplified form):

(44) $start(j, wp)$
$\&\ finish(t, wp)$
$\&\ \neg last(j, wp)$
$\&\ \forall lb: LBook.finish(j, \pi_1(lb))$

where $LBook \equiv \Sigma b : Book.long(b)$ is the type that interprets the CN 'long book' and π_1 is the first projection operator that takes a long book and returns the book itself. In the coercive subtyping framework, (44) is coerced into (and equal to) the following:

(45) $start(j, c(j, wp))$
$\&\ finish(t, c(t, wp))$
$\&\ \neg last(j, c(j, wp))$
$\&\ \forall lb: LBook.\ finish(j, c(j, \pi_1(lb)))$

which is (equal to)

(46) $start(j, read(j, wp))$
$\&\ finish(t, write(t, wp))$
$\&\ \neg last(j, read(j, wp))$
$\&\ \forall lb: LBook.\ finish(j, c(j, \pi_1(lb)))$

Note that, in the last conjunct, the coercion c is still present – $c(j, \pi_1(lb))$ cannot be reduced furthermore because lb is a variable.

5 Conclusions

In this paper we proposed to deal with NLI by making use of proof-assistant technology, in particular the proof-assistant Coq. It was shown that the combination of MTT semantics as well as the use of a proof-assistant that 'understands' so to say MTT semantics can provide us with encouraging results as regards the computational treatment of NLI. More specifically, the paper has concentrated on the importance and expressivity of MTTs as regards typing by exemplifying the use of a rich typing system in order to deal with a number of inference cases ranging from adjectival and adverbial modification to conjoined/disjoined NPs, comparatives as well as factive/implicative verbs and type coercions.

References

N. Asher and Z. Luo. 2012. Formalisation of coercions in lexical semantics. *Sinn und Bedeutung 17, Paris*, 223.

P. Boldini. 2000. Formalizing context in intuitionistic type theory. *Fundamenta Informaticae*, 42(2):1–23.

S. Chatzikyriakidis and Z. Luo. 2012. An account of natural language coordination in type theory with coercive subtyping. In Y. Parmentier and D. Duchier, editors, *Proc. of Constraint Solving and Language Processing (CSLP12). LNCS 8114*, pages 31–51, Orleans.

S. Chatzikyriakidis and Z. Luo. 2013a. Adjectives in a modern type-theoretical setting. In G. Morrill and J.M Nederhof, editors, *Proceedings of Formal Grammar 2013. LNCS 8036*, pages 159–174.

S. Chatzikyriakidis and Z. Luo. 2013b. Natural language inference in coq. Submitted.

S. Chatzikyriakidis and Z. Luo. 2014. Hyperintensionality in modern type theories. Submitted manuscript.

A. Church. 1940. A formulation of the simple theory of types. *J. Symbolic Logic*, 5(1).

R. Cooper, D. Crouch, J. van Eijck, C. Fox, J. van Genabith, J. Jaspars, H. Kamp, D. Milward, M. Pinkal, M. Poesio, and S. Pulman. 1996. Using the framework. *Technical Report LRE 62-051r*. http://www.cogsci.ed.ac.uk/ fracas/.

R. Cooper. 2005. Records and record types in semantic theory. *J. Logic and Compututation*, 15(2).

The Coq Development Team, 2007. *The Coq Proof Assistant Reference Manual (Version 8.1), INRIA*.

C. Fox and S. Lappin. 2005. *Foundations of Intensional Semantics*. Blackwell.

J. Ginzburg and R. Cooper. forthcoming. Ttr for natural language semantics. In C. Fox and S. Lappin, editors, *Handbook of Contemporary Semantic Theory*. Blackwell.

J.-Y. Girard. 1971. Une extension de l'interpretation fonctionelle de gödel à l'analyse et son application à l'élimination des coupures dans et la thèorie des types'. *Proc. 2nd Scandinavian Logic Symposium*. North-Holland.

H. Goguen. 1994. *A Typed Operational Semantics for Type Theory*. Ph.D. thesis, University of Edinburgh.

Z. Luo, S. Soloviev, and T. Xue. 2012. Coercive subtyping: theory and implementation. *Information and Computation*, 223:18–42.

Z. Luo. 1994. *Computation and Reasoning: A Type Theory for Computer Science*. Oxford Univ Press.

Z. Luo. 1999. Coercive subtyping. *Journal of Logic and Computation*, 9(1):105–130.

Z. Luo. 2010. Type-theoretical semantics with coercive subtyping. *Semantics and Linguistic Theory 20 (SALT20), Vancouver*, 84(2):28–56.

Z. Luo. 2011a. Contextual analysis of word meanings in type-theoretical semantics. In *Logical Aspects of Computational Linguistics (LACL'2011). LNAI 6736*, pages 159–174.

Zhaohui Luo. 2011b. Adjectives and adverbs in type-theoretical semantics. Notes.

Z. Luo. 2012a. Common nouns as types. In D. Bechet and A. Dikovsky, editors, *Logical Aspects of Computational Linguistics (LACL'2012). LNCS 7351*, pages 173–185.

Z. Luo. 2012b. Formal semantics in modern type theories with coercive subtyping. *Linguistics and Philosophy*, 35(6):491–513.

B. MacCartney. 2009. *Natural Language Inference*. Ph.D. thesis, Stanford Universisty.

P. Martin-Löf. 1975. An intuitionistic theory of types: predicative part. In H.Rose and J.C.Shepherdson, editors, *Logic Colloquium'73*.

P. Martin-Löf. 1984. *Intuitionistic Type Theory*. Bibliopolis.

R. Montague. 1974. *Formal Philosophy*. Yale University Press.

A. Ranta. 1994. *Type-Theoretical Grammar*. Oxford University Press.

C. Retoré. 2013. The Montagovian generative lexicon $\lambda\mathsf{Ty}_n$: an integrated type-theoretical framework for compositional semantics and lexical pragmatics.

G. Sundholm. 1989. Constructive generalized quantifiers. *Synthese*, 79(1):1–12.

A Type-Driven Tensor-Based Semantics for CCG

Jean Maillard
University of Cambridge
Computer Laboratory
jm864@cam.ac.uk

Stephen Clark
University of Cambridge
Computer Laboratory
sc609@cam.ac.uk

Edward Grefenstette
University of Oxford
Department of Computer Science
edward.grefenstette@cs.ox.ac.uk

Abstract

This paper shows how the tensor-based semantic framework of Coecke et al. can be seamlessly integrated with Combinatory Categorial Grammar (CCG). The integration follows from the observation that tensors are linear maps, and hence can be manipulated using the combinators of CCG, including type-raising and composition. Given the existence of robust, wide-coverage CCG parsers, this opens up the possibility of a practical, type-driven compositional semantics based on distributional representations.

1 Intoduction

In this paper we show how tensor-based distributional semantics can be seamlessly integrated with Combinatory Categorial Grammar (CCG, Steedman (2000)), building on the theoretical discussion in Grefenstette (2013). Tensor-based distributional semantics represents the meanings of words with particular syntactic types as tensors whose semantic type matches that of the syntactic type (Coecke et al., 2010). For example, the meaning of a transitive verb with syntactic type $(S\backslash NP)/NP$ is a 3rd-order tensor from the tensor product space $N \otimes S \otimes N$. The seamless integration with CCG arises from the (somewhat trivial) observation that tensors are linear maps — a particular kind of function — and hence can be manipulated using CCG's combinatory rules.

Tensor-based semantics arises from the desire to enhance distributional semantics with some compositional structure, in order to make distributional semantics more of a complete semantic theory, and to increase its utility in NLP applications. There are a number of suggestions for how to add compositionality to a distributional semantics (Clarke, 2012; Pulman, 2013; Erk, 2012). One approach is to assume that the meanings of all words are represented by context vectors, and then combine those vectors using some operation, such as vector addition, element-wise multiplication, or tensor product (Clark and Pulman, 2007; Mitchell and Lapata, 2008). A more sophisticated approach, which is the subject of this paper, is to adapt the compositional process from formal semantics (Dowty et al., 1981) and attempt to build a distributional representation in step with the syntactic derivation (Coecke et al., 2010; Baroni et al., 2013). Finally, there is a third approach using neural networks, which perhaps lies in between the two described above (Socher et al., 2010; Socher et al., 2012). Here compositional distributed representations are built using matrices operating on vectors, with all parameters learnt through a supervised learning procedure intended to optimise performance on some NLP task, such as syntactic parsing or sentiment analysis. The approach of Hermann and Blunsom (2013) conditions the vector combination operation on the syntactic type of the combinands, moving it a little closer to the more formal semantics-inspired approaches.

The remainder of the Introduction gives a short summary of distributional semantics. The rest of the paper introduces some mathematical notation from multi-linear algebra, including Einstein notation, and then shows how the combinatory rules of CCG, including type-raising and composition, can be applied directly to tensor-based semantic representations. As well as describing a tensor-based semantics for CCG, a further goal of this paper is to present the compositional framework of Coecke et al. (2010), which is based on category theory, to a computational linguistics audience using only the mathematics of multi-linear algebra.

1.1 Distributional Semantics

We assume a basic knowledge of distributional semantics (Grefenstette, 1994; Schütze, 1998). Recent inroductions to the topic include Turney and Pantel (2010) and Clark (2014).

A potentially useful distinction for this paper, and one not commonly made, is between *distributional* and *distributed* representations. Distributional representations are inherently *contextual*, and rely on the frequently quoted dictum from Firth that "you shall know a word from the company it keeps" (Firth, 1957; Pulman, 2013). This leads to the so-called distributional hypothesis that words that occur in similar contexts tend to have similar meanings, and to various proposals for how to implement this hypothesis (Curran, 2004), including alternative definitions of context; alternative weighting schemes which emphasize the importance of some contexts over others; alternative similarity measures; and various dimensionality reduction schemes such as the well-known LSA technique (Landauer and Dumais, 1997). An interesting conceptual question is whether a similar distributional hypothesis can be applied to phrases and larger units: is it the case that sentences, for example, have similar meanings if they occur in similar contexts? Work which does extend the distributional hypothesis to larger units includes Baroni and Zamparelli (2010), Clarke (2012), and Baroni et al. (2013).

Distributed representations, on the other hand, can be thought of simply as vectors (or possibly higher-order tensors) of real numbers, where there is no *a priori* interpretation of the basis vectors. Neural networks can perhaps be categorised in this way, since the resulting vector representations are simply sequences of real numbers resulting from the optimisation of some training criterion on a training set (Collobert and Weston, 2008; Socher et al., 2010). Whether these distributed representations can be given a contextual interpretation depends on how they are trained.

One important point for this paper is that *the tensor-based compositional process makes no assumptions about the interpretation of the tensors*. Hence in the remainder of the paper we make no reference to how noun vectors or verb tensors, for example, can be acquired (which, for the case of the higher-order tensors, is a wide open research question). However, in order to help the reader who would prefer a more grounded discussion, one possibility is to obtain the noun vectors using standard *distributional* techniques (Curran, 2004), and learn the higher-order tensors using recent techniques from "recursive" neural networks (Socher et al., 2010). Another possibility is suggested by Grefenstette et al. (2013), extending the learning technique based on linear regression from Baroni and Zamparelli (2010) in which "gold-standard" distributional representations are assumed to be available for some phrases and larger units.

2 Mathematical Preliminaries

The tensor-based compositional process relies on taking dot (or inner) products between vectors and higher-order tensors. Dot products, and a number of other operations on vectors and tensors, can be conveniently written using Einstein notation (also referred to as the Einstein summation convention). In the rest of the paper we assume that the vector spaces are over the field of real numbers.

2.1 Einstein Notation

The squared amplitude of a vector $\boldsymbol{v} \in \mathbb{R}^n$ is given by:

$$|\boldsymbol{v}|^2 = \sum_{i=1}^{n} v_i v_i$$

Similarly, the dot product of two vectors $\boldsymbol{v}, \boldsymbol{w} \in \mathbb{R}^n$ is given by:

$$\boldsymbol{v} \cdot \boldsymbol{w} = \sum_{i=1}^{n} v_i w_i$$

Denote the components of an $m \times n$ real matrix $\mathbf{A}$ by A_{ij} for $1 \leq i \leq m$ and $1 \leq j \leq n$. Then the matrix-vector product of $\mathbf{A}$ and $\boldsymbol{v} \in \mathbb{R}^n$ gives a vector $\mathbf{A}\boldsymbol{v} \in \mathbb{R}^m$ with components:

$$(\mathbf{A}\boldsymbol{v})_i = \sum_{j=1}^{n} A_{ij} v_j$$

We can also multiply an $n \times m$ matrix $\mathbf{A}$ and an $m \times o$ matrix $\mathbf{B}$ to produce an $n \times o$ matrix $\mathbf{AB}$ with components:

$$(\mathbf{AB})_{ij} = \sum_{k=1}^{m} A_{ik} B_{kj}$$

The previous examples are some of the most common operations in linear algebra, and they all involve sums over repeated indices. They can be simplified by introducing the *Einstein summation convention*: summation over the relevant range is implied on every component index that occurs twice. Pairs of indices that are summed over are known as *contracted*, while the remaining indices are known as *free*. Using this convention, the above operations can be written as:

$|\boldsymbol{v}|^2 = v_i v_i$

$\boldsymbol{v} \cdot \boldsymbol{w} = v_i w_i$

$(\mathbf{A}\boldsymbol{v})_i = A_{ij} v_j$, i.e. the contraction of $\boldsymbol{v}$ with the second index of $\mathbf{A}$

$(\mathbf{AB})_{ij} = A_{ik} B_{kj}$, i.e. the contraction of the second index of $\mathbf{A}$ with the first of $\mathbf{B}$

Note how the number of free indices is always conserved between the left- and right-hand sides in these examples. For instance, while the last equation has two indices on the left and four on the right, the two extra indices on the right are contracted. Hence *counting the number of free indices* can be a quick way of determining what type of object is given by a certain mathematical expression in Einstein notation: no free indices means that an operation yields a scalar number, one free index means a vector, two a matrix, and so on.

2.2 Tensors

Linear Functionals Given a finite-dimensional vector space $\mathbb{R}^n$ over $\mathbb{R}$, a *linear functional* is a linear map $a : \mathbb{R}^n \to \mathbb{R}$.

Let a vector $\boldsymbol{v}$ have components v_i in a fixed basis. Then the result of applying a linear functional a to $\boldsymbol{v}$ can be written as:

$$a(\boldsymbol{v}) = a_1 v_1 + \cdots + a_n v_n = \begin{pmatrix} a_1 & \cdots & a_n \end{pmatrix} \begin{pmatrix} v_1 \\ \vdots \\ v_n \end{pmatrix}$$

The numbers a_i are the components of the linear functional, which can also be pictured as a row vector. Since there is a one-to-one correspondence between row and column vectors, the above equation is equivalent to:

$$v(\boldsymbol{a}) = a_1 v_1 + \cdots + a_n v_n = \begin{pmatrix} v_1 & \cdots & v_n \end{pmatrix} \begin{pmatrix} a_1 \\ \vdots \\ a_n \end{pmatrix}$$

Using Einstein convention, the equations above can be written as:

$$a(\boldsymbol{v}) = v_i a_i = v(\boldsymbol{a})$$

Thus every finite-dimensional vector is a linear functional, and vice versa. Row and column vectors are examples of *first-order tensors*.

Definition 1 (First-order tensor)**.** *Given a vector space V over the field $\mathbb{R}$, a first-order tensor T can be defined as:*

- *an element of the vector space V,*
- *a linear map $T : V \to \mathbb{R}$,*
- *a $|V|$-dimensional array of numbers T_i, for $1 \leq i \leq |V|$.*

These three definitions are all equivalent. Given a first-order tensor described using one of these definitions, it is trivial to find the two other descriptions.

Matrices An $n \times m$ matrix $\mathbf{A}$ over $\mathbb{R}$ can be represented by a two-dimensional array of real numbers A_{ij}, for $1 \leq i \leq n$ and $1 \leq j \leq m$.

Via matrix-vector multiplication, the matrix $\mathbf{A}$ can be seen as a linear map $\mathbf{A} : \mathbb{R}^m \to \mathbb{R}^n$. It maps a vector $\boldsymbol{v} \in \mathbb{R}^m$ to a vector

$$\begin{pmatrix} A_{11} & \cdots & A_{1m} \\ \vdots & \ddots & \vdots \\ A_{n1} & \cdots & A_{nm} \end{pmatrix} \begin{pmatrix} v_1 \\ \vdots \\ v_m \end{pmatrix},$$

with components

$$\mathbf{A}(\boldsymbol{v})_i = A_{ij} v_j.$$

We can also contract a vector with the first index of the matrix, which gives us a map $\mathbf{A} : \mathbb{R}^n \to \mathbb{R}^m$. This corresponds to the operation

$$\begin{pmatrix} w_1 & \cdots & w_n \end{pmatrix} \begin{pmatrix} A_{11} & \cdots & A_{1m} \\ \vdots & \ddots & \vdots \\ A_{n1} & \cdots & A_{nm} \end{pmatrix},$$

resulting in a vector with components

$$(\boldsymbol{w}^T \mathbf{A})_i = A_{ji} w_j.$$

We can combine the two operations and see a matrix as a map $\mathbf{A} : \mathbb{R}^n \times \mathbb{R}^m \to \mathbb{R}$, defined by:

$$\boldsymbol{w}^T \mathbf{A} \boldsymbol{v} = \begin{pmatrix} w_1 & \cdots & w_n \end{pmatrix} \begin{pmatrix} A_{11} & \cdots & A_{1m} \\ \vdots & \ddots & \vdots \\ A_{n1} & \cdots & A_{nm} \end{pmatrix} \begin{pmatrix} v_1 \\ \vdots \\ v_m \end{pmatrix}$$

In Einstein notation, this operation can be written as

$$w_i A_{ij} v_j,$$

which yields a scalar (constant) value, consistent with the fact that all the indices are contracted.

Finally, matrices can also be characterised in terms of Kronecker products. Given two vectors $\boldsymbol{v} \in \mathbb{R}^n$ and $\boldsymbol{w} \in \mathbb{R}^m$, their Kronecker product $\boldsymbol{v} \otimes \boldsymbol{w}$ is a matrix

$$\boldsymbol{v} \otimes \boldsymbol{w} = \begin{pmatrix} v_1 w_1 & \cdots & v_1 w_m \\ \vdots & \ddots & \vdots \\ v_n w_1 & \cdots & v_n w_m \end{pmatrix},$$

with components

$$(\boldsymbol{v} \otimes \boldsymbol{w})_{ij} = v_i w_j.$$

It is a general result in linear algebra that any $n \times m$ matrix can be written as a finite sum of Kronecker products $\sum_k \boldsymbol{x}^{(k)} \otimes \boldsymbol{y}^{(k)}$ of a set of vectors $\boldsymbol{x}^{(k)}$ and $\boldsymbol{y}^{(k)}$. Note that the sum over k is written explicitly as it would not be implied by Einstein notation: this is because the index k does not range over vector/matrix/tensor components, but over a set of vectors, and hence that index appears in brackets.

An $n \times m$ matrix is an element of the tensor space $\mathbb{R}^n \otimes \mathbb{R}^m$, and it can also be seen as a linear map $\mathbf{A} : \mathbb{R}^n \otimes \mathbb{R}^m \rightarrow \mathbb{R}$. This is because, given a matrix $\mathbf{B}$ with decomposition $\sum_k \boldsymbol{x}^{(k)} \otimes \boldsymbol{y}^{(k)}$, the matrix $\mathbf{A}$ can act as follows:

$$\begin{aligned} \mathbf{A}(\mathbf{B}) &= A_{ij} \sum_k x_i^{(k)} y_j^{(k)} \\ &= \sum_k \begin{pmatrix} x_1^{(k)} & \cdots & x_n^{(k)} \end{pmatrix} \begin{pmatrix} A_{11} & \cdots & A_{1m} \\ \vdots & \ddots & \vdots \\ A_{n1} & \cdots & A_{nm} \end{pmatrix} \begin{pmatrix} y_1^{(k)} \\ \vdots \\ y_m^{(k)} \end{pmatrix} \\ &= A_{ij} B_{ij}. \end{aligned}$$

Again, counting the number of free indices in the last line tells us that this operation yields a scalar.

Matrices are examples of *second-order tensors*.

Definition 2 (Second-order tensor)**.** *Given vector spaces V, W over the field $\mathbb{R}$, a second-order tensor T can be defined as:*

- *an element of the vector space $V \otimes W$,*
- *a $|V| \times |W|$-dimensional array of numbers T_{ij}, for $1 \leq i \leq |V|$ and $1 \leq j \leq |W|$,*
- *a (multi-) linear map:*
  - $T : V \rightarrow W$,
  - $T : W \rightarrow V$,
  - $T : V \times W \rightarrow \mathbb{R}$ *or* $T : V \otimes W \rightarrow \mathbb{R}$.

Again, these definitions are all equivalent. Most importantly, the four types of maps given in the definition are isomorphic. Therefore specifying one map is enough to specify all the others.

Tensors We can generalise these definitions to the more general concept of *tensor*.

Definition 3 (Tensor)**.** *Given vector spaces $V_1, \ldots, V_k$ over the field $\mathbb{R}$, a kth-order tensor T is defined as:*

- *an element of the vector space $V_1 \otimes \cdots \otimes V_k$,*
- *a $|V_1| \times \cdots \times |V_k|$, k^{th}-dimensional array of numbers $T_{i_1 \cdots i_k}$, for $1 \leq i_j \leq |V_j|$,*
- *a multi-linear map $T : V_1 \times \cdots \times V_k \rightarrow \mathbb{R}$.*

3 Tensor-Based CCG Semantics

In this section we show how CCG's syntactic types can be given tensor-based meaning spaces, and how the combinator's employed by CCG to combine syntactic categories carry over to those meaning spaces, maintaining what is often described as CCG's "transparent interface" between syntax and semantics. Here are some example syntactic types, and the corresponding tensor spaces containing the meanings of the words with those types (using the notation *syntactic type* : *semantic type*).

We first assume that all atomic types have meanings living in distinct vector spaces:

- noun phrases, NP : N
- sentences, S : S

The recipe for determining the meaning space of a complex syntactic type is to replace each atomic type with its corresponding vector space and the slashes with tensor product operators:

- Intransitive verb, $S\backslash NP : \mathsf{S} \otimes \mathsf{N}$
- Transitive verb, $(S\backslash NP)/NP : \mathsf{S} \otimes \mathsf{N} \otimes \mathsf{N}$
- Ditransitive verb, $((S\backslash NP)/NP)/NP$: $\mathsf{S} \otimes \mathsf{N} \otimes \mathsf{N} \otimes \mathsf{N}$
- Adverbial modifier, $(S\backslash NP)\backslash(S\backslash NP)$: $\mathsf{S} \otimes \mathsf{N} \otimes \mathsf{S} \otimes \mathsf{N}$
- Preposition modifying NP, $(NP\backslash NP)/NP$: $\mathsf{N} \otimes \mathsf{N} \otimes \mathsf{N}$

Hence the meaning of an intransitive verb, for example, is a matrix in the tensor product space $\mathsf{S} \otimes \mathsf{N}$. The meaning of a transitive verb is a "cuboid", or 3rd-order tensor, in the tensor product space $\mathsf{S} \otimes \mathsf{N} \otimes \mathsf{N}$. In the same way that the syntactic type of an intransitive verb can be thought of as a function — taking an NP and returning an S — the meaning of an intransitive verb is also a function (linear map) — taking a vector in N and returning a vector in S. Another way to think of this function is that each element of the matrix specifies, for a pair of basis vectors (one from N and one from S), what the result is on the S basis vector given a value on the N basis vector.

Now we describe how the combinatory rules carry over to the meaning spaces.

3.1 Application

The function application rules of CCG are forward ($>$) and backward ($<$) application:

$$\begin{array}{llll} X/Y & Y & \Longrightarrow X & (>) \\ Y & X\backslash Y & \Longrightarrow X & (<) \end{array}$$

In a traditional semantics for CCG, if function application is applied in the syntax, then function application applies also in the semantics (Steedman, 2000). This is also true of the tensor-based semantics. For example, the meaning of a subject NP combines with the meaning of an intransitive verb via matrix multiplication, which is equivalent to applying the linear map corresponding to the matrix to the vector representing the meaning of the NP. Applying (multi-)linear maps in (multi-)linear algebra is equivalent to applying tensor contraction to the combining tensors. Here is the case for an intransitive verb:

$$\begin{array}{cc} \textit{Pat} & \textit{walks} \\ NP & S\backslash NP \\ \mathsf{N} & \mathsf{S} \otimes \mathsf{N} \end{array}$$

Let *Pat* be assigned a vector $P \in \mathsf{N}$ and *walks* be assigned a second-order tensor $W \in \mathsf{S} \otimes \mathsf{N}$. Using the backward application combinator corresponds to feeding P, an element of N, into W, seen as a function $\mathsf{N} \rightarrow \mathsf{S}$. In terms of tensor contraction, this is the following operation:

$$W_{ij}P_j.$$

Here we use the convention that the indices maintain the same order as the syntactic type. Therefore, in the tensor of an object of type X/Y, the first index corresponds to the type X and the second to the type Y. That is why, when performing the contraction corresponding to *Pat walks*, $P \in \mathsf{N}$ is contracted with the *second* index of $W \in \mathsf{S} \otimes \mathsf{N}$, and not the first.[1] The first index of W is then the only free index, telling us that the above operation yields a first-order tensor (vector). Since this index corresponds to S, we know that applying backward application to *Pat walks* yields a meaning vector in S.

Forward application is performed in the same manner. Consider the following example:

$$\begin{array}{ccc} \textit{Pat} & \textit{kisses} & \textit{Sandy} \\ NP & (S\backslash NP)/NP & NP \\ \mathsf{N} & \mathsf{S} \otimes \mathsf{N} \otimes \mathsf{N} & \mathsf{N} \end{array}$$

with corresponding tensors $P \in \mathsf{N}$ for *Pat*, $K \in \mathsf{S} \otimes \mathsf{N} \otimes \mathsf{N}$ for *kisses* and $Y \in \mathsf{N}$ for *Sandy*.

The forward application deriving the type of *kisses Sandy* corresponds to

$$K_{ijk}Y_k,$$

where Y is contracted with the third index of K because we have maintained the order defined by the type $(S\backslash NP)/NP$: the third index then corresponds to an argument NP coming from the right.

Counting the number of free indices in the above expression tells us that it yields a second-order tensor. Looking at the types corresponding to the free indices tells us that this second-order tensor is of type $\mathsf{S} \otimes \mathsf{N}$, which is the semantic type of a verb phrase (or intransitive verb), as we have already seen in the *walks* example.

3.2 Composition

The forward ($>_\mathbf{B}$) and backward ($<_\mathbf{B}$) composition rules are:

$$\begin{array}{llll} X/Y & Y/Z & \Longrightarrow X/Z & (>_\mathbf{B}) \\ Y\backslash Z & X\backslash Y & \Longrightarrow X\backslash Z & (<_\mathbf{B}) \end{array}$$

Composition in the semantics also reduces to a form of tensor contraction. Consider the following example, in which *might* can combine with *kiss* using forward composition:

$$\begin{array}{cccc} \textit{Pat} & \textit{might} & \textit{kiss} & \textit{Sandy} \\ NP & (S\backslash NP)/(S\backslash NP) & (S\backslash NP)/NP & NP \\ \mathsf{N} & \mathsf{S} \otimes \mathsf{N} \otimes \mathsf{S} \otimes \mathsf{N} & \mathsf{S} \otimes \mathsf{N} \otimes \mathsf{N} & \mathsf{N} \end{array}$$

[1]The particular order of the indices is not important, as long as a convention such as this one is decided upon and consistently applied to all types (so that tensor contraction contracts the relevant tensors from each side when a combinator is used).

with tensors $M \in \mathsf{S} \otimes \mathsf{N} \otimes \mathsf{S} \otimes \mathsf{N}$ for *might* and $K \in \mathsf{S} \otimes \mathsf{N} \otimes \mathsf{N}$ for *kiss*. Combining the meanings of *might* and *kiss* corresponds to the following operation:

$$M_{ijkl} K_{klm},$$

yielding a tensor in $\mathsf{S} \otimes \mathsf{N} \otimes \mathsf{N}$, which is the correct semantic type for a phrase with syntactic type $(S\backslash NP)/NP$. Backward composition is performed analogously.

3.3 Backward-Crossed Composition

English also requires the use of backward-crossed composition (Steedman, 2000):

$$X/Y \quad Z\backslash X \quad \Longrightarrow Z/Y \qquad (<_{\mathbf{B}_\times})$$

In tensor terms, this is the same as forward composition; we just need to make sure that the contraction matches up the correct parts of each tensor correctly. Consider the following backward-crossed composition:

$$(S\backslash NP)/NP \quad (S\backslash NP)\backslash(S\backslash NP) \quad \Rightarrow_{<_{\mathbf{B}_\times}} (S\backslash NP)/NP$$

Let the two items on the left-hand side be represented by tensors $A \in \mathsf{S} \otimes \mathsf{N} \otimes \mathsf{N}$ and $B \in \mathsf{S} \otimes \mathsf{N} \otimes \mathsf{S} \otimes \mathsf{N}$. Then, combining them with backward-crossed composition in tensor terms is

$$B_{ijkl} A_{klm},$$

resulting in a tensor in $\mathsf{S} \otimes \mathsf{N} \otimes \mathsf{N}$ (corresponding to the indices i, j and m). Note that we have reversed the order of tensors in the contraction to make the matching of the indices more transparent; however, tensor contraction is commutative (since it corresponds to a sum over products) so the order of the tensors does not affect the result.

3.4 Type-raising

The forward ($>_\mathbf{T}$) and backward ($<_\mathbf{T}$) type-raising rules are:

$$\begin{array}{lll} X & \Longrightarrow T/(T\backslash X) & (>_\mathbf{T}) \\ X & \Longrightarrow T\backslash(T/X) & (<_\mathbf{T}) \end{array}$$

where T is a variable ranging over categories.

Suppose we are given an item of atomic type Y, with corresponding vector $A \in \mathsf{Y}$. If we apply forward type-raising to it, we get a new tensor of type $A' \in \mathsf{T} \otimes \mathsf{T} \otimes \mathsf{Y}$. Now suppose the item of type Y is followed by another item of type $X\backslash Y$, with tensor $B \in \mathsf{X} \otimes \mathsf{Y}$. A phrase consisting of two words with types Y and $X\backslash Y$ can be parsed in two different ways:

- $Y \ X\backslash Y \Rightarrow X$, by backward application;
- $Y \ X\backslash Y \Rightarrow_\mathbf{T} X/(X\backslash Y) \ X\backslash Y$, by forward type-raising, and $X/(X\backslash Y) \ X\backslash Y \Rightarrow X$, by forward application.

Both ways of parsing this sentence yield an item of type X, and crucially the meaning of the resulting item should be the same in both cases.[2] This property of type-raising provides an avenue into determining what the tensor representation for the type-raised category should be, since the tensor representations must also be the same:

$$A_j B_{ij} = A'_{ijk} B_{jk}.$$

Moreover, this equation must hold for all items, B. As a concrete example, the requirement says that a subject NP combining with a verb phrase $S\backslash NP$ must produce the same meaning for the two alternative derivations, irrespective of the verb phrase. This is equivalent to the requirement that

$$A_j B_{ij} = A'_{ijk} B_{jk}, \quad \forall B \in \mathsf{X} \otimes \mathsf{Y}.$$

So to arrive at the tensor representation, we simply have to solve the tensor equation above. We start by renaming the dummy index j on the left-hand side:

$$A_k B_{ik} = A'_{ijk} B_{jk}.$$

We then insert a Kronecker delta ($\delta_{ij} = 1$ if $i = j$ and 0 otherwise):

$$A_k B_{jk} \delta_{ij} = A'_{ijk} B_{jk}.$$

Since the equation holds for all B, we are left with

$$A'_{ijk} = \delta_{ij} A_k,$$

which gives us a recipe for performing type-raising in a tensor-based model. The recipe is particularly simple and elegant: it corresponds to inserting the vector being type-raised into the 3rd-order tensor at all places where the first two indices are equal (with the rest of the elements in the 3rd-order tensor being zero). For example, to type-raise a subject NP, its meaning vector in N is placed in the 3rd-order tensor $\mathsf{S} \otimes \mathsf{S} \otimes \mathsf{N}$ at all places where the indices of the two S dimensions are the same. Visually, the 3rd-order tensor corresponding to the meaning of the type-raised category is

[2] This property of CCG resulting from the use of type-raising and composition is sometimes referred to as "spurious ambiguity".

a cubiod in which the noun vector is repeated a number of times (once for each sentence index), resulting in a series of "steps" progressing diagonally from the bottom of the cuboid to the top (assuming a particular orientation).

The discussion so far has been somewhat abstract, so to finish this section we include some more examples with CCG categories, and show that the tensor contraction operation has an intuitive similarity with the "cancellation law" of categorial grammar which applies in the syntax.

First consider the example of a subject NP with meaning A, combining with a verb phrase $S\backslash NP$ with meaning B, resulting in a sentence with meaning C. In the syntax, the two NPs cancel. In the semantics, for each basis of the sentence space S we perform an inner product between two vectors in N:

$$C_i = A_j B_{ij}$$

Hence, *inner products in the tensor space correspond to cancellation in the syntax.*

This correspondence extends to complex arguments, and also to composition. Consider the subject type-raising case, in which a subject NP with meaning A in $\mathsf{S} \otimes \mathsf{S} \otimes \mathsf{N}$ combines with a verb phrase $S\backslash NP$ with meaning B, resulting in a sentence with meaning C. Again we perform inner product operations, but this time the inner product is between two matrices:[3]

$$C_i = A_{ijk} B_{jk}$$

Note that two matrices are "cancelled" for each basis vector of the sentence space (i.e. for each index i in C_i).

As a final example, consider the forward composition from earlier, in which a modal verb with meaning A in $\mathsf{S} \otimes \mathsf{N} \otimes \mathsf{S} \otimes \mathsf{N}$ combines with a transitive verb with meaning B in $\mathsf{S} \otimes \mathsf{N} \otimes \mathsf{N}$ to give a transitive verb with meaning C in $\mathsf{S} \otimes \mathsf{N} \otimes \mathsf{N}$. Again the cancellation in the syntax corresponds to inner products between matrices, but this time we need an inner product for each combination of 3 indices:

$$C_{ijk} = A_{ijlm} B_{lmk}$$

[3]To be more precise, the two matrices can be thought of as vectors in the tensor space $\mathsf{S} \otimes \mathsf{N}$ and the inner product is between these vectors. Another way to think of this operation is to "linearize" the two matrices into vectors and then perform the inner product on these vectors.

For each i, j, k, two matrices — corresponding to the l, m indices above — are "cancelled".

This intuitive explanation extends to arguments with any number of slashes. For example, a composition where the cancelling categories are $(N/N)/(N/N)$ would require inner products between 4th-order tensors in $\mathsf{N} \otimes \mathsf{N} \otimes \mathsf{N} \otimes \mathsf{N}$.

4 Related Work

The tensor-based semantics presented in this paper is effectively an extension of the Coecke et al. (2010) framework to CCG, re-expressing in Einstein notation the existing categorical CCG extension in Grefenstette (2013), which itself builds on an earlier Lambek Grammar extension to the framework by Coecke et al. (2013).

This work also bears some similarity to the treatment of categorial grammars presented by Baroni et al. (2013), which it effectively encompasses by expressing the tensor contractions described by Baroni *et al.* as Einstein summations. However, this paper also covers CCG-specific operations not discussed by Baroni *et al.*, such as type-raising and composition.

One difference between this paper and the original work by Coecke et al. (2010) is that they use pregroups as the syntactic formalism (Lambek, 2008), a context-free variant of categorial grammar. In pregroups, cancellation in the syntax is always between two atomic categories (or more precisely, between an atomic category and its "adjoint"), whereas in CCG the arguments in complex categories can be complex categories themselves. To what extent this difference is significant remains to be seen. For example, one area where this may have an impact is when non-linearities are added after contractions. Since the CCG contractions with complex arguments happen "in one go", whereas the corresponding pregroup cancellation in the semantics would be a series of contractions, many more non-linearities would be added in the pregroup case.

Krishnamurthy and Mitchell (2013) is based on a similar insight to this paper – that CCG provides combinators which can manipulate functions operating over vectors. Krishnamurthy and Mitchell consider the function application case, whereas we have shown how the type-raising and composition operators apply naturally in this setting also.

5 Conclusion

This paper provides a theoretical framework for the development of a compositional distributional semantics for CCG. Given the existence of robust, wide-coverage CCG parsers (Clark and Curran, 2007; Hockenmaier and Steedman, 2002), together with various techniques for learning the tensors, the opportunity exists for a practical implementation. However, there are significant engineering difficulties which need to be overcome.

Consider adapting the neural-network learning techniques of Socher et al. (2012) to this problem.[4] In terms of the number of tensors, the lexicon would need to contain a tensor for every word-category pair; this is at least an order of magnitude more tensors then the number of matrices learnt in existing work (Socher et al., 2012; Hermann and Blunsom, 2013). Furthermore, the order of the tensors is now higher. Syntactic categories such as $((N/N)/(N/N))/((N/N)/(N/N))$ are not uncommon in the wide-coverage grammar of Hockenmaier and Steedman (2007), which in this case would require an 8th-order tensor. This combination of many word-category pairs and higher-order tensors results in a huge number of parameters.

As a solution to this problem, we are investigating ways to reduce the number of parameters, for example using tensor decomposition techniques (Kolda and Bader, 2009). It may also be possible to reduce the size of some of the complex categories in the grammar. Many challenges remain before a type-driven compositional distributional semantics can be realised, similar to the work of Bos for the model-theoretic case (Bos et al., 2004; Bos, 2005), but in this paper we have set out the theoretical framework for such an implementation.

Finally, we repeat a comment made earlier that the compositional framework makes no assumptions about the underlying vector spaces, or how they are to be interpreted. On the one hand, this flexibility is welcome, since it means the framework can encompass many techniques for building word vectors (and tensors). On the other hand, it means that a description of the framework is necessarily abstract, and it leaves open the question of what the meaning spaces represent. The latter question is particularly pressing in the case of the sentence space, and providing an interpretation of such spaces remains a challenge for the distributional semantics community, as well as relating distributional semantics to more traditional topics in semantics such as quantification and inference.

[4] Non-linear transformations are inherent to neural networks, whereas the framework in this paper is entirely linear. However, as hinted at earlier in the paper, non-linear transformations can be applied to the output of each tensor, turning the linear networks in this paper into extensions of those in Socher et al. (2012) (extensions in the sense that the tensors in Socher et al. (2012) do not extend beyond matrices).

Acknowledgments

Jean Maillard is supported by an EPSRC MPhil studentship. Stephen Clark is supported by ERC Starting Grant DisCoTex (306920) and EPSRC grant EP/I037512/1. Edward Grefenstette is supported by EPSRC grant EP/I037512/1. We would like to thank Tamara Polajnar, Laura Rimell, Nal Kalchbrenner and Karl Moritz Hermann for useful discussion.

References

M. Baroni and R. Zamparelli. 2010. Nouns are vectors, adjectives are matrices: Representing adjective-noun constructions in semantic space. In *Conference on Empirical Methods in Natural Language Processing (EMNLP-10)*, Cambridge, MA.

M. Baroni, R. Bernardi, and R. Zamparelli. 2013. Frege in space: A program for compositional distributional semantics (to appear). *Linguistic Issues in Language Technologies.*

Johan Bos, Stephen Clark, Mark Steedman, James R. Curran, and Julia Hockenmaier. 2004. Wide-coverage semantic representations from a CCG parser. In *Proceedings of COLING-04*, pages 1240–1246, Geneva, Switzerland.

Johan Bos. 2005. Towards wide-coverage semantic interpretation. In *Proceedings of the Sixth International Workshop on Computational Semantics (IWCS-6)*, pages 42–53, Tilburg, The Netherlands.

Stephen Clark and James R. Curran. 2007. Wide-coverage efficient statistical parsing with CCG and log-linear models. *Computational Linguistics*, 33(4):493–552.

Stephen Clark and Stephen Pulman. 2007. Combining symbolic and distributional models of meaning. In *Proceedings of AAAI Spring Symposium on Quantum Interaction*, Stanford, CA. AAAI Press.

Stephen Clark. 2014. Vector space models of lexical meaning (to appear). In Shalom Lappin and Chris Fox, editors, *Handbook of Contemporary Semantics second edition*. Wiley-Blackwell.

Daoud Clarke. 2012. A context-theoretic framework for compositionality in distributional semantics. *Computational Linguistics*, 38(1):41–71.

B. Coecke, M. Sadrzadeh, and S. Clark. 2010. Mathematical foundations for a compositional distributional model of meaning. In J. van Bentham, M. Moortgat, and W. Buszkowski, editors, *Linguistic Analysis (Lambek Festschrift)*, volume 36, pages 345–384.

Bob Coecke, Edward Grefenstette, and Mehrnoosh Sadrzadeh. 2013. Lambek vs. Lambek: Functorial vector space semantics and string diagrams for Lambek calculus. *Annals of Pure and Applied Logic*.

R. Collobert and J. Weston. 2008. A unified architecture for natural language processing: Deep neural networks with multitask learning. In *International Conference on Machine Learning, ICML*, Helsinki, Finland.

James R. Curran. 2004. *From Distributional to Semantic Similarity*. Ph.D. thesis, University of Edinburgh.

D.R. Dowty, R.E. Wall, and S. Peters. 1981. *Introduction to Montague Semantics*. Dordrecht.

Katrin Erk. 2012. Vector space models of word meaning and phrase meaning: a survey. *Language and Linguistics Compass*, 6(10):635–653.

J. R. Firth. 1957. A synopsis of linguistic theory 1930-1955. In *Studies in Linguistic Analysis*, pages 1–32. Oxford: Philological Society.

Edward Grefenstette, Georgiana Dinu, YaoZhong Zhang, Mehrnoosh Sadrzadeh, and Marco Baroni. 2013. Multistep regression learning for compositional distributional semantics. In *Proceedings of the 10th International Conference on Computational Semantics (IWCS-13)*, Potsdam, Germany.

Gregory Grefenstette. 1994. *Explorations in Automatic Thesaurus Discovery*. Kluwer.

Edward Grefenstette. 2013. *Category-Theoretic Quantitative Compositional Distributional Models of Natural Language Semantics*. Ph.D. thesis, University of Oxford.

Karl Moritz Hermann and Phil Blunsom. 2013. The role of syntax in vector space models of compositional semantics. *Proceedings of ACL, Sofia, Bulgaria, August. Association for Computational Linguistics*.

Julia Hockenmaier and Mark Steedman. 2002. Generative models for statistical parsing with Combinatory Categorial Grammar. In *Proceedings of the 40th Meeting of the ACL*, pages 335–342, Philadelphia, PA.

Julia Hockenmaier and Mark Steedman. 2007. CCGbank: a corpus of CCG derivations and dependency structures extracted from the Penn Treebank. *Computational Linguistics*, 33(3):355–396.

T. G. Kolda and B. W. Bader. 2009. Tensor decompositions and applications. *SIAM Review*, 51(3):455–500.

Jayant Krishnamurthy and Tom M. Mitchell. 2013. Vector space semantic parsing: A framework for compositional vector space models. In *Proceedings of the 2013 ACL Workshop on Continuous Vector Space Models and their Compositionality*, Sofia, Bulgaria.

Joachim Lambek. 2008. *From Word to Sentence. A Computational Algebraic Approach to Grammar*. Polimetrica.

T. K. Landauer and S. T. Dumais. 1997. A solution to Plato's problem: the latent semantic analysis theory of acquisition, induction and representation of knowledge. *Psychological Review*, 104(2):211–240.

Jeff Mitchell and Mirella Lapata. 2008. Vector-based models of semantic composition. In *Proceedings of ACL-08*, pages 236–244, Columbus, OH.

Stephen Pulman. 2013. Distributional semantic models. In Sadrzadeh Heunen and Grefenstette, editors, *Compositional Methods in Physics and Linguistics*. Oxford University Press.

Hinrich Schütze. 1998. Automatic word sense discrimination. *Computational Linguistics*, 24(1):97–124.

Richard Socher, Christopher D. Manning, and Andrew Y. Ng. 2010. Learning continuous phrase representations and syntactic parsing with recursive neural networks. In *Proceedings of the NIPS Deep Learning and Unsupervised Feature Learning Workshop*, Vancouver, Canada.

Richard Socher, Brody Huval, Christopher D. Manning, and Andrew Y. Ng. 2012. Semantic compositionality through recursive matrix-vector spaces. In *Proceedings of the Conference on Empirical Methods in Natural Language Processing*, pages 1201–1211, Jeju, Korea.

Mark Steedman. 2000. *The Syntactic Process*. The MIT Press, Cambridge, MA.

Peter D. Turney and Patrick Pantel. 2010. From frequency to meaning: Vector space models of semantics. *Journal of Artificial Intelligence Research*, 37:141–188.

From Natural Language to RDF Graphs with Pregroups

Antonin Delpeuch
École Normale Supérieure
45 rue d'Ulm
75005 Paris, France
antonin.delpeuch@ens.fr

Anne Preller
LIRMM
161 rue Ada
34392 Montpellier Cedex 5, France
preller@lirmm.fr

Abstract

We define an algorithm translating natural language sentences to the formal syntax of RDF, an existential conjunctive logic widely used on the Semantic Web. Our translation is based on pregroup grammars, an efficient type-logical grammatical framework with a transparent syntax-semantics interface. We introduce a restricted notion of side effects in the semantic category of finitely generated free semimodules over $\{0, 1\}$ to that end. The translation gives an intensional counterpart to previous extensional models. We establish a one-to-one correspondence between extensional models and RDF models such that satisfaction is preserved. Our translation encompasses the expressivity of the target language and supports complex linguistic constructions like relative clauses and unbounded dependencies.

1 Introduction

There is a general agreement that Natural Language Processing has two aspects. One is syntax, rules how words are put together to form a grammatical string. The other is semantics, rules how meanings of strings are computed from the meanings of words. To this we add a third aspect, namely that semantics must include rules of logic how to compute the truth of the whole string from the truth of its parts.

The Resource Description Framework (RDF) (Hayes and McBride, 2004) is an artificial language that takes the intuitive form of knowledge graphs. Its semantics has the expressive power of the fragment of multisorted first order logic that uses conjunction and existential quantification only. This restricted expressive power limits the statements of natural language that can be interpreted as RDF graphs. Typically, statements with negation words are excluded.

We use pregroup grammars as the linguistic and mathematical tool to recognise and interpret natural language strings in RDF. Pregroup Calculus, also known as Compact Bilinear Logic (Lambek, 1993) (Lambek, 1999), is a simplification of Lambek's Syntactic Calculus, (Lambek, 1958). Pregroup grammars are based on a lexicon like all categorial grammars. Syntactical analysis consists in the construction of a proof (derivation) in the calculus.

All semantics proposed so far use functors from the lexical category of (Preller and Lambek, 2007) into some symmetric compact closed category. They include the compositional distributional vector space models of (Clark et al., 2008), (Kartsaklis et al., 2013) based on context and the functional logical models of (Preller, 2012).

We proceed as follows. Recalling that words and grammatical strings recognised by the grammar are represented by meaning-morphisms in the lexical category, we propose a "syntactic" functor from the latter into a symmetric monoidal category $\mathcal{C}_S$ of 'morphisms with side effects' over the category $\mathcal{C}$ of finite dimensional semimodules over the lattice $\mathbb{B} = \{0, 1\}$. The elements of the semimodule S identify with RDF graphs. The value of the syntactic functor at a statement is the RDF graph of the statement. The extensional models of logic are recast as "semantic" functors from the lexical category to $\mathcal{C}$. We associate to any semantic functor an RDF interpretation and show that a statement is true in the semantic functor if and only if the corresponding RDF graph is true in the RDF interpretation.

2 Preliminaries

2.1 RDF graphs

RDF is a widely-adopted framework introduced in (Hayes and McBride, 2004) as a standard for linked information representation on the Web. Informally, an RDF graph is a set of labeled links between objects, which represent statements concerning the linked objects.

Throughout this article we will simply consider that they are represented by strings of characters without spaces, written in a mono-spaced font: the entity *John* is denoted by the string `John`.

A link between two objects is a triple, made of one entity (the subject of the predicate), a property (the type of the link, also represented by a string) and a second entity (the object of the predicate). Graphically, we represent a triple as a directed property from the subject to the object, labeled by the predicate.

RDF allows to use nodes without labels, called blank nodes. Concretely, this means that we can always pick a fresh node, named `blank-n` where `n` is some number, such that this node is not involved in any triple yet.

An example We can represent the sentence *John owns a white boat* using a fresh blank node for *a white boat*:

```
John owns blank-1
blank-1 rdf:type boat
blank-1 is_white true
```

Here, `rdf:type` is a special RDF predicate indicating the type of its subject. The graph representing this set of triples is

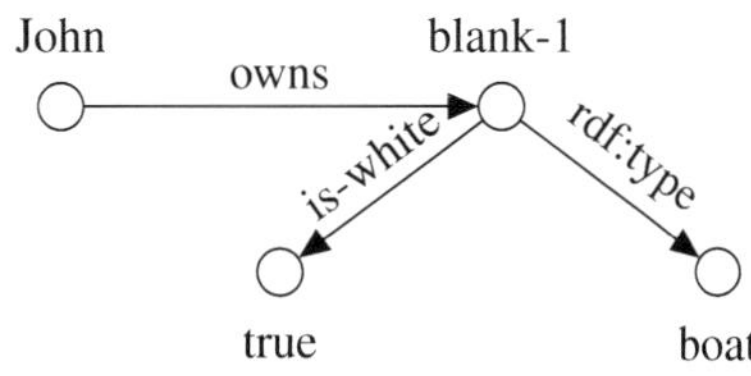

Figure 1: A graph with a blank node

Recall that our goal is to translate natural language sentences to graphs. Graphs can indeed be seen as semantic representations of sentences, in the sense that they can be used to assign a truth value to a sentence, trough the notion of entailment (Hayes and McBride, 2004).

A graph $\mathcal{H}$ is an *instance* of $\mathcal{G}$ when $\mathcal{H}$ can be obtained from $\mathcal{G}$ by assigning labels to some blank nodes (possibly none of them). A graph $\mathcal{G}_0$ *entails* another graph $\mathcal{G}$ if an instance of $\mathcal{G}$ is a subgraph of $\mathcal{G}_0$. With these definitions, we can define true RDF graphs as the graphs entailed by some reference graph, storing all the true facts.

2.2 Pregroup grammars

A pregroup grammar (Lambek, 1999), consists of the free pregroup $\mathcal{C}(\mathcal{B})$ generated by a partially ordered set $\mathcal{B}$ and a lexicon $\mathcal{D}_\mathcal{B}$. By 'free pregroup' we mean the free compact closed category $\mathcal{C}(\mathcal{B})$ generated by $\mathcal{B}$ following the version given in (Preller and Lambek, 2007)[1]. The lexicon $\mathcal{D}_\mathcal{B}$ introduces the monoidal category $\mathcal{L}_\mathcal{B}$, freely generated by the inequalities and the lexical morphisms given by the lexicon. Lexical entries have "formal meanings" in the *lexical category*, the free compact closed category generated by $\mathcal{B}$ and the morphisms introduced by the words. They are analogue to the lambda-terms intervening in categorial grammars, (Steedman, 1996).

The working of pregroup grammars can be described without explicit use of category theory. The main result of this section however, the decomposition lemma, invokes properties of the graphs proved in (Preller and Lambek, 2007).

[1]Semantics requires more than one morphism between objects, whereas the partial preorder of the free pregroup of (Lambek, 1999) confounds all morphisms with identical domain and codomain.

We start with the formal definition of a monoidal category followed by the condition it must satisfy to be compact closed.

Definition 1. *A category $\mathcal{C}$ is*

1. ***monoidal*** *if there is a bifunctor $\otimes : \mathcal{C} \times \mathcal{C} \to \mathcal{C}$, a distinguished object I, the* unit *of $\otimes$, satisfying $(A \otimes B) \otimes C = A \otimes (B \otimes C)$, $(f \otimes g) \otimes h = f \otimes (g \otimes h)$* [2]
2. ***compact closed*** *if it is monoidal and there are contravariant endofunctors $(\ )^r$ and $(\ )^\ell$, called* right adjoint *and* left adjoint, *such that for every object A and every morphism $f : A \to B$ there are morphisms $\eta_f : I \to A^r \otimes A$, the* name *of f, and $\epsilon_f : A \otimes B^r \to I$, the* coname *of f, satisfying for any $g : B \to C$*

$$(A \otimes B)^r = B^r \otimes A^r, \quad (A \otimes B)^\ell = B^\ell \otimes A^\ell$$
$$(\epsilon_f \otimes 1_C) \circ (1_A \otimes \eta_g) = g \circ f$$
$$(1_{A^r} \otimes \epsilon_g) \circ (\eta_f \otimes 1_{C^r}) = (f \circ g)^r .$$

3. ***symmetric*** *if it is monoidal and there is a natural isomorphism $\sigma_{AB} : A \otimes B \to B \otimes A$ such that $\sigma_{AB}^{-1} = \sigma_{BA}$.*

Recall that $\otimes$ is a bifunctor if and only if the following equalities are satisfied for all objects A, B and all morphisms $f_i : A_i \to B_i, g_i : B_i \to C_i, i = 1, 2$

$$\begin{array}{l} 1_A \otimes 1_B = 1_{A \otimes B} \\ \textit{Interchange Law} \\ (f_2 \circ f_1) \otimes (g_2 \circ g_1) = (f_2 \otimes g_2) \circ (f_1 \otimes g_1) \end{array} \qquad (1)$$

The morphisms of $\mathcal{C}(\mathcal{B})$ and $\mathcal{L}_\mathcal{B}$ identify with graphs, which we now describe without invoking category theory.

The objects of $\mathcal{C}(\mathcal{B})$ are called *types*. They include the elements of $\mathcal{B}$, called *basic types*. For instance, the set $\mathcal{B}$ may include the basic types $\boldsymbol{s}$ for statements, $\boldsymbol{d}$ for determiners, $\boldsymbol{n}$ for noun phrases, $\boldsymbol{o}$ for direct objects with corresponding types in relatives clauses $\boldsymbol{r}$, $\hat{\boldsymbol{n}}$ and $\hat{\boldsymbol{o}}$. There is only one strict inequality $\boldsymbol{n} < \boldsymbol{o}$. Assimilating $\mathcal{B}$ to a category, we write $i_{\boldsymbol{ab}} : \boldsymbol{a} \to \boldsymbol{b}$ instead of $\boldsymbol{a} \leq \boldsymbol{b}$ and $1_{\boldsymbol{a}}$ for $i_{\boldsymbol{aa}}$. A *simple* type is an iterated left adjoint or right adjoint of a basic type $\ldots, \boldsymbol{a}^{\ell\ell} = \boldsymbol{a}^{(-2)}, \boldsymbol{a}^\ell = \boldsymbol{a}^{(-1)}, \boldsymbol{a} = \boldsymbol{a}^{(0)}, \boldsymbol{a}^r = \boldsymbol{a}^{(1)}, \boldsymbol{a}^{rr} = \boldsymbol{a}^{(2)}, \ldots$. The *iterator* of $t = \boldsymbol{a}^{(z)}$ is the integer z. An arbitrary type is a string of simple types separated by the symbol $\otimes$. In particular, the empty string is a type, denoted I.

The *lexicon* of a pregroup grammar consists of a set of pairs *word* : T where the type $T \in \mathcal{C}(\mathcal{B})$ captures the different grammatical roles a word may play. For

[2]Strictly speaking, these equalities hold up to natural isomorphisms, but the coherence theorem of (Mac Lane, 1971) makes it possible to replace the isomorphisms by equalities without loss of generality.

instance

proper name	: $\boldsymbol{n}$
transitive verb	: $\boldsymbol{n}^r \otimes \boldsymbol{s} \otimes \boldsymbol{o}^\ell$
transitive verb	: $\hat{\boldsymbol{n}}^r \otimes \boldsymbol{r} \otimes \boldsymbol{o}^\ell$
transitive verb	: $\boldsymbol{n}^r \otimes \hat{\boldsymbol{o}}^r \otimes \boldsymbol{r}$
determiner	: $\boldsymbol{d}$
adjective	: $\boldsymbol{d}^r \otimes \boldsymbol{d}$
countnoun	: $\boldsymbol{d}^r \otimes \boldsymbol{n}$
relpronoun	: $\boldsymbol{n}^r \otimes \boldsymbol{n} \otimes \boldsymbol{r}^\ell \otimes \hat{\boldsymbol{n}}$
relpronoun	: $\boldsymbol{n}^r \otimes \boldsymbol{n} \otimes \boldsymbol{r}^\ell \otimes \hat{\boldsymbol{o}}$

A pregroup grammars analyses a string of words by constructing a graph: choose an entry $w_i : T_i$ for each word w_i and align the types in the order of the words. Place non-crossing oriented underlinks such that the tail of an underlink is a basic type with an even number of iterations, say $t = \boldsymbol{a}^{(z)}$, where $z = \pm 2n$. If the head is to the left of the tail then it is the left adjoint $\boldsymbol{b}^{(z)\ell} = \boldsymbol{b}^{(z-1)}$, for some basic type $\boldsymbol{b} \geq \boldsymbol{a}$. If it is to the right then its a right adjoint $\boldsymbol{b}^{(z)r} = \boldsymbol{b}^{(z+1)}$. Complete the graph by repeating the nodes that are not head or tail of an underlink in a line below and adding a vertical link between corresponding nodes.

The string is said to be *grammatical* if exactly one simple type remains that is not the tail or head of an underlink and if it is a basic type. The resulting graph is called a *reduction* and denotes a unique morphism $r : T_1 \otimes \ldots \otimes T_n \to \boldsymbol{b}$ of $\mathcal{C}(\mathcal{B})$. More generally, graphs standing for morphisms align the domain above and the codomain below.

For instance, the graph below exhibits a reduction to the sentence type $\boldsymbol{s}$

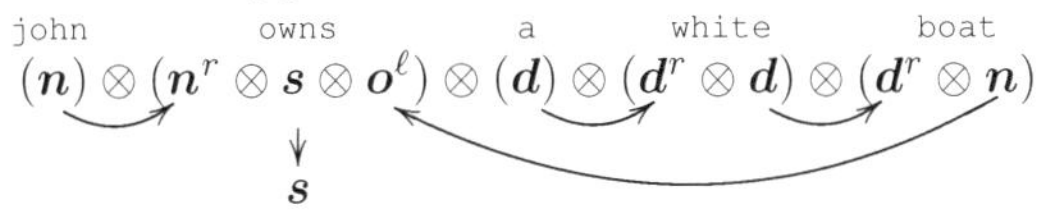

The following two graphs are reductions to the noun phrase type $\boldsymbol{n}$. The first graph corresponds to the case where the relative pronoun is the object of the verb in the relative clause whereas it is the subject in the second graph

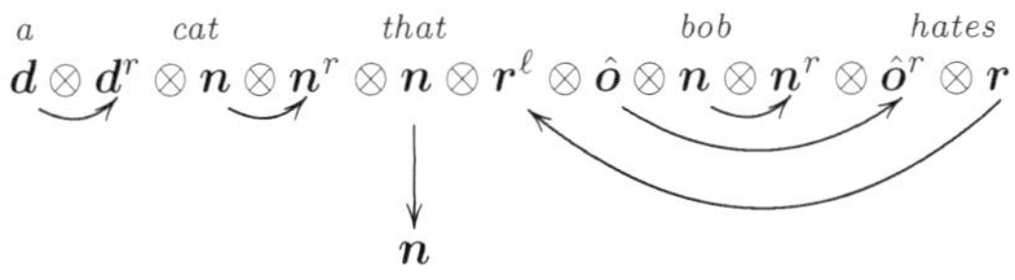

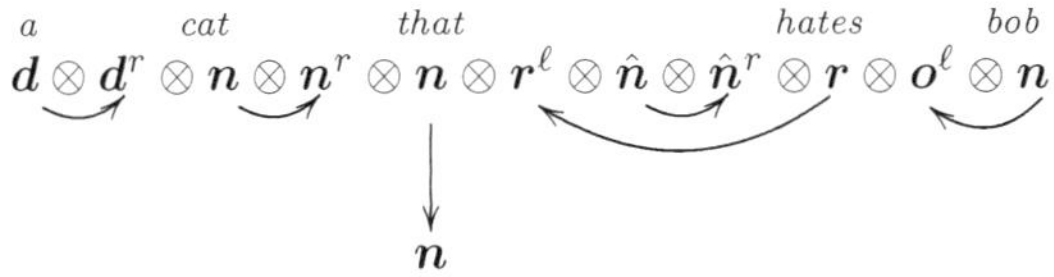

The meanings of words are also represented by graphs that correspond to morphisms of the lexical category $\mathcal{L}_\mathcal{B}$. In fact, every entry $w : T$ in the lexicon gives rise to a *meaning morphism* $\overline{\mathtt{w}}_T : I \to T$ and a *lexical morphism* $\mathtt{w}_T$ represented by the following oriented labelled graphs

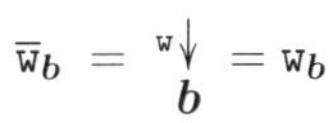

$T = \boldsymbol{a}^r \otimes \boldsymbol{b}$

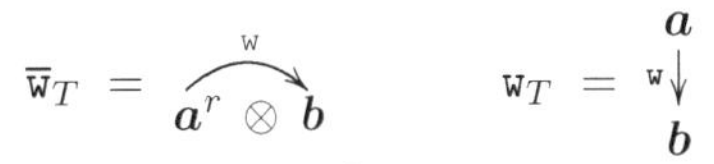

$T = \boldsymbol{a}^r \otimes \boldsymbol{b} \otimes \boldsymbol{c}^\ell$

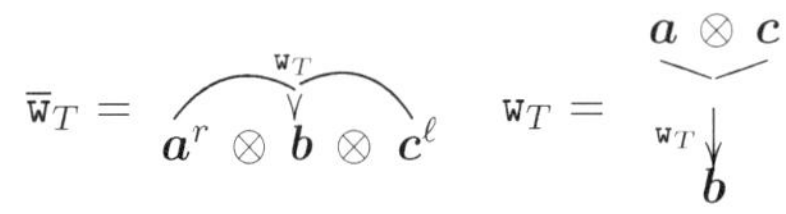

$T = \boldsymbol{a}^r \otimes \boldsymbol{c}^r \otimes \boldsymbol{b}$

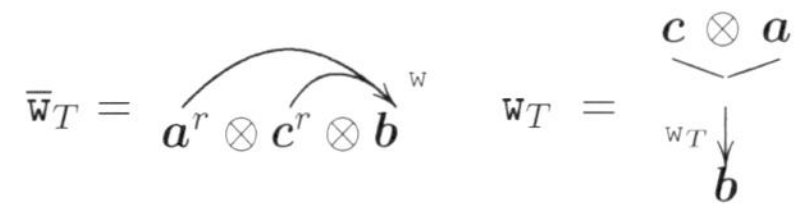

If T has two factors that are basic types, there is besides the main lexical morphism w_T an auxiliary lexical morphism j_T.

$T = \boldsymbol{n}^r \otimes \boldsymbol{n} \otimes \boldsymbol{r}^\ell \otimes \boldsymbol{d},\ \boldsymbol{d} = \hat{\boldsymbol{n}}, \hat{\boldsymbol{o}}$

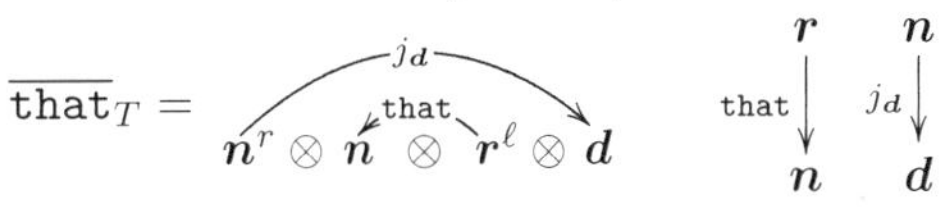

We omit the subscript T if this does not lead to confusion.

The nodes of the meaning graphs are the simple types of T. They form the lower line of the graph, the upper line is the empty string I. The corresponding morphism has domain I and codomain T. An overlink may have several tails but only one head. The tails of overlinks are right or left adjoints of basic types, the head is a basic type[3].

The *lexical category* $\mathcal{L}_\mathcal{B}$ generated by the lexicon $\mathcal{D}_\mathcal{B}$ is the compact closed category freely generated by $\mathcal{B}$, the symmetry morphisms $\sigma_{\boldsymbol{ab}}$ and the lexical morphisms introduced by $\mathcal{D}_\mathcal{B}$.

Strings of words also have meaning(s) in the lexical category. The *lexical meaning* of a grammatical string $word_1 \ldots word_n$ *recognised by the reduction* $r : T_1 \ldots T_n \to \boldsymbol{b}$ is, by definition, the composite of the tensor product of the word meanings and the chosen reduction.

$$r \circ (\overline{\mathtt{word}_1}_{T_1} \otimes \ldots \otimes \overline{\mathtt{word}_n}_{T_n}) : I \to \boldsymbol{b}\,.$$

The meaning of a composite morphism $g \circ f$ can be simplified graphically. Stack the graph of f above the graph of g and walk the paths of the graph starting at a node that is not the head of a link until you arrive at a node that is not the tail of a link. Compose the labels in the order they are encountered along the path. Replace the whole path by a single link labelling it by the composite label of the path. The resulting graph represents the morphism $g \circ f$, (Selinger, 2011).

For instance, the grammatical strings mentioned

[3] "basic type" is replaced by simple type with an even iterator in the general case

above above simplify to

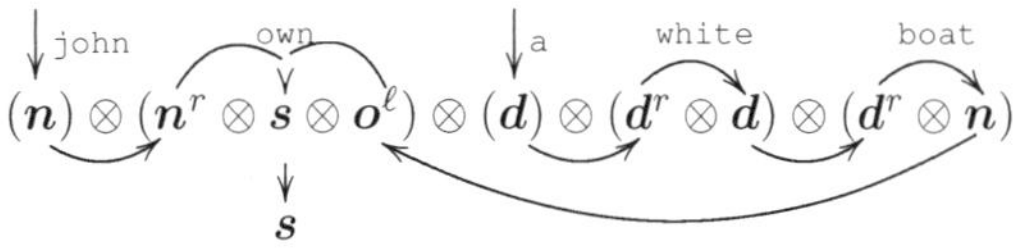

$T = \hat{\boldsymbol{n}}^r \otimes \boldsymbol{r} \otimes \boldsymbol{o}^\ell$

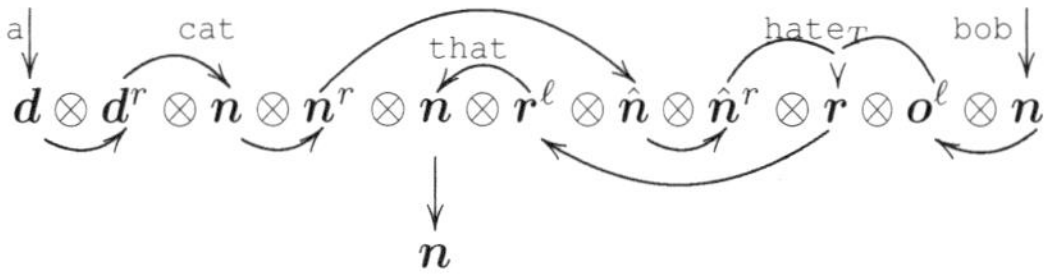

$\texttt{that} \circ \texttt{hate}_T \circ ((\texttt{cat} \circ \texttt{a}) \otimes \texttt{bob})] : I \otimes I \to \boldsymbol{n}$

$T' = \boldsymbol{n}^r \otimes \hat{\boldsymbol{o}}^r \otimes \boldsymbol{r}$

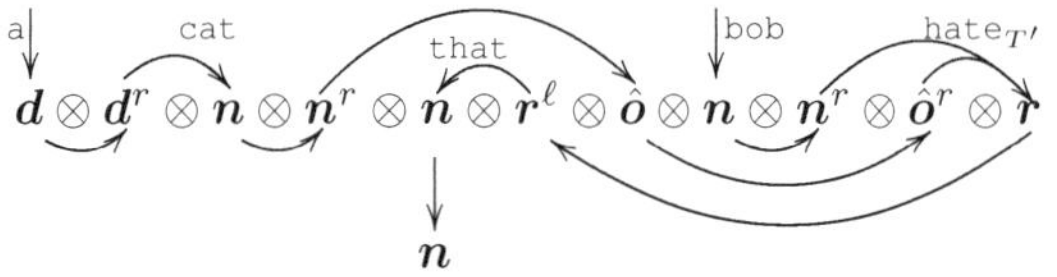

$= \texttt{that} \circ \texttt{hate}_{T'} \circ ((\texttt{cat} \circ \texttt{a}) \otimes \texttt{bob})] : I \otimes I \to \boldsymbol{n}$

All unlabelled links in the graph above correspond to inequalities of basic types. Inserting the strict inequalities at the appropriate place and applying the interchange law, we decompose the label into minimal building blocks that correspond one-to-one to the resources occurring in the RDF graph associated to the statement. For example,

$$\begin{aligned}&\texttt{own} \circ (\texttt{john} \otimes (\texttt{boat} \circ \texttt{white} \circ \texttt{a})) \\ &= \texttt{own} \circ (1_{\boldsymbol{n}} \otimes in) \circ (1_{\boldsymbol{n}} \otimes \texttt{boat}) \circ (1_{\boldsymbol{n}} \otimes \texttt{white}) \\ &\circ (\texttt{john} \otimes \texttt{a}) .\end{aligned} \tag{2}$$

The expression after the equality symbol above is a composite of tensor products the factors of which are either inequalities between basic objects or lexical morphisms. Only the rightmost tensor product contains more than one lexical morphism. In fact, all factors are lexical morphisms with domain I.

The translation of statements to RDF graphs rests on the existence of this decomposition. Borrowing the terminology of RDF graphs, call any lexical morphism with domain I a *node word* and any other lexical morphism a *property word.*

Lemma 1 (Decomposition). *Let* $word_1 \dots word_n$ *be a grammatical string with lexical morphisms* $\texttt{word}_1, \dots, \texttt{word}_n$ *and a reduction* $r : T_1 \dots T_n \to \boldsymbol{b}$*. Then there is an enumeration of the node words* $\texttt{word}_{i_1} : I \to \boldsymbol{b}_1, \dots, \texttt{word}_{i_m} : I \to \boldsymbol{b}_m$ *such that the lexical meaning of the string satisfies*

$$\begin{aligned}&r \circ (\overline{\texttt{word}}_1 \otimes \dots \otimes \overline{\texttt{word}}_n) \\ &= p_1 \circ \dots \circ p_{m'} \circ (\texttt{word}_{i_1} \otimes \dots \otimes \texttt{word}_{i_m}) ,\end{aligned}$$

where each p_k *is either a tensor product of inequalities of basic types or a tensor product of inequalities and one property word* $\texttt{word}_{j_k}$*. Moreover,* $k < k'$ *implies* $j_k < j_{k'}$.

In particular, the meaning of the string belongs to the monoidal category generated by the lexicon

This is a straightforward consequence of the characterisation of morphisms as normal graphs in the free category, (Preller and Lambek, 2007) and the interchange law.

We map lexical morphisms to "unfinished" RDF triples

lexical morphism	RDF triple
$\texttt{noun} : \boldsymbol{d} \to \boldsymbol{n}$	? `rdf : type` `noun`
$\texttt{adjective} : \boldsymbol{d} \to \boldsymbol{d}$	? `is-adjective` `true`
$\texttt{verb} : \boldsymbol{a} \otimes \boldsymbol{b} \to \boldsymbol{c}$	? `verb` ?
$\texttt{determiner} : I \to \boldsymbol{d}$	`blank` ? ?, ? ? `blank`
$\texttt{propername} : I \to \boldsymbol{n}$	`propername` ? ?, ? ? `propername`

(3)

The question marks designate unoccupied positions in the triple. Node words occupy either the subject or the object position, unary property words leave only the subject position open, binary property words occupy the centre position leaving subject and object position unoccupied. Finally, the noun phrases *a cat that hates Bob* and *a cat that Bob hates* are respectively translated to the following graphs :

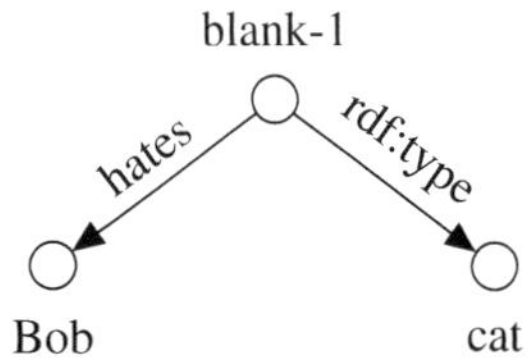

(a) A cat that hates Bob

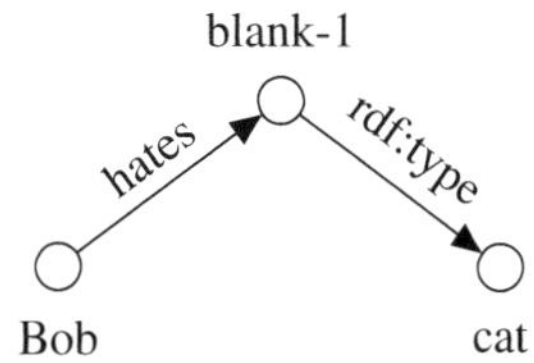

(b) A cat that Bob hates

3 The Translation

Let $\mathbb{B} = \langle \{0, 1\}, +, \cdot \rangle$ be the commutative semiring in which the addition, $+$, is the lattice operator $\vee$ and the multiplication, $\cdot$, the lattice operator $\wedge$ on $\{0, 1\}$.

The *semantic* category which hosts the RDF graphs and our models of grammatical strings is the category $\mathcal{C}$ of finitely generated semimodules over $\mathbb{B}$. It is compact closed satisfying $A^\ell = A = A^r$ for each object A. Every object A has a'canonical' basis $(e_i)_i$ such that every element $v \in A$ can be written uniquely as $v = \sum_i \alpha_i e_i$, where $\alpha_i \in \mathbb{B}$. We refer to elements of$A$ as *vectors*. Morphisms of $\mathcal{C}$ are maps that commute with addition and scalar multiplication.

We interpret RDF graphs as elements of a semimodule S determined by the RDF vocabulary, see below.

The translation of grammatical strings is given by a functor from the monoidal category generated by the lexical morphisms into a *category of morphisms with side effects* mapping the decomposition of a grammatical string to a vector of S.

Let L be a set of *labels* that includes the property words and a 'very large', but finite number n_0 of labels $\texttt{blank}_i$, for $i = 1, \ldots n_0$[4]. The other elements of L are node names and property names of an RDF vocabulary.

Define N as the semimodule over the semi-ring $\mathbb{B}$ freely generated by L and denote $e_{\texttt{label}}$ the basis vector of N corresponding to $\texttt{label} \in L$. We present RDF triples by basis vectors of $S = N \otimes N \otimes N$ and RDF graphs by sums of basis vectors of S, for instance $e_{\texttt{bob}} \otimes e_{\texttt{hate}} \otimes e_{\texttt{blank}} + e_{\texttt{blank}} \otimes e_{\texttt{rdf-type}} \otimes e_{\texttt{cat}}$. Hence, the vector sum models the union of RDF graphs.

We want to interpret the lexical morphisms such that they construct a triple when applied to an argument and add it to the vector of S already constructed. Composition of the category $\mathcal{C}$ alone is not powerful enough to achieve this. We define a new category $\mathcal{C}_S$ in which the entity *a white boat* will be denoted by the pair $(e_{\text{blank-1}}, e_{\text{blank-1}} \otimes e_{\text{rdf:type}} \otimes e_{\text{boat}} + e_{\text{blank-1}} \otimes e_{\text{is-white}} \otimes e_{\text{true}})$.

Therefore we switch from $\mathcal{C}$ to the monoidal category $\mathcal{C}_S$ below in which arrows have two components. The first component creates the triple and the second component adds the new triple to the graph as a 'side effect'.

Definition 2 (Category with Side Effects). *Let $\{a_1, \ldots, a_m\}$ and $\{b_1, \ldots, b_n\}$ be the basis[5] of A and B. For any $p \in \mathcal{C}(A, S)$, $q \in \mathcal{C}(B, S)$, define $p \otimes_+ q \in \mathcal{C}(A \otimes B, S)$ as the unique linear map satisfying for an arbitrary basis vector $a_i \otimes b_j$ of $A \otimes B$*

$$(p \otimes_+ q) : a_i \otimes b_j \mapsto p(a_i) + q(b_j)\,.$$

The category $\mathcal{C}_S$ of morphisms with side effects in S has:

- *objects as in $\mathcal{C}$*
- *morphisms $(f, p) : A \to B$ where $f \in \mathcal{C}(A, B)$, $\mathrm{Ker}(f) = \{0\}$ and $p \in \mathcal{C}(A, S)$.*
- *arrows $1_A = (1_A, 0)$.*
- *an operation $\circ$ defined by $(f, p) \circ (h, q) = (f \circ h, p \circ h + q)$.*
- *an operation $\otimes$ on objects defined as in $\mathcal{C}$*
- *an operation $\otimes$ on arrows defined by $(f, p) \otimes (h, q) = (f \otimes h, p \otimes_+ q)$.*

Examples of morphisms in the first component are the symmetry $\sigma : N \otimes N \to N \otimes N$, $\pi_1, \pi_2 : N \otimes N \to N$ defined by $\sigma(a_i \otimes b_j) = b_j \otimes a_i$, $\pi_1(a_i \otimes b_j) = a_i$ and $\pi_2(a_i \otimes b_j) = b_j$.

The new operation $\otimes_+$ introduced above concerns the second component only. The morphism $p \otimes_+ q$ computes at $a_i \otimes b_j$ the union of the RDF graphs $p(a_i)$ and $q(b_j)$, computed separately by p and q.

As an illustration, consider the following morphisms of $\mathcal{C}_S$

$$m_{\texttt{john}} = (e_{\texttt{john}}, 0), \; m_{\texttt{blank}_i} = (e_{\texttt{blank}_i}, 0)$$

The arrow of a proper noun consists of the node representing this entity, e.g. e_{john}, paired with the empty graph represented by $0 \in S$. Choosing the empty graph means that nothing is said about this node. A similar remark holds for determiners.

$$m_{\texttt{white}} = (1_N, 1_N \otimes e_{\texttt{is-white}} \otimes e_{\texttt{true}}),$$
$$m_{\texttt{boat}} = (1_N, 1_N \otimes e_{\texttt{rdf-type}} \otimes e_{\texttt{boat}})$$

An adjective or a noun is a morphism that maps a node word to itself and to the empty slot in the corresponding triple. As a side effect, it adds this triple to the second component.

$$m_{\texttt{own}} = (1_N \otimes e_{\texttt{own}} \otimes 1_N, 1_N \otimes e_{\texttt{own}} \otimes 1_N)$$

A transitive verb is a morphism that maps an ordered pair of nodes to a triple making the first the subject and the second the object of the triple.

Compose the morphisms

$$\begin{aligned}
&m_{\texttt{white}} \circ m_{\texttt{blank}_i} = (e_{\texttt{blank}_i}, t_1) \\
&\quad t_1 = (e_{\texttt{blank}_i} \otimes e_{\texttt{is-white}} \otimes e_{\texttt{true}}) \\
&m_{\texttt{boat}} \circ m_{\texttt{white}} \circ m_{\texttt{blank}_i} = (e_{\texttt{blank}_i}, t_2 + t_1) \\
&\quad t_2 = (e_{\texttt{blank}_i} \otimes e_{\texttt{rdf-type}} \otimes e_{\texttt{boat}}) \\
&m_{\texttt{own}} \circ (m_{\texttt{john}} \otimes (m_{\texttt{boat}} \circ m_{\texttt{white}} \circ m_{\texttt{blank}_i})) = \\
&m_{\texttt{own}} \circ (e_{\texttt{john}} \otimes e_{\texttt{blank}_i}, 0 + t_2 + t_1) = \\
&(e_{\texttt{john}} \otimes e_{\texttt{own}} \otimes e_{\texttt{blank}_i}, t_3 + t_2 + t_1) \\
&\quad t_3 = e_{\texttt{john}} \otimes e_{\texttt{own}} \otimes e_{\texttt{blank}_i}
\end{aligned} \tag{4}$$

The effect of composition is to create a new triple on the left of the comma and to store it on the right.

Proposition 1. *The category with side effects $\mathcal{C}_S$ is a monoidal category.*

The proof of this proposition is given in appendix A.

Define a monoidal structure preserving functor $\mathcal{F}$ from the monoidal category generated by the lexical morphisms to $\mathcal{C}_S$ thus

- $\mathcal{F}(\boldsymbol{s}) = S = N \otimes N \otimes N$
- $\mathcal{F}(\boldsymbol{a}) = N$ if $\boldsymbol{a} \neq \boldsymbol{s}$
- $\mathcal{F}(1_{\boldsymbol{a}}) = \mathcal{F}(i_{\boldsymbol{a}\,\boldsymbol{b}}) = \mathcal{F}(j_{\boldsymbol{a}\,\boldsymbol{b}}) = 1_{\mathcal{F}}(\boldsymbol{a})$, for all basic types $\boldsymbol{a}, \boldsymbol{b} \in \mathcal{B}$
- $\mathcal{F}(\textbf{that} : \boldsymbol{r} \to \boldsymbol{n}) = (1, 0)$
- $\mathcal{F}(\texttt{name} : I \to \boldsymbol{d}) = (e_{name}, 0)$
- $\mathcal{F}(\texttt{determiner} : I \to \boldsymbol{d}) = (e_{\texttt{blank}_i}, 0)$
- $\mathcal{F}(\texttt{word} : \boldsymbol{d}^r \otimes \boldsymbol{n}) = (1, 1 \otimes e_{\texttt{rdf-type}} \otimes e_{\texttt{word}})$
- $\mathcal{F}(\texttt{word} : \boldsymbol{d}^r \otimes \boldsymbol{d}) = (1, 1 \otimes e_{\texttt{is-word}} \otimes e_{\texttt{true}})$
- $\mathcal{F}(\texttt{word}_{\boldsymbol{n}^r \otimes \boldsymbol{s} \otimes \boldsymbol{o}^l}) = (1 \otimes e_{\texttt{word}} \otimes 1, 1 \otimes e_{\texttt{word}} \otimes 1)$
  $\mathcal{F}(\texttt{word}_{\hat{\boldsymbol{n}}^r \otimes \boldsymbol{r} \otimes \boldsymbol{o}^l}) = (\pi_1, 1 \otimes e_{\texttt{word}} \otimes 1)$
  $\mathcal{F}(\texttt{word}_{\boldsymbol{n}^r \otimes \hat{\boldsymbol{o}}^r \otimes \boldsymbol{r}}) = (\pi_2, (1 \otimes e_{\texttt{word}} \otimes 1) \circ \sigma)$.

Note that the morphisms in the example above satisfy $m_{\texttt{word}} = \mathcal{F}(\texttt{word})$. Computation (4) shows that $\mathcal{F}$ maps the lexical meaning of *john owns a white boat* to the three RDF triples t_1, t_2, t_3.

[4]it suffices that n_0 exceeds the number of occurrences of determiners in the set of digitalised documents

[5]In $\mathcal{C}$, every object has a unique basis: the canonical one.

Lemma 2. *Let $word_1 \ldots word_n$ be a statement with corresponding lexical entries $word_1 : T_1 \ldots word_n : T_n$ and $r : T_1 \ldots T_n \to \boldsymbol{s}$ a reduction to the sentence type. Then second component of*

$$\mathcal{F}(r \circ (\overline{\mathtt{word_1}} \otimes \ldots \otimes \overline{\mathtt{word_n}})) = (f, t_1 + \cdots + t_m) \in \mathcal{C}_S(I, S)$$

is a sum of RDF triples $t_i \in S$, for $k = 1, \ldots, m$. Moreover, t_k has the form (3) *determined by the property word $\mathtt{word}_{j_k}$ such that the unlabelled nodes are filled by node words of the statement.*

The proof is given in Appendix B.

Definition 3 (RDF Translation)**.** *The* RDF graph translating the statement *$word_1 \ldots word_n$ with reduction $r : T_1 \ldots T_n \to \boldsymbol{s}$ is the second component of $\mathcal{F}(r \circ (\overline{\mathtt{word_1}} \otimes \ldots \otimes \overline{\mathtt{word_n}}))$.*

For instance, the translation of the statement *John owns a white boat* is

$$e_{\mathtt{john}} \otimes e_{\mathtt{own}} \otimes e_{\mathtt{blank}_i} + e_{\mathtt{blank}_i} \otimes e_{\mathtt{is\text{-}white}} \otimes e_{\mathtt{true}} + e_{\mathtt{blank}_i} \otimes e_{\mathtt{rdf\text{-}type}} \otimes e_{\mathtt{boat}}\,,$$

because

$$\mathcal{F}(\mathtt{own} \circ (\mathtt{john} \otimes (\mathtt{boat} \circ \mathtt{white} \circ \mathtt{a})) = m_{\mathtt{own}} \circ (m_{\mathtt{john}} \otimes (m_{\mathtt{boat}} \circ m_{\mathtt{white}} \circ m_{\mathtt{blank}_i}))\,.$$

The translation algorithm from text to RDF graphs starts with a parsing algorithm of pregroup grammars that chooses a type for each word of the statement and provides a reduction to the sentence type. Next it computes the decomposition of the formal meaning in the lexical category by 'yanking'. Finally it computes the RDF graph by applying the translation functor $\mathcal{F}$ to the decomposition. The parsing algorithm is cubic polynomial in the number of words. Decomposition is linear, because the number of links is proportional to the number of words. Finally, translation again is linear, because the sum of the number of property words and of the number of node words in the decomposition is proportional to the number of words.

4 $\mathcal{C}$-Models and RDF Interpretations

In this section, we establish the connection between the extensional models of meaning of (Preller, 2012) with the RDF interpretations of (Hayes, 2004) via the translation $\mathcal{F}$ from natural language to RDF graphs. We show that a statement is true in an extensional model if and only if the RDF graph computed by $\mathcal{F}$ is true in the RDF interpretation associated to the extensional model.

Choose an object U of $\mathcal{C}$, the 'universe of discourse' of the fragment of natural language. The basis vectors of U stand for individuals or concepts. Properties are represented by maps that test (n-tuples of) entities and let (part of) them pass if the test succeeds.

Let $1 \leq i_1 < \cdots < i_m \leq n$ be a strictly increasing sequence. A linear map $q : U_1 \otimes \ldots \otimes U_n \to U_{i_1} \otimes \ldots \otimes U_{i_m}$ is said to be a *selector* if for any basis vector $e_1 \otimes \ldots \otimes e_n \in U_1 \otimes \ldots \otimes U_n$

$$q(e_1 \otimes \ldots \otimes e_n) = e_{i_1} \otimes \ldots \otimes e_{i_m} \text{ or } q(e_1 \otimes \ldots \otimes e_n) = 0\,.$$

We say that q *selects the i-th factor* if $m = 1$ and $i = i_1$ and that it is a *projector* if $m = n$. If the latter is the case then q is an idempotent and self-adjoint endomorphism, hence a 'property' in quantum logic, see (Abramsky and Coecke, 2004).

If the domain V and the codomain $U_{i_1} \otimes \ldots \otimes U_{i_m}$ are fixed then the selectors are in a one-to-one correspondence with the 'truth-value' functions $p : A \to \{\top, \bot\}$ on the set A of basis vectors of V related by the condition

$$p(a) = \top \text{ if and only if } q(a) \neq 0$$

for all $a \in A$.

Let $v = \sum_{l=1}^{k} a_{j_l}$ be an arbitrary vector of V. A selector $q : V \to W$ is said to be *true at v* if $q(a_{j_l}) \neq 0$, for $l = 1, \ldots, k$.

Lemma 3. *Selectors are closed under composition and the tensor product. Every identity is a selector.*

Let $p : V \to W$ and $q : W \to X$ be selectors and $v \in V$. Then $q \circ p$ is true at v if and only if p is true at v and q is true at $w = p(v)$.

Proof. The first assertion is straight forward. To show the second, assume that a is a basis vector for which $(q \circ p)(a) \neq 0$. Then $p(a) \neq 0$ because $q(0) = 0$. Hence $p(a)$ is a basis vector of W selected by p. The property now follows for an arbitrary vector from the definitions. □

Definition 4. *A compact closed structure preserving functor $\mathcal{M} : \mathcal{L}_{\mathcal{B}} \to \mathcal{C}$ is a $\mathcal{C}$-*model *with universe U if it satisfies*

- $\mathcal{M}(\boldsymbol{s}) = U \otimes U$
- $\mathcal{M}(\boldsymbol{a}) = U$ *for any basic type $\boldsymbol{a} \neq \boldsymbol{s}$*
- $\mathcal{M}(1_{\boldsymbol{a}}) = \mathcal{M}(i_{\boldsymbol{a}\,\boldsymbol{b}}) = \mathcal{M}(j_{\boldsymbol{a}\,\boldsymbol{b}}) = 1_{\mathcal{M}}(\boldsymbol{a})$, *for all basic types $\boldsymbol{a}, \boldsymbol{b} \in \mathcal{B}$*
- $\mathcal{M}(\mathtt{that}) = 1_U$
- $\mathcal{M}(\mathtt{word}_{\boldsymbol{a}^r \otimes \boldsymbol{b}})$ *and* $\mathcal{M}(\mathtt{word}_{\boldsymbol{n}^r \otimes \boldsymbol{s} \otimes \boldsymbol{o}^l})$ *are projectors*
- $\mathcal{M}(\mathtt{word}_{\hat{\boldsymbol{n}} \otimes \boldsymbol{r} \otimes \boldsymbol{o}^l}) = \pi_1 \circ \mathcal{M}(\mathtt{word}_{\boldsymbol{n}^r \otimes \boldsymbol{s} \otimes \boldsymbol{o}^l})$
  $\mathcal{M}(\mathtt{word}_{\boldsymbol{n}^r \otimes \hat{\boldsymbol{o}}^r \otimes \boldsymbol{r}}) = \pi_2 \circ \mathcal{M}(\mathtt{word}_{\boldsymbol{n}^r \otimes \boldsymbol{s} \otimes \boldsymbol{o}^l}) \circ \sigma$
- $\mathcal{M}$ *maps determiners and proper names in the singular to basis vectors.*

The last condition guarantees that the interpretations of a transitive verb in a statement and in a relative clause are equal if the relative pronoun is the subject of the verb in the relative clause and that they differ only by the symmetry isomorphism if the relative pronoun is the object.

Definition 5. *A statement $word_1 \ldots word_n$ with reduction $r : T_1 \otimes \ldots \otimes T_n \to \boldsymbol{b}$ is* true *in $\mathcal{M}$ if $\mathcal{M}(r \circ (\overline{\mathtt{word}}_1 \otimes \ldots \otimes \overline{\mathtt{word}}_n) \neq 0$.*

Truth in a model can be reformulated in terms of selector truth with the help of Lemma 1.

Lemma 4. *Let* $p_1 \circ \cdots \circ p_{m'} \circ (\mathtt{word}_{i_1} \otimes \ldots \otimes \mathtt{word}_{i_m})$ *be the decomposition of the formal meaning of the statement* $word_1 \ldots word_n$. *Then* $\mathcal{M}(p_l)$ *is a selector and* $\mathcal{M}(\mathtt{word}_{i_k})$ *a vector in U, for* $1 \leq l \leq m'$, $1 \leq k \leq m$.

Moreover, the statement is true in $\mathcal{M}$ *if and only if the selector* $\mathcal{M}(p_l)$ *is true at* $\mathcal{M}(p_{l+1}) \circ \cdots \circ \mathcal{M}(p_{m'}) \circ (\mathcal{M}(\mathtt{word}_{i_1}) \otimes \ldots \otimes \mathcal{M}(\mathtt{word}_{i_m}))$ *for* $1 \leq l \leq m'$.

Proof. $\mathcal{M}$ maps the meaning of the string to $\mathcal{M}(p_1) \circ \cdots \circ \mathcal{M}(p_{m'}) \circ (\mathcal{M}(\mathtt{word}_{i_1}) \otimes \ldots \otimes \mathcal{M}(\mathtt{word}_{i_m}))$. Note that for $k = 1, \ldots, m'$ any factor of $\mathcal{M}(p_k)$ is the identity of U unless it is $\mathcal{M}(\mathtt{word}_{j_k}) = q_k$. Thus $\mathcal{M}(p_k)$ is a tensor product of selectors. Hence both assertions follow from Lemma 3. □

Any $\mathcal{C}$-model $\mathcal{M}$ defines an RDF interpretation. The *vocabulary* consists of the basis vectors $e_{\mathtt{label}} \in N$, see previous section. The set of property symbols is given by

$$P = \{e_{\textit{is-adjective}} : \textit{adjective} \in \mathcal{D}\} \cup \{\mathtt{rdf:type}\} \cup \{e_{\textit{verb}} : \textit{verb} \in \mathcal{C}\}$$

Define an RDF interpretation $\mathrm{I}_{\mathcal{M}}$ as follows

- set of properties
$$\mathrm{IP} = \{\mathcal{M}(\mathtt{word}) : e_{\mathtt{word}} \in P\} \cup \{\mathtt{rdf:type}\}$$

- set of resources
$$\mathrm{IR} = \mathrm{IP} \cup U \cup \{\mathtt{true}\}$$

- mapping IS and its extension to blank nodes
$$\mathrm{IS}(e_{\mathtt{word}}) = \mathcal{M}(\mathtt{word}),$$
$$\mathrm{IS}(e_{\mathtt{blank}_i}) = \mathcal{M}(\mathtt{determiner}_i)$$

- mapping IEXT from IP into the power set of IR × IR
$$\mathrm{IEXT}(\mathtt{rdf\text{-}type}) = \{\langle e, \mathcal{M}(\mathtt{noun})\rangle : \mathcal{M}(\mathtt{noun}) \text{ is true at } e\}$$
$$\mathrm{IEXT}(\mathrm{IS}(e_{\mathtt{is\text{-}adjective}})) = \{\langle e, \mathtt{true}\rangle : \mathcal{M}(\mathtt{adjective}) \text{ is true at } e\}$$
$$\mathrm{IEXT}(\mathrm{IS}(e_{\mathtt{verb}})) = \{\langle e_1, e_2\rangle : \mathcal{M}(\mathtt{verb}) \text{ is true at } e_1 \otimes e_2\}.$$

Proposition 2. *A statement* $word_1 \ldots word_n$ *is true in a* $\mathcal{C}$*-model* $\mathcal{M}$ *if and only if every triple of its RDF translation G is true in the RDF interpretation* $I_{\mathcal{M}}$

The proof is given in Appendix B.

5 Conclusion

The modelling of natural language by RDF graphs remains limited by the expressivity of RDF. The latter goes way beyond the few examples presented here. So far, we have only considered the extensional branch of a word. Future work will take advantage of the distinction between a property and its extension in RDF to introduce the conceptual branch of a plural, which does not refer to an extension, e.g *Tom likes* books, or capture the difference between Eve and John *own a boat* and *Eve and John* are athletes.

Acknowledgments

This work was supported by the École Normale Supérieure and the LIRMM. The first author wishes to thank David Naccache, Alain Lecomte, Antoine Amarilli, Hugo Vanneuville and both authors the members of the TEXTE group at the LIRMM for their interest in the project.

References

Samson Abramsky and Bob Coecke. 2004. A categorical semantics of quantum protocols. In *Proceedings of the 19th Annual IEEE Symposium on Logic in Computer Science*, pages 415–425.

Stephen Clark, Bob Coecke, and Mehrnoosh Sadrzadeh. 2008. A compositional distributional model of meaning. In W. Lawless P. Bruza and J. van Rijsbergen, editors, *Proceedings of Conference on Quantum Interactions*. University of Oxford, College Publications.

Patrick Hayes and Brian McBride. 2004. Rdf semantics. Technical report, Hewlett Packard Labs.

Patrick Hayes. 2004. Rdf semantics. Technical report, W3C Recommendation, W3C.

Dimitri Kartsaklis, Mehrnoosh Sadrzadeh, Stephen Pulman, and Bob Coecke, 2013. *Reasoning about Meaning in Natural Language with Compact Closed Categories and Frobenius Algebras*. Cambridge University Press.

Joachim Lambek. 1958. The mathematics of sentence structure. *American Mathematical Monthly*, 65:154–170.

Joachim Lambek, 1993. *Substructural Logics*, chapter From categorial grammar to bilinear logic, pages 207–237. Oxford University Press.

Joachim Lambek. 1999. Type grammar revisited. In Alain Lecomte, editor, *Logical Aspects of Computational Linguistics*, volume 1582 of *LNAI*, pages 1–27, Heidelberg. Springer.

Saunders Mac Lane. 1971. *Categories for the Working Mathematician*. Springer.

Anne Preller and Joachim Lambek. 2007. Free compact 2-categories. *Mathematical Structures for Computer Sciences*, 17(1):1–32.

Anne Preller, 2012. *From Sentence to Concept: Predicate Logic and Quantum Logic in Compact Closed Categories*, pages 00–29. Oxford University Press.

Peter Selinger. 2011. A survey of graphical languages for monoidal categories. In *New Structures for Physics*, volume 813 of *Lecture Notes in Physics*, pages 289–233. Springer.

Mark Steedman. 1996. *Surface Structure and Interpretation*, volume 30 of *Linguistic Inquiry Monograph*. MIT Press, Cambridge, Massachusetts.

A Proof of proposition 1

Note first that composition and the tensor are well defined.

Assume $(f,p) : A \to B$ and $(g,q) : B \to C$. Then $q \circ f : A \to S$ and $p : A \to S$, so $q \circ f + p : A \to S$. Therefore $(g,q) \circ (f,p) = (g \circ f, q \circ f + p) : A \to C$ is well defined. Similarly, if $(f_i, p_i) : A_i \to B_i$ for $i = 1,2$ then $p_1 \otimes_+ p_2 : A_1 \otimes A_2 \to S$ and therefore $(f_1 \otimes f_2, p_1 \otimes_+ p_2) : A_1 \otimes A_2 \to B_1 \otimes B_2$ as required.

The operation $\otimes_+$ is associative on arrows. Indeed, let $(a_i)_i$, $(b_j)_j$ and $(c_k)_k$ be the basis of A, B and C, respectively. Then for $r : C \to S$

$$
\begin{aligned}
&((p \otimes_+ q) \otimes_+ r)(a_i \otimes b_j \otimes c_k) \\
=&(p \otimes_+ q)(a_i \otimes b_j) + r(c_k) \\
=&p(a_i) + q(b_j) + r(c_k) \\
=&(p \otimes_+ (q \otimes_+ r))(a_i \otimes b_j \otimes c_k).
\end{aligned}
$$

Hence the tensor product on arrows of $\mathcal{C}_S$ is associative.

To show the interchange law (1), we need a lemma:

Lemma 5. *Let* $p : C \to S, q : D \to S$ *and* $f : A \to C, g : B \to D$ *with* $\mathrm{Ker}(f) = \mathrm{Ker}(g) = \{0\}$. *Then*

$$(p \otimes_+ q) \circ (f \otimes g) = (p \circ f) \otimes_+ (q \circ g)$$

Indeed, let $(a_i)_i$, $(b_i)_i$, $(c_i)_i$ and $(d_i)_i$ be the bases of A, B, C and D respectively. For all i and j, we decompose $f(a_i)$ on the basis $(c_i)_i$ and similarly for $g(b_j)$ on $(d_i)_i$:

$$f(a_i) = \sum_r c_{i_r} \text{ and } g(b_j) = \sum_s d_{i_s}$$

Each family of indices $(i_r)_r$ and $(i_s)_s$ is non empty, because $\mathrm{Ker}(f) = \mathrm{Ker}(g) = \{0\}$. Hence,

$$
\begin{aligned}
&((p \otimes_+ q) \circ (f \otimes g))(a_i \otimes b_j) \\
=&(p \otimes_+ q)(f(a_i) \otimes g(b_j)) \\
=&(p \otimes_+ q)((\sum_r c_{i_r}) \otimes (\sum_s d_{i_s})) \\
=&(p \otimes_+ q)(\sum_{r,s} c_{i_r} \otimes d_{i_s}) \\
=&\sum_{r,s} p(c_{i_r}) + q(d_{i_s}) \\
=&\sum_r p(c_{i_r}) + \sum_s q(d_{i_s}) \\
=&p(f(a_i)) + q(g(b_j)) \\
=&((p \circ f) \otimes_+ (q \circ g))(a_i \otimes b_j)
\end{aligned}
$$

The fifth equality uses the fact that $1 + 1 = 1$ and the sum is non empty. This terminates the proof of the lemma.

Now let $(f_1, p_1) : A \to C$, $(f_2, p_2) : C \to E$, $(g_1, q_1) : B \to D$ and $(g_2, q_2) : D \to F$. We show first the following equality

$$(f_1 \otimes_+ g_1) + (f_2 \otimes_+ g_2) = (f_1 + f_2) \otimes_+ (g_1 + g_2). \quad (5)$$

Indeed, let $(e_i)_i$ and $(f_j)_j$ be the bases of A and B respectively. Then, for all i and j,

$$
\begin{aligned}
&((f_1 \otimes_+ g_1) + (f_2 \otimes_+ g_2))(e_i \otimes f_j) \\
=&(f_1 \otimes_+ g_1)(e_i \otimes f_j) + (f_2 \otimes_+ g_2)(e_i \otimes f_j) \\
=&f_1(e_i) + g_1(f_j) + f_2(e_i) + g_2(f_j) \\
=&((f_1 + f_2) \otimes_+ (g_1 + g_2))(e_i \otimes f_j).
\end{aligned}
$$

Finally, the Interchange Law follows from (5) and the definitions thus

$$
\begin{aligned}
&((f_2, p_2) \otimes (g_2, q_2)) \circ ((f_1, p_1) \otimes (g_1, q_1)) \\
=&(f_2 \otimes g_2, p_2 \otimes_+ q_2) \circ (f_1 \otimes g_1, p_1 \otimes_+ q_1) \\
=&((f_2 \otimes g_2) \circ (f_1 \otimes g_1), (p_2 \otimes_+ q_2) \circ (f_1 \otimes g_1) + (p_1 \otimes_+ q_1)) \\
=&((f_2 \circ f_1) \otimes (g_2 \circ g_1), (p_2 \circ f_1) \otimes_+ (q_2 \circ g_1) + (p_1 \otimes_+ q_1)) \\
=&((f_2 \circ f_1) \otimes (g_2 \circ g_1), (p_2 \circ f_1 + p_1) \otimes_+ (q_2 \circ g_1 + q_1)) \\
=&(f_2 \circ f_1, p_2 \circ f_1 + p_1) \otimes (g_2 \circ g_1, q_2 \circ g_1 + q_1) \\
=&((f_2, p_2) \circ (f_1, p_1)) \otimes ((g_2, q_2) \circ (g_1, q_1)).
\end{aligned}
$$

Therefore $\mathcal{C}_S$ is a monoidal category.

B Proof of Lemma 2 and Proposition 2

Proof. Note that both $\mathcal{F}$ and $\mathcal{M}$ map inequalities of basic types to identities, hence also any atom without a lexical morphism to an identity. Let $\mathtt{word}_{j_l}$ be the property word occurring in p_l, say as the k_l-th factor, $q_l = \mathcal{M}(\mathtt{word}_{j_l})$ and $m_l = \mathcal{F}(\mathtt{word}_{j_l})$, for $l = 1, \ldots, m$. Then $\mathcal{M}(p_l) = 1_U \otimes \ldots q_l \ldots \otimes 1_U$ and $\mathcal{F}(p_l) = 1_N \otimes \ldots m_l \ldots \otimes 1_N$. Suppose that e_i is a basis vector of U and $e_{\mathtt{node}_i}$ a basis vector of N satisfying $e_i = I(e_{\mathtt{node}_i})$.

Use induction on $n - m - l$ and assume that $e_1 \otimes \ldots \otimes e_{r_l} = \mathcal{M}(p_{l+1}) \circ \cdots \circ \mathcal{M}(p_{n-m}) \circ (\mathcal{M}(\mathtt{node}_{i_1}) \otimes \ldots \otimes \mathcal{M}(\mathtt{node}_{i_m}))$ and $(e_{\mathtt{node}_1}, 0) \otimes \ldots \otimes (e_{\mathtt{node}_{r_l}}, 0) = \mathcal{F}(p_{l+1}) \circ \cdots \circ \mathcal{F}(p_{n-m}) \circ (\mathcal{F}(e_{\mathtt{node}_{i_1}}) \otimes \ldots \otimes \mathcal{F}(e_{\mathtt{node}_{i_m}}))$.[6]

Let t_l be the triple created when composing $\mathcal{F}(p_l)$ with $(e_{\mathtt{node}_1}, 0) \otimes \ldots \otimes (e_{\mathtt{node}_{r_l}}, 0)$. We want the show that t_l is true in $\mathrm{I}_{\mathcal{M}}$ if and only if $\mathcal{M}(p_l)$ is true at $e_1 \otimes \ldots \otimes e_{r_l}$.

Consider the case where $\mathtt{word}_{j_l} : \boldsymbol{d} \to \boldsymbol{d}$. The other cases are shown similarly. Recall that $m_l \circ (e_{\mathtt{node}_{k_l}}, 0) = (e_{\mathtt{node}_{k_l}}, t_l)$, with $t_l = e_{\mathtt{node}_{k_l}} \otimes e_{\mathtt{is\text{-}word}_{j_l}} \otimes e_{\mathtt{true}}$. Hence, $\mathcal{F}(p_l)((e_{\mathtt{node}_1}, 0) \otimes \ldots \otimes (e_{\mathtt{node}_r}, 0)) = ((e_{\mathtt{node}_1}, 0) \otimes \ldots (e_{\mathtt{node}_{k_l}}, t_l) \ldots \otimes (e_{\mathtt{node}_r}, 0) = (e_{\mathtt{node}_1} \otimes \ldots \otimes e_{\mathtt{node}_r}, t_l)$. Then t_l is true in $\mathrm{I}_{\mathcal{M}}$ if and only if $(\mathrm{I}(e_{\mathtt{node}_{k_l}}), \mathtt{true}) \in \mathrm{IEXT}(\mathrm{I}(e_{\mathtt{is\text{-}word}}))$ if and only if q_l is true at e_{k_l}, by definition of I. On the other hand, $1_U \otimes \ldots q_l \ldots \otimes 1_U$ is true at $e_1 \otimes \ldots e_{k_l} \ldots \otimes e_r$ if and only if q_l is true at e_{k_l}. If that is the case then $\mathcal{M}(p_l)(e_1 \otimes \ldots e_{k_l} \ldots \otimes e_r) = e_1 \otimes \ldots e_{k_l} \ldots \otimes e_r$. $\square$

[6] 0 can be replaced by any vector of S without changing the proof.

Incremental semantic scales by strings

Tim Fernando
Computer Science Department
Trinity College Dublin
Dublin, Ireland
Tim.Fernando@tcd.ie

Abstract

Scales for natural language semantics are analyzed as moving targets, perpetually under construction and subject to adjustment. Projections, factorizations and constraints are described on strings of bounded but refinable granularities, shaping types by the processes that put semantics in flux.

1 Introduction

An important impetus for recent investigations into type theory for natural language semantics is the view of "semantics in flux," correcting "the impression" from, for example, Montague 1973 "of natural languages as being regimented with meanings determined once and for all" (Cooper 2012, page 271). The present work concerns scales for temporal expressions and gradable predicates. Two questions that loom large from the perspective of semantics in flux are: how to construct scales and align them against one another (e.g. Klein and Rovatsos 2011). The formal study carried out below keeps scales as simple as possible, whilst allowing for necessary refinements and adjustments. The basic picture is that a scale is a moving target finitely approximable as a string over an alphabet which we can expand to refine granularity. Reducing a scale to a string comes, however, at a price; indivisible points must give way to refinable intervals (embodying underspecification).

Arguments for a semantic reorientation around intervals (away from points) are hardly new. Best known within linguistic semantics perhaps are those in tense and aspect from Bennett and Partee 1972, which seem to have met less resistance than arguments in the degree literature from Kennedy 2001 and Schwarzschild and Wilkinson 2002 (see Solt 2013). At the center of the present argument for intervals is a notion of finite approximability, plausibly related to cognition. What objection might there be to it? The fact that no finite linear order is dense raises the issue of compatibility between finite approximability and density — no small worry, given the popularity of dense linear orders for time (e.g. Kamp and Reyle 1993, Pratt-Hartmann 2005, Klein 2009) as well as measurement (e.g. Fox and Hackl 2006).

Fortunately, finite linear orders can be organized into a system of approximations converging at the limit to a dense linear order. The present work details ways to form such systems and limits, with density reanalyzed as refinability of arbitrary finite approximations. A familiar example provides some orientation.

Example A (calendar) We can represent a calendar year as the string

$$s_{mo} := \boxed{\text{Jan}}\boxed{\text{Feb}}\boxed{\text{Mar}}\cdots\boxed{\text{Dec}}$$

of length 12, or, were we interested also in days d1,d2. . .,d31, the string

$$s_{mo,dy} := \boxed{\text{Jan,d1}}\boxed{\text{Jan,d2}}\cdots\boxed{\text{Jan,d31}}$$
$$\boxed{\text{Feb,d1}}\cdots\boxed{\text{Dec,d31}}$$

of length 365 for a non-leap year (Fernando 2011).[1] In contrast to the points in the real line $\mathbb{R}$, a box can split, as $\boxed{\text{Jan}}$ in s_{mo} does (30 times) to

$$\boxed{\text{Jan,d1}}\boxed{\text{Jan,d2}}\cdots\boxed{\text{Jan,d31}}$$

in $s_{mo,dy}$, on introducing days d1, d2,. . ., d31 into the picture. Reversing direction and generalizing from

$$mo := \{\text{Jan,Feb,}\ldots\text{Dec}\}$$

[1] We draw boxes (instead of the usual curly braces { and }) around sets-as-symbols, stringing together "snapshots" much like a cartoon/film strip.

to any set A, we define the function ρ_A on strings (of sets) to componentwise intersect with A

$$\rho_A(\alpha_1 \cdots \alpha_n) \ := \ (\alpha_1 \cap A) \cdots (\alpha_n \cap A)$$

(throwing out non-A's from each box) so that

$$\rho_{mo}(s_{mo,dy}) \ = \ \boxed{\text{Jan}}^{31}\boxed{\text{Feb}}^{28} \cdots \boxed{\text{Dec}}^{31}.$$

Next, the *block compression* $bc(s)$ *of* a string s compresses all repeating blocks α^n (for $n \geq 1$) of a box α in a string s to α for

$$bc(s) \ := \ \begin{cases} bc(\alpha s') & \text{if } s = \alpha\alpha s' \\ \alpha \ bc(\beta s') & \text{if } s = \alpha\beta s' \text{ with } \\ & \qquad \alpha \neq \beta \\ s & \text{otherwise} \end{cases}$$

so that if $bc(s) = \alpha_1 \cdots \alpha_n$ then $\alpha_i \neq \alpha_{i+1}$ for i from 1 to $n-1$. In particular,

$$bc(\boxed{\text{Jan}}^{31}\boxed{\text{Feb}}^{28} \cdots \boxed{\text{Dec}}^{31}) \ = \ s_{mo}.$$

Writing bc_A for the function mapping s to $bc(\rho_A(s))$, we have

$$bc_{mo}(s_{mo,dy}) \ = \ s_{mo}.$$

In general, we can refine a string s_A of granularity A to one $s_{A'}$ of granularity $A' \supseteq A$ with $bc_A(s_{A'}) = s_A$. Iterating over a chain

$$A \subseteq A' \subseteq A'' \subseteq \cdots,$$

we can glue together strings $s_A, s_{A'}, s_{A''}, \ldots$ such that

$$bc_X(s_{X'}) \ = \ s_X \ \text{ for } X \in \{A, A', A'', \ldots\}.$$

Details in section 2.

We shall refer to the expressions we can put in a box as *fluents* (short for temporal propositions), and assume they are the elements of a set Φ. While the set Φ of fluents might be infinite, we restrict the boxes that we string together to finite sets of fluents. Writing $Fin(\Phi)$ for the set of finite subsets of Φ and 2^X for the powerset of X (i.e. the set of X's subsets), we will organize the strings over the infinite alphabet $Fin(\Phi)$ around finite alphabets 2^A, for $A \in Fin(\Phi)$

$$Fin(\Phi)^* \ = \ \bigcup_{A \in Fin(\Phi)} (2^A)^*.$$

In addition to projecting $Fin(\Phi)$ down to 2^A for some $A \in Fin(\Phi)$, we can build up, forming the componentwise unions of strings $\alpha_1 \cdots \alpha_n$ and $\beta_1 \cdots \beta_n$ of the same number n of sets for their *superposition*

$$\alpha_1 \cdots \alpha_n \ \& \ \beta_1 \cdots \beta_n \ := \ (\alpha_1 \cup \beta_1) \cdots (\alpha_n \cup \beta_n)$$

and superposing languages L and L' over $Fin(\Phi)$ by superposing strings in L and L' of the same length

$$L \ \& \ L' \ := \ \{s \& s' \mid s \in L, \ s' \in L' \text{ and } \\ \text{length}(s) = \text{length}(s')\}$$

(Fernando 2004). For example,

$$s_{mo,dy} \ = \ \rho_{mo}(s_{mo,dy}) \ \& \ \rho_{dy}(s_{mo,dy})$$

where $dy := \{\text{d1}, \text{d2} \ldots, \text{d31}\}$. More generally, writing L_A for the image of L under ρ_A

$$L_A \ := \ \{\rho_A(s) \mid s \in L\},$$

observe that for $L \subseteq (2^B)^*$ and $A \subseteq B$, L is included in the superposition of L_A and L_{B-A}

$$L \ \subseteq \ L_A \ \& \ L_{B-A}.$$

The next step is to identify a language L' such that

$$L \ = \ (L_A \ \& \ L_{B-A}) \cap L' \qquad (1)$$

other than $L' = L$. For a decomposition (1) of L into (generic) contextual constraints L' separate from the (specific) components L_A and L_{B-A}, it will be useful to sharpen L_A, L_{B-A} and $\&$, factoring in bc and variants of bc (not to mention $\cap$). Measurements ranging from crude comparisons (of order) to quantitative judgments (multiplying unit magnitudes with real numbers) can be expressed through fluents in Φ. We interpret the fluents relative to suitable strings in $Fin(\Phi)^*$, presented below in category-theoretic terms connected to type theory (e.g. Mac Lane and Moerdijk 1992). Central to this presentation is the notion of a *presheaf on* $Fin(\Phi)$ — a functor from the opposite category $Fin(\Phi)^{op}$ (a morphism in which is a pair (B, A) of finite subsets of Φ such that $A \subseteq B$) to the category **Set** of sets and functions. The $Fin(\Phi)$-indexed family of functions bc_A (for $A \in Fin(\Phi)$) provides an important example that we generalize in section 2.

An example of linguistic semantic interest to which block compression bc applies is

Example B (continuous change) The pair (a), (b) below superposes two events, soup cooling and an hour passing, in different ways (Dowty 1979).

(a) The soup cooled in an hour.

(b) The soup cooled for an hour.

A common intuition is that *in an hour* requires an event that culminates, while *for an hour* requires a homogeneous event. In the case of (a), the culmination may be that some threshold temperature (supplied by context) was reached, while in (b), the homogeneity may be the steady drop in temperature over that hour. We might track soup cooling by a descending sequence of degrees, $d_1 > d_2 > \cdots > d_n$, with d_1 at the beginning of the hour, and d_n at the end. But *no* sample of finite size n can be complete. To overcome this limitation, it is helpful to construe the ith box in a string as a description of an interval I_i over the real line $\mathbb{R}$. We call a sequence $I_1 \cdots I_n$ of intervals a *segmentation* if $\bigcup_{i=1}^{n} I_i$ is an interval and for $1 \le i < n$, $I_i < I_{i+1}$, where $<$ is *full precedence*

$$I < I' \quad \text{iff} \quad (\forall r \in I)(\forall r' \in I')\; r < r'.$$

Now, assuming an assignment of degrees $sDg(r)$ to real numbers r representing temporal instants, the idea is to define satisfaction $\models$ between intervals I and fluents $sDg < d$ according to

$$I \models sDg < d \quad \text{iff} \quad (\forall r \in I)\; sDg(r) < d$$

and similarly for $d \le sDg$. We then lift $\models$ to segmentations $I_1 \cdots I_n$ and strings $\alpha_1 \cdots \alpha_n \in Fin(\Phi)^n$ of the same length n such that

$$I_1 \cdots I_n \models \alpha_1 \cdots \alpha_n \quad \text{iff} \quad \text{whenever } 1 \le i \le n \text{ and } \varphi \in I_i,\; I_i \models \varphi_i$$

and analyze (a) above as (c) below, where d is the contextually given threshold required by *in an hour*, and x is the start of that hour, the end of which is marked by hour(x).

(c) $\boxed{x, d \le sDg}\boxed{d \le sDg}\boxed{\text{hour}(x), sDg < d}$

All fluents φ in (c) have the stative property

(†) for all intervals I and I' whose union $I \cup I'$ is an interval,

$$I \cup I' \models \varphi \quad \text{iff} \quad I \models \varphi \text{ and } I' \models \varphi$$

(Dowty 1979). (†) holds also for the fluents in the string (d) below for (b), where the subinterval relation $\sqsubseteq$ is inclusion restricted to intervals,

$$I \models [\sqsupseteq]\varphi \quad \text{iff} \quad (\forall I' \sqsubseteq I)\; I' \models \varphi$$

and $sDg_{\downarrow}$ is the fluent

$$\exists x\, (sDg < x \wedge \text{Prev}(x \le sDg))$$

saying the degree drops (with $I \models \text{Prev}(\varphi)$ iff $I'I \models \boxed{\varphi}\boxed{}$ for some $I' < I$ such that $I \cup I'$ is an interval).

(d) $\boxed{x}\boxed{[\sqsupseteq]sDg_{\downarrow}}\boxed{\text{hour}(x), [\sqsupseteq]sDg_{\downarrow}}$

(†) is intimately related to block compression bc (Fernando 2013b), supporting derivations of (c) and (d) by a modification $\&_{bc}$ of $\&$ defined in §2.3 below.

Our third example directly concerns computational processes, which we take up in section 3.

Example C (finite automata) Given a finite alphabet A, a (non-deterministic) *finite automaton* $\mathcal{A}$ *over* A is a quadruple (Q, δ, F, q_0) consisting of a finite set Q of states, a transition relation $\delta \subseteq Q \times A \times Q$, a subset F of Q consisting of final (accepting) states, and an initial state $q_0 \in Q$. $\mathcal{A}$ *accepts* a string $a_1 \cdots a_n \in A^*$ precisely if there is a string $q_1 \cdots q_n \in Q^n$ such that

$$q_n \in F \text{ and } \delta(q_{i-1}, a_i, q_i) \text{ for } 1 \le i \le n \qquad (2)$$

(where q_0 is $\mathcal{A}$'s designated initial state). The *accepting runs of* $\mathcal{A}$ are strings of the form

$$\boxed{a_1, q_1}\cdots\boxed{a_n, q_n} \in (2^{A \cup Q})^*$$

satisfying (2). While we can formulate such runs as strings over the alphabet $A \times Q$, we opt for the alphabet $2^{A \cup Q}$ (formed from $A \cup Q \in Fin(\Phi)$) to link up smoothly with examples where more than one automata may be running, not all necessarily known nor in perfect harmony with others. Such examples are arguably of linguistic interest, the so-called *Imperfective Paradox* (Dowty 1979) being a case in point (Fernando 2008). That said, the attention below is largely on certain category-theoretic preliminaries for type theory.[2]

We adopt the following notational conventions. Given a function f and a set X, we write

[2]Only the most rudimentary category-theoretic notions are employed; explanations can be found in any number of introductions to category theory available online (and in print).

- $f \upharpoonright X$ for f restricted to $X \cap \mathit{domain}(f)$

- $\mathit{image}(f)$ for $\{f(x) \mid x \in \mathit{domain}(f)\}$

- fX for $\mathit{image}(f \upharpoonright X)$

- $f^{-1}X$ for $\{x \in \mathit{domain}(f) \mid f(x) \in X\}$

and if g is a function for which $\mathit{image}(f) \subseteq \mathit{domain}(g)$,

- $f; g$ for f composed (left to right) with g

$$(f; g)(x) \ := \ g(f(x))$$

  for all $x \in \mathit{domain}(f)$.

We say f is a function *on* X if

$$\mathit{domain}(f) = X \supseteq \mathit{image}(f)$$

— i.e., $f : X \to X$. The *kernel of* f, $\mathit{ker}(f)$, is the equivalence relation on $\mathit{domain}(f)$ that holds between s, s' such that $f(s) = f(s')$. Clearly,

$$\mathit{ker}(f) \ \subseteq \ \mathit{ker}(f; g)$$

when $f; g$ is defined.

2 Some presheaves on $Fin(\Phi)$

Given a function f on $Fin(\Phi)^*$ and $A \in Fin(\Phi)$, let us write f_A for the function $\rho_A; f$ on $Fin(\Phi)^*$

$$f_A(s) \ := \ f(\rho_A(s))$$

(recalling $\rho_A(\alpha_1 \cdots \alpha_n) := (\alpha_1 \cap A) \cdots (\alpha_n \cap A)$ and generalizing bc_A from Example A). To extract a presheaf on $Fin(\Phi)$ from the $Fin(\Phi)$-indexed family of functions f_A, certain requirements on f are helpful. Toward that end, let us agree that

- f *preserves* a function g with domain $Fin(\Phi)^*$ if $g = f; g$

- f is *idempotent* if f preserves itself (i.e., $f = f; f$)

- the *vocabulary* $\mathit{voc}(s)$ *of* $s \in Fin(\Phi)^*$ is the set of fluents that occur in s

$$\mathit{voc}(\alpha_1 \cdots \alpha_n) \ := \ \bigcup_{i=1}^{n} \alpha_i$$

  whence $s \in \mathit{voc}(s)^*$.

Note that for idempotent f, $\mathit{image}(f)$ consists of canonical representatives $f(s)$ of $\mathit{ker}(f)$'s equivalence classes $\{s' \in Fin(\Phi)^* \mid f(s') = f(s)\}$.

2.1 Φ-preserving functions

A function f on $Fin(\Phi)^*$ is Φ*-preserving* if f preserves *voc* and f_A, for all $A \in Fin(\Phi)$. Note that bc is Φ-preserving, as is the identity function id on $Fin(\Phi)^*$.

Proposition 1. *If f is Φ-preserving then f is idempotent and*

$$f_B; f_A \ = \ f_{A \cap B}$$

for all $A, B \in Fin(\Phi)$.

Let $\mathbf{P}_f$ be the function with domain

$$Fin(\Phi) \cup \{(B, A) \in Fin(\Phi) \times Fin(\Phi) \mid A \subseteq B\}$$

mapping $A \in Fin(\Phi)$ to $f(2^A)^*$

$$\mathbf{P}_f(A) \ := \ \{f(s) \mid s \in (2^A)^*\}$$

and a $Fin(\Phi)^{op}$-morphism (B, A) to the restriction of f_A to $\mathbf{P}_f(B)$

$$\mathbf{P}_f(B, A) \ := \ f_A \upharpoonright \mathbf{P}_f(B).$$

Corollary 2. *If f is Φ-preserving then $\mathbf{P}_f$ is a presheaf on $Fin(\Phi)$.*

Apart from bc, we get a Φ-preserving function by stripping off any initial or final empty boxes $\square$

$$\mathit{unpad}(s) \ := \ \begin{cases} \mathit{unpad}(s') & \text{if } s = \square s' \text{ or} \\ & \text{else } s = s'\square \\ s & \text{otherwise} \end{cases}$$

so that $\mathit{unpad}(s)$ neither begins nor ends with $\square$. Notice that $bc; \mathit{unpad} = \mathit{unpad}; bc$.

Proposition 3. *If f and g are Φ-preserving and $f; g = g; f$, then $f; g$ is Φ-preserving.*

2.2 The Grothendieck construction

Given a presheaf F on $Fin(\Phi)$, the *category* $\int F$ *of elements of* F (also known as the *Grothendieck construction* for F) has

- objects $(A, s) \in Fin(\Phi) \times F(A)$ (making $\sum_{X \in Fin(\Phi)} F(X)$ the set of objects in $\int F$)

- morphisms (B, s', A, s) from objects (B, s') to (A, s) when $A \subseteq B$ and $F(B, A)(s') = s$

(e.g. Mac Lane and Moerdijk 1992). Let π_f be the left projection

$$\pi_f(A, s) \ = \ A$$

from $\int \mathbf{P}_f$ back to $Fin(\Phi)$. The *inverse limit of* $\mathbf{P}_f$, $\varprojlim \mathbf{P}_f$, is the set of $(\int \mathbf{P}_f)$-valued presheaves p on $Fin(\Phi)$ (i.e. functors $p : Fin(\Phi)^{op} \to \int \mathbf{P}_f$) that are inverted by π_f

$$\pi_f(p(A)) \;=\; A \qquad \text{for all } A \in Fin(\Phi).$$

That is, $p(A) = (A, s_A)$ for some $s_A \in f(2^A)^*$ such that

$$(\ddagger)\;\; s_A = f_A(s_B) \text{ whenever } A \subseteq B \in Fin(\Phi).$$

$(\ddagger)$ is the essential restriction that $\varprojlim \mathbf{P}_f$ adds to objects $\{s_X\}_{X \in Fin(\Phi)}$ of the dependent type $\prod_{X \in Fin(\Phi)} \mathbf{P}_f(X)$.

2.3 Superposition and non-determinism

Taking the presheaf $\mathbf{P}_{id}$ induced by the identity function id on $Fin(\Phi)^*$, observe that in $\int \mathbf{P}_{id}$, there is a product of

$$(\emptyset, \boxed{\,}\boxed{\,}) \text{ and } (\{\varphi\}, \boxed{\varphi}\boxed{\,})$$

but not of

$$(\{\varphi\}, \boxed{\,}\boxed{\,}) \text{ and } (\{\varphi\}, \boxed{\varphi}\boxed{\,}).$$

The tag A in (A, s) differentiating $(\emptyset, \boxed{\,}\boxed{\,})$ from $(\{\varphi\}, \boxed{\,}\boxed{\,})$ cannot be ignored when forming products in $\int \mathbf{P}_{id}$. A necessary and sufficient condition for (A, s) and (B, s') to have a product is

$$\rho_B(s) \;=\; \rho_A(s')$$

presupposed by the pullback of

$$(A, s) \;\to\; (A \cap B, \rho_B(s)) \;\leftarrow\; (B, s').$$

By comparison, the superposition $s \& s'$ exists (as a string) if and only if

$$\rho_\emptyset(s) \;=\; \rho_\emptyset(s')$$

for

$$(\mathit{voc}(s), s) \;\to\; (\emptyset, \rho_\emptyset(s)) \;\leftarrow\; (\mathit{voc}(s'), s')$$

(or length(s) = length(s') as $\rho_\emptyset(s) = \square^{length(s)}$). Products in $\int \mathbf{P}_{id}$ are superpositions, but superpositions need not be products.

Next, we step from id to other Φ-preserving functions f such as bc and $\mathit{bc}; \mathit{unpad}$. A pair (A, s) and (B, s') of $\int \mathbf{P}_f$-objects may fail to have a product *not* because there is *no* $\int \mathbf{P}_f$-object $(A \cup B, s'')$ such that

$$(A, s) \;\leftarrow\; (A \cup B, s'') \;\to\; (B, s')$$

but too many non-isomorphic choices for such s''. Consider the case of $\mathit{bc}; \mathit{unpad}$, with $(\emptyset, \epsilon)$ terminal in $\int \mathbf{P}_{\mathit{bc};\mathit{unpad}}$ (where ϵ is the null string of length 0). For distinct fluents a and $b \in \Phi$, there are 13 strings $s \in \mathbf{P}_{\mathit{bc};\mathit{unpad}}(\{a, b\})$ such that

$$(\{a\}, \boxed{a}) \leftarrow (\{a, b\}, s) \to (\{b\}, \boxed{b})$$

corresponding to the 13 interval relations in Allen 1983 (Fernando 2007).

The explosion of solutions $s'' \in \mathbf{P}_f(A \cup B)$ to the equations

$$f_A(s'') = s \;\text{ and }\; f_B(s'') = s'$$

given

$$(A, s) \;\to\; (A \cap B, f_B(s)) \;\leftarrow\; (B, s')$$

(i.e., $f_B(s) = f_A(s')$) is paralleled by the transformation, under f, of a language L to

$$L_f \;:=\; f^{-1} f L$$

used to turn the superposition $L \& L'$ of languages L and L' into

$$L \;\&_f\; L' \;:=\; f(L_f \;\&\; L'_f).$$

For $f := \mathit{bc}; \mathit{unpad}$, the set $\boxed{a} \;\&_f\; \boxed{b}$ consists of the 13 strings mentioned above. (We follow the usual practice of conflating a string s with the singleton language $\{s\}$ whenever convenient.)

Stepping from strings to languages, we lift the presheaf $\mathbf{P}_f$ to the presheaf $\mathbf{Q}_f$ mapping $A \in Fin(\Phi)$ to

$$\mathbf{Q}_f(A) \;:=\; \{fL \mid L \subseteq (2^A)^*\}$$

and a $Fin(\Phi)^{op}$-morphism (B, A) to the function

$$\mathbf{Q}_f(B, A) \;:=\; (\lambda L \in \mathbf{Q}_f(B))\; f_A L$$

sending $L \in \mathbf{Q}_f(B)$ to $f_A L \in \mathbf{Q}_f(A)$. Then, for non-identity morphisms between $\int \mathbf{Q}_f$-objects (A, L) and (A, L') where $L \subseteq L'$, we add inclusions from (A, L) to (A, L') to the $\int \mathbf{Q}_f$-morphisms for the category $\mathfrak{C}(\Phi, f)$ with

- objects the same as those in $\int \mathbf{Q}_f$, and
- morphisms (B, L', A, L) from objects (B, L') to (A, L) whenever $A \subseteq B$ and $f_A L' \subseteq L$.

As is the case with $\int \mathbf{Q}_f$-morphisms, the sources (domains) of $\mathfrak{C}(\Phi, f)$-morphisms entail their targets (codomains). To make these entailments precise, we can identify the space of possible worlds with the inverse limit of $\mathbf{P}_f$, and reduce (A, L) to

$$[\![A, L]\!]_f := \{p \in \varprojlim \mathbf{P}_f \mid (\exists s \in L)\ p(A) = (A, s)\}.$$

The inclusion

$$[\![B, L']\!]_f \subseteq [\![A, L]\!]_f$$

can then be pronounced: (B, L') *f-entails* (A, L).

Proposition 4. *Let f be a Φ-preserving function and (A, L) and (B, L') be $\int \mathbf{Q}_f$-objects such that $A \subseteq B$. (B, L') f-entails (A, L) iff there is a $\mathfrak{C}(\Phi, f)$-morphism from (B, L') to (A, L).*

Relaxing the assumption $A \subseteq B$, one can also check that for $f \in \{bc, unpad, (bc; unpad)\}$, pullbacks of

$$(A, L) \rightarrow (A \cap B, (f_{\emptyset}L) \cap f_{\emptyset}L') \leftarrow (B, L')$$

in $\mathfrak{C}(\Phi, f)$ are given by

$$(A, L) \leftarrow (A \cup B, L \&_f L') \rightarrow (B, L') \quad (3)$$

although (3) need not hold for $L \&_f L'$ to be well-defined.

3 Constraints and finite automata

We now bring finite automata into the picture, recalling from section 1 Example C's superpositions

$$\boxed{a_1} \cdots \boxed{a_n} \ \& \ \boxed{q_1} \cdots \boxed{q_n} \quad (4)$$

where $a_1 \cdots a_n$ is accepted by a finite automaton $\mathcal{A}$ going through the sequence $q_1 \cdots q_n$ of (internal) states. We can assume the tape alphabet $A \supseteq \{a_1, \ldots, a_n\}$ and the state set $Q \supseteq \{q_1, \ldots, q_n\}$ are two disjoint subsets of the set Φ of fluents; fluents in A are "observable" (on a tape), while fluents in Q are "hidden" (inside a black box). Disjoint though they may be, A and Q are tightly coupled by $\mathcal{A}$'s transition table $\delta \subseteq Q \times A \times Q$ (not to mention the other components of $\mathcal{A}$, its initial and final states). That coupling can hardly be recreated by superposition $\&$ (or some simple modification $\&_f$) without the help of some machinery encoding δ. But first, there is the small matter of formulating the map $a_1 \cdots a_n \mapsto \boxed{a_1} \cdots \boxed{a_n}$ implicit in (4) above as a natural transformation.

3.1 Bottom $\perp$ naturally

If the function η_A such that for $a_1 \cdots a_n \in A^*$,

$$\eta_A(a_1 \cdots a_n) = \boxed{a_1} \cdots \boxed{a_n}$$

is to be the A-th component of a natural transformation $\eta : \mathbf{S} \Rightarrow \mathbf{P}_{id}$, we need to specify the presheaf $\mathbf{S}$ on $Fin(\Phi)$. To form a function $\mathbf{S}(B, A) : \mathbf{S}(B) \rightarrow \mathbf{S}(A)$ for $A \subseteq B \in Fin(\Phi)$ with $B^* \subseteq \mathbf{S}(B)$ and $A^* \subseteq \mathbf{S}(A)$, it is handy to introduce a bottom $\perp$ for $B - A$, adjoining $\perp$ to a finite subset X of Φ for $X_\perp := X + \{\perp\}$ before forming the strings in $\mathbf{S}(X) := {X_\perp}^*$. We then set $\mathbf{S}(B, A) : {B_\perp}^* \rightarrow {A_\perp}^*$

$$\mathbf{S}(B, A)(\epsilon) := \epsilon$$

$$\mathbf{S}(B, A)(\beta \mathsf{s}) := \begin{cases} \beta\, \mathbf{S}(B, A)(\mathsf{s}) & \text{if } \beta \in A_\perp \\ \perp \mathbf{S}(B, A)(\mathsf{s}) & \text{otherwise} \end{cases}$$

(e.g. $\mathbf{S}(\{a, b\}, \{a\})(ba\perp) = \perp a \perp$) and let $\eta_A : {A_\perp}^* \rightarrow (2^A)^*$ map ϵ to itself, and

$$\eta_A(\alpha \mathsf{s}) := \begin{cases} \boxed{}\, \eta_A(\mathsf{s}) & \text{if } \alpha = \perp \\ \boxed{\alpha}\, \eta_A(\mathsf{s}) & \text{otherwise} \end{cases}$$

(e.g. $\eta_{\{a\}}(\perp a \perp) = \boxed{}\boxed{a}\boxed{}$).

Proposition 5. *η is a natural transformation from $\mathbf{S}$ to $\mathbf{P}_{id}$.*

3.2 Another presheaf and category

Turning now to finite automata, we recall a fundamental result about languages that are regular (i.e., accepted by finite automata),[3] the Büchi-Elgot-Trakhtenbrot theorem (e.g. Thomas 1997)

> *for every finite alphabet $A \neq \emptyset$, a language $L \subseteq A^+$ is regular iff there is a sentence φ of MSO$_A$ such that*
>
> $$L = \{\mathsf{s} \in A^+ \mid \mathsf{s} \models_A \varphi\} .$$

MSO$_A$ is Monadic Second Order logic with a unary relation symbol U_a for each $a \in A$, plus a binary relation symbol S for successors. The predicate $\models_A$ treats a string $a_1 a_2 \cdots a_n$ over A as an MSO$_A$-model with universe $\{1, 2, \ldots, n\}$, U_a as its subset $\{i \mid a_i = a\}$, and S as

$$\{(1, 2), (2, 3), \ldots, (n-1, n)\}$$

[3] Whether or not this sense of *regular* has an interesting connection with regular categories (which are, among other things, finitely complete), I do not know.

so that, for instance,

$$a_1 \cdots a_n \models_A \exists x \exists y\ \mathsf{S}(x,y) \ \text{ iff } \ n \geq 2 \qquad (5)$$

for all finite $A \neq \emptyset$. Notice that no $a \in A$ is required to interpret $\exists x \exists y\ \mathsf{S}(x,y)$, which after all is an MSO$_\emptyset$-sentence suited to strings $\bot^n \in \mathbf{S}(\emptyset)$. Furthermore, for $a \neq b$ and $\{a,b\} \subseteq A$,

$$\textit{no} \text{ string in } A^+ \text{ satisfies } \exists x\ \mathsf{U}_a(x) \wedge \mathsf{U}_b(x) \qquad (6)$$

which makes it awkward to extend $\models_A$ to formulas with free variables (requiring variable assignments on top of strings in A^+).

A simple way to accommodate variables is to include them in A and interpret MSO$_A$-formulas not over A^+ but over $(2^A)^+$, lifting $\models_A$ from strings s over A to a predicate $\models^A$ on strings over 2^A such that

$$\mathsf{s} \models_A \varphi \ \text{ iff } \ \eta_A(\mathsf{s}) \models^A \varphi \qquad (7)$$

for every MSO$_A$-sentence φ (Fernando 2013a). For all $s \in (2^A)^+$, we set

$$s \models^A \mathsf{S}(x,y) \ \text{ iff } \ \rho_{\{x,y\}}(s) \in \fbox{$\ $}^* \fbox{$x$}\fbox{$y$}\fbox{$\ $}^* \qquad (8)$$

for $A \supseteq \{x,y\}$, and

$$s \models^A \mathsf{U}_a(x) \ \text{ iff } \ \rho_{\{a,x\}}(s) \in E_a \fbox{a, x} E_a \qquad (9)$$

for $A \supseteq \{a,x\}$, where $E_a := (\fbox{$\ $}+\fbox{$a$})^*$. We must be careful to incorporate into the clauses defining $s \models^A \varphi$ the presupposition that each first-order variable x free in φ occurs uniquely in s — i.e. $s \models^A x = x$ where

$$s \models^A x = y \ \text{ iff } \ \rho_{\{x,y\}}(s) \in \fbox{$\ $}^* \fbox{$x, y$}\fbox{$\ $}^* \qquad (10)$$

for $x, y \in A$. In particular, we restrict negation $\neg\varphi$ to strings $\models^A$-satisfying $x = x$, for each first-order variable x free in φ. We can then put

$$s \models^A \exists x\ \varphi \ \text{ iff } \ (\exists s')\ \rho_A(s') = \rho_A(s) \ \text{ and } s' \models^{A \cup \{x\}} \varphi$$

and similarly for second-order existential quantification. The equivalence (5) above then becomes

$$s \models^A \exists x \exists y\ \mathsf{S}(x,y) \ \text{ iff } \ \rho_\emptyset(s) \in \fbox{$\ $}\fbox{$\ $}^+ \qquad (11)$$

and in place of (6), we have

$$s \models^A \exists x\ \mathsf{U}_a(x) \wedge \mathsf{U}_b(x) \ \text{ iff } \ \rho_{\{a,b\}}(s) \in (2^{\{a,b\}})^* \fbox{a, b} (2^{\{a,b\}})^* \qquad (12)$$

for $a, b \in A$.

Working back from (7)

$$\mathsf{s} \models_A \varphi \ \text{ iff } \ \eta_A(\mathsf{s}) \models^A \varphi$$

to the Büchi-Elgot-Trakhtenbrot theorem, one can check that for every finite A and MSO$_A$-formula φ, the set

$$\mathcal{L}_A(\varphi) \ := \ \{s \in (2^A)^+ \mid s \models^A \varphi\}$$

of strings over 2^A that $\models^A$-satisfy φ is regular, using the fact that for all $A' \subseteq A$, the restriction of $\rho_{A'}$ to $(2^A)^*$ is computable by a finite state transducer. But for $A \subseteq \Phi$,[4] $\rho_{A'} \upharpoonright (2^A)^*$ is just $\mathbf{P}_{id}(A, A')$. In recognition of the role of these functions in $\models^A$, we effectivize the presheaf $\mathbf{Q}_{id}$ from §2.3 as follows. Let $\mathbf{R}_\Phi$ be the presheaf on $Fin(\Phi)$ mapping

- $A \in Fin(\Phi)$ to the set of languages over the alphabet 2^A that are regular

$$\mathbf{R}_\Phi(A) \ := \ \{L \in \mathbf{Q}_{id}(A) \mid L \text{ is regular}\}$$

and

- a $Fin(\Phi)^{op}$-morphism (B, A) to the restriction of $\mathbf{Q}_{id}(B, A)$ to $\mathbf{R}_\Phi(B)$

$$\mathbf{R}_\Phi(B, A) \ := \ (\lambda L \in \mathbf{R}_\Phi(B))\ \rho_A L.$$

$\int \mathbf{R}_\Phi$-objects are then pairs (A, L) where $A \in Fin(\Phi)$ and L is a regular language over the alphabet 2^A, while $\int \mathbf{R}_\Phi$-morphisms are quadruples $(B, L, A, \rho_A L)$ from (B, L) to $(A, \rho_A L)$ for $A \subseteq B \in Fin(\Phi)$. To account for the Boolean operations in MSO (as opposed to the predications (8)– (10) involving ρ_A), we add inclusions for a category $\mathfrak{R}(\Phi)$ with

- the same objects as $\int \mathbf{R}_\Phi$
- morphisms all of those in $\mathfrak{C}(\Phi, id)$ between objects in $\int \mathbf{R}_\Phi$ — i.e., quadruples (B, L', A, L) such that $A \subseteq B \in Fin(\Phi)$, $L' \subseteq (2^B)^*$ is regular, $L \subseteq (2^A)^*$ is regular, and $\rho_A L' \subseteq L$.

Let us agree to write

$$(B, L') \rightsquigarrow (A, L)$$

[4]Note an MSO$_A$-formula φ is *not* strictly a fluent in Φ but is formed in part from fluents.

to mean (B, L', A, L) is a $\mathfrak{R}(\Phi)$-morphism. Clearly, for $s \in (2^A)^+$, $A' \subseteq A$ and $L \subseteq (2^{A'})^+$,

$$\rho_{A'}(s) \in L \text{ iff } (A, \{s\}) \rightsquigarrow (A', L).$$

In particular, for $x \in A$ and $s \in (2^A)^+$,

$$s \models^A x = x \text{ iff } (A, \{s\}) \rightsquigarrow (\{x\}, \boxed{}^* \boxed{x} \boxed{}^*)$$

and similarly for $x = x$ replaced by the different MSO$_A$-formulas specified in clauses (8)–(12) above. The MSO$_A$-sentence

$$spec(A) \ := \ \forall x \bigvee_{a \in A} (\mathsf{U}_a(x) \wedge \bigwedge_{b \in A - \{a\}} \neg \mathsf{U}_b(x))$$

associating a unique $a \in A$ with each string position (presupposed in $\models_A$ but not in $\models^A$) fits the same pattern

$$\begin{aligned} s \models^A spec(A) \ & \text{iff } \ \rho_A(s) \in \{\boxed{a} \mid a \in A\}^+ \\ & \text{iff } \ (A \cup voc(s), \{s\}) \rightsquigarrow \\ & \qquad (A, \{\boxed{a} \mid a \in A\}^+) \\ & \text{iff } \ \rho_A(s) \in \eta_A A^+. \end{aligned}$$

Let us define a string $s \in Fin(\Phi)^+$ to be

- *A-specified* if $s \models^A spec(A)$
- *A-underspecified* if $\rho_A(s) \in \eta_A(A_\perp{}^+ - A^+)$
- *A-overspecified* if $\rho_A(s) \notin image(\eta_A)$

so that for $a \neq a'$ and $A = \{a, a'\}$, $\boxed{a}\boxed{a}$ is A-specified, $\boxed{a}\boxed{}$ is A-underspecified, and $\boxed{a, a'}\boxed{a}$ is A-overspecified. Given a finite automaton $\mathcal{A}$ over A with set Q of states, its set $AcRun(\mathcal{A})$ of accepting runs (Example C) is both A-specified and Q-specified, provided $A \cap Q = \emptyset$ (and otherwise risks being A-overspecified). The language accepted by $\mathcal{A}$ is the η_A^{-1}-image of the language $\rho_A AcRun(\mathcal{A})$ that is Q-underspecified, in accordance with the intuition that the states are hidden. From the regularity of $AcRun(\mathcal{A})$, however, it is clear that we can make these states visible, with $AcRun(\mathcal{A})$ as the language accepted by a finite automaton $\mathcal{A}'$ (over $2^{A \cup Q}$) that may (or may not) have the same set Q of states.

The maps ρ_A and inclusions $\subseteq$ underlying the morphisms of $\mathfrak{R}(\Phi)$ represent the two ways information may grow from $\int \mathbf{R}_\Phi$-objects (A, L) to (B, L') — *expansively* with $A \subseteq B$ and $L = \rho_A L'$, and *eliminatively* with $L' \subseteq L$ and $A = B$. The same notion of f-entailment defined in §2.3 through the sets $[\![A, L]\!]_f$ applies, but we have been careful here to fix f to id, in view of

Proposition 6. *For $A \subseteq B \in Fin(\Phi)$, φ an MSO$_A$-formula and $s \in (2^B)^+$,*

$$s \models^B \varphi \text{ iff } \rho_A(s) \models^A \varphi.$$

Proposition 6 says that $s \models^B \varphi$ depends only on the part $\rho_A(s)$ of s mentioned in φ. It is a particular instance of the *satisfaction condition* in *institutions*, expressing the invariance of truth under change of notation (Goguen and Burstall 1992). Proposition 6 breaks down if we replace ρ_A by bc_A or $unpad_A$, as can be seen with $A = \emptyset$, and $\varphi = \exists x \exists y\, \mathsf{S}(x, y)$, for which recall (11).

3.3 Varying grain and span

Troublesome as they are, the maps bc_A and $unpad_A$ have some use. Just as we can vary temporal grain through bc (Examples A and B in section 1), we can vary temporal span through *unpad*. For instance, we can combine runs of automata $\mathcal{A}_1$ over A_1 and $\mathcal{A}_2$ over A_2 in

$$L(\mathcal{A}_1, \mathcal{A}_2) \ := \ AcRun(\mathcal{A}_1) \,\&_{unpad}\, AcRun(\mathcal{A}_2)$$

with the subscript *unpad* on & relaxing the requirement that $\mathcal{A}_1$ and $\mathcal{A}_2$ start and finish together (running in lockstep throughout). For $i \in \{1, 2\}$, and Q_i the state set for $\mathcal{A}_i$,

$$AcRun(\mathcal{A}_i) \ = \ unpad_{A_i \cup Q_i} L(\mathcal{A}_1, \mathcal{A}_2)$$

assuming the sets A_1, A_2, Q_1 and Q_2 are pairwise disjoint. The disjointness assumption rules out any communication (or interference) between $\mathcal{A}_1$ and $\mathcal{A}_2$. As subsets of one large set Φ of fluents, however, it is perfectly natural for these sets to intersect (and communicate through a common vocabulary), and we might express very partial constraints involving them through, for example, MSO-formulas. Recalling the definition $\mathcal{L}_A(\varphi) := \{s \in (2^A)^+ \mid s \models^A \varphi\}$, we can rewrite the satisfaction condition

$$s \models^B \varphi \text{ iff } f_A(s) \models^A \varphi$$

on MSO$_A$-formulas φ, $A \subseteq B \in Fin(\Phi)$ and $s \in (2^B)^+$ as

$$\mathcal{L}_B(\varphi) \ = \ \{s \in (2^B)^+ \mid f_A(s) \in \mathcal{L}_A(\varphi)\}.$$

This equation lifts any regular language $\mathcal{L}_A(\varphi)$ to a regular language $\mathcal{L}_B(\varphi)$, provided f is computed by a finite-state transducer (as in the case of bc or *unpad*). Inverse images under such relations are a useful addition to the stock of operations constituting MSO-formulas as well as regular expressions.

References

James F. Allen. 1983. Maintaining knowledge about temporal intervals. *C. ACM*, 26(11):832–843.

Michael Bennett and Barbara Partee. 1972. Toward the logic of tense and aspect in English. Technical report, System Development Corporation, Santa Monica, California. Reprinted in Partee 2008.

Robin Cooper. 2012. Type theory and semantics in flux. In *Handbook of the Philosophy of Science*. Volume 14: Philosophy of Linguistics. pages 271–323.

David R. Dowty. 1979. *Word Meaning and Montague Grammar*. Reidel, Dordrecht.

Tim Fernando. 2004. A finite-state approach to events in natural language semantics. *J. Logic and Computation*, 14(1):79–92.

Tim Fernando. 2007. Observing events and situations in time. *Linguistics and Philosophy* 30(5):527–550.

Tim Fernando. 2008. Branching from inertia worlds. *J. Semantics* 25(3):321–344.

Tim Fernando. 2011. Regular relations for temporal propositions. *Natural Language Engineering* 17(2): 163–184.

Tim Fernando. 2013a. Finite state methods and description logics *Proceedings of the 11th International Conference on Finite State Methods and Natural Language Processing*, pages 63 – 71.

Tim Fernando. 2013b. Dowty's aspect hypothesis segmented. *Proceedings of the 19th Amsterdam Colloquium*, pages 107 – 114.

Danny Fox and Martin Hackl. 2006. The universal density of measurement. *Linguistics and Philosophy* 29(5): 537 – 586.

Joseph Goguen and Rod Burstall. 1992., Institutions: Abstract model theory for specification and programming, *J. ACM*, 39(1):95–146.

Hans Kamp and Uwe Reyle. 1993. *From Discourse to Logic*. Kluwer.

Christopher Kennedy. 2001. Polar opposition and the ontology of degrees. *Linguistics and Philosophy* 24. 33 – 70.

Ewan Klein and Michael Rovatsos. 2011. Temporal Vagueness, Coordination and Communication In *Vagueness in Communication 2009*, LNAI 6517, pages 108–126.

Wolfgang Klein. 2009. How time is encoded. In W. Klein and P. Li, editors, *The Expression of Time*, pages 39 – 81, Mouton De Gruyter.

Saunders Mac Lane and Ieke Moerdijk. 1992. *Sheaves in Geometry and Logic: A First Introduction to Topos Theory*. Springer.

Richard Montague. 1973. The proper treatment of quantification in ordinary English. In *Approaches to Natural Language*, pages 221 – 42. D. Reidel, Dordrecht.

Ian Pratt-Hartmann. 2005. Temporal prepositions and their logic. *Artificial Intelligence* 166: 1–36.

Roger Schwarzschild and Karina Wilkinson. 2002. Quantifiers in comparatives: A semantics of degree based on intervals. *Natural Language Semantics* 10(1):1–41.

Stephanie Solt. 2013. Scales in natural language. Manuscript.

Wolfgang Thomas. 1997. Languages, automata and logic. In *Handbook of Formal Languages: Beyond Words*, volume 3, pages 389 – 455. Springer-Verlag.

A Probabilistic Rich Type Theory for Semantic Interpretation

Robin Cooper[1], **Simon Dobnik**[1], **Shalom Lappin**[2], **and Staffan Larsson**[1]
[1]University of Gothenburg, [2]King's College London
{cooper,sl}@ling.gu.se, simon.dobnik@gu.se, shalom.lappin@kcl.ac.uk

Abstract

We propose a probabilistic type theory in which a situation s is judged to be of a type T with probability p. In addition to basic and functional types it includes, *inter alia*, record types and a notion of typing based on them. The type system is intensional in that types of situations are not reduced to sets of situations. We specify the fragment of a compositional semantics in which truth conditions are replaced by probability conditions. The type system is the interface between classifying situations in perception and computing the semantic interpretations of phrases in natural language.

1 Introduction

Classical semantic theories (Montague, 1974), as well as dynamic (Kamp and Reyle, 1993) and underspecified (Fox and Lappin, 2010) frameworks use categorical type systems. A type T identifies a set of possible denotations for expressions in T, and the system specifies combinatorial operations for deriving the denotation of an expression from the values of its constituents.

These theories cannot represent the gradience of semantic properties that is pervasive in speakers' judgements concerning truth, predication, and meaning relations. In general, predicates do not have determinate extensions (or intensions), and so, in many cases, speakers do not make categorical judgements about the interpretation of an expression. Attributing gradience effects to performance mechanisms offers no help, unless one can show precisely how these mechanisms produce the observed effects.

Moreover, there is a fair amount of evidence indicating that language acquisition in general crucially relies on probabilistic learning (Clark and Lappin, 2011). It is not clear how a reasonable account of semantic learning could be constructed on the basis of the categorical type systems that either classical or revised semantic theories assume. Such systems do not appear to be efficiently learnable from the primary linguistic data (with weak learning biases), nor is there much psychological data to suggest that they provide biologically determined constraints on semantic learning.

A semantic theory that assigns probability rather than truth conditions to sentences is in a better position to deal with both of these issues. Gradience is intrinsic to the theory by virtue of the fact that speakers assign values to declarative sentences in the continuum of real numbers [0,1], rather than Boolean values in $\{0,1\}$. In addition, a probabilistic account of semantic learning is facilitated if the target of learning is a probabilistic representation of meaning. Both semantic representation and learning are instances of reasoning under uncertainty.

Probability theorists working in AI often describe probability judgements as involving distributions over worlds. In fact, they tend to limit such judgements to a restricted set of outcomes or events, each of which corresponds to a partial world which is, effectively, a type of situation (Halpern, 2003). A classic example of the reduction of worlds to situation types in probability theory is the estimation of the likelihood of heads vs tails in a series of coin tosses. Here the world is held constant except along the dimension of a binary choice between a particular set of possible outcomes. A slightly more complex case is the probability distribution for possible results of throwing a single die, which allows for six possibilities corresponding to each of its numbered faces. This restricted range of outcomes constitutes the sample space.

We are making explicit the assumption, common to most probability theories used in AI, with clearly defined sample spaces, that probability is distributed over situation types (Barwise and Perry, 1983), rather than over sets of entire worlds. An Austinian proposition is a judgement that a situation is of a particular type, and we treat it as probabilistic. In fact, it expresses a subjective probability in that it encodes the belief of an agent concerning the likelihood that a situation is of that type. The core of an Austinian proposition is a type judgement of the form $s : T$, which states that a situation s is of type T. On our account this judgement is expressed probabilistically as $p(s : T) = r$, where $r \in [0,1]$.[1]

On the probabilistic type system that we propose situation types are intensional objects over which probability distributions are specified. This allows us to reason about the likelihood of alternative states of affairs without invoking possible worlds.

Complete worlds are not tractably representable. Assume that worlds are maximal consistent sets of propositions (Carnap, 1947). If the logic of propositions is higher-order, then the problem of determining membership in such a set is not complete. If the logic is classically first-order, then the membership problem is complete, but undecidable.

Alternatively, we could limit ourselves to propositional logic, and try to generate a maximally consistent set of propositions from a single finite proposition P in Conjunctive Normal Form (CNF, a conjunction of disjunctions), by simply adding conjuncts to P. But it is not clear what (finite) set of rules or procedures we could use to decide which propositions to add in order to generate a full description of a world in a systematic way. Nor is it obvious at what point the conjunction will constitute a complete description of the world.

Moreover, all the propositions that P entails must be added to it, and all the propositions with which P is inconsistent must be excluded, in order to obtain the maximal consistent set of propositions that describe a world. But then testing the satisfiability of P is an instance of the $ksat$ problem, which, in the general case, is NP-complete.[2]

[1] Beltagy et al. (2013) propose an approach on which classical logic-based representations are combined with distributional lexical semantics and a probabilistic Markov logic, in order to select among the set of possible inferences from a sentence. Our concern here is more foundational. We seek to replace classical semantic representations with a rich probabilistic type theory as the basis of both lexical and compositional interpretation.

[2] The $ksat$ problem is to determine whether a formula in propositional logic has a satisfying set of truth-value assignments. For the complexity results of different types of $ksat$ problem see Papadimitriou (1995).

By contrast situation types can be as large or as small as we need them to be. They are not maximal in the way that worlds are, and so the issue of completeness of specification does not arise. Therefore, they can, in principle, be tractably represented.

2 Rich Type Theory and Probability

Central to standard formulations of rich type theories (for example, (Martin-Löf, 1984)) is the notion of a judgement $a : T$, that object a is of type T. We represent the probability of this judgement as $p(a : T)$. Our system (based on Cooper (2012)) includes the following types.

Basic Types are not constructed out of other objects introduced in the theory. If T is a basic type, $p(a : T)$ for any object a is provided by a probability model, an assignment of probabilities to judgements involving basic types.

PTypes are constructed from a *predicate* and an appropriate sequence of arguments. An example is the predicate 'man' with arity $\langle Ind, Time \rangle$ where the types *Ind* and *Time* are the basic type of individuals and of time points respectively. Thus *man(john,18:10)* is the type of situation (or eventuality) where John is a man at time 18:10. A probability model provides probabilities $p(e : r(a_1, \ldots, a_n))$ for ptypes $r(a_1, \ldots, a_n)$. We take both common nouns and verbs to provide the components out of which PTypes are constructed.

Meets and Joins give, for T_1 and T_2, the meet, $T_1 \wedge T_2$ and the join $T_1 \vee T_2$, respectively. $a : T_1 \wedge T_2$ just in case $a : T_1$ and $a : T_2$. $a : T_1 \vee T_2$ just in case either $a : T_1$ or $a : T_2$ (possibly both).[3] The probabilities for meet and joint types are defined by the classical (Kolmogorov, 1950) equations $p(a : T_1 \wedge T_2) = p(a : T_1)p(a : T_2 \mid a : T_1)$ (equivalently, $p(a : T_1 \wedge T_2) = p(a : T_1, a : T_2)$), and $p(a : T_1 \vee T_2) = p(a : T_1) + p(a : T_2) - p(a : T_1 \wedge T_2)$, respectively.

Subtypes A type T_1 is a subtype of type T_2, $T_1 \sqsubseteq T_2$, just in case $a : T_1$ implies $a : T_2$ no matter what we assign to the basic types. If $T_1 \sqsubseteq T_2$ then $a : T_1 \wedge T_2$ iff $a : T_1$ and $a : T_1 \vee T_2$ iff $a : T_2$. Similarly, if $T_2 \sqsubseteq T_1$ then $a : T_1 \wedge T_2$ iff $a : T_2$ and $a : T_1 \vee T_2$ iff $a : T_1$.

If $T_2 \sqsubseteq T_1$, then $p(a : T_1 \wedge T_2) = p(a : T_2)$, and $p(a : T_1 \vee T_2) = p(a : T_1)$. If $T_1 \sqsubseteq T_2$,

[3] This use of intersection and union types is not standard in rich type theories, where product and disjoint union are preferred following the Curry-Howard correspondence for conjunction and disjunction.

then $p(a : T_1) \leq p(a : T_2)$. These definitions also entail that $p(a : T_1 \wedge T_2) \leq p(a : T_1)$, and $p(a : T_1) \leq p(a : T_1 \vee T_2)$.

We generalize probabilistic meet and join types to probabilities for unbounded conjunctive and disjunctive type judgements, again using the classical equations.

Let $\bigwedge_p(a_0 : T_0, \ldots, a_n : T_n)$ be *the conjunctive probability of judgements* $a_0 : T_0, \ldots, a_n : T_n$. Then $\bigwedge_p(a_0 : T_0, \ldots, a_n : T_n) = \bigwedge_p(a_0 : T_0, \ldots, a_{n-1} : T_{n-1})p(a_n : T_n \mid a_0 : T_0, \ldots, a_{n-1} : T_{n-1})$. If $n = 0$, $\bigwedge_p(a_0 : T_0, \ldots, a_n : T_n) = 1$.

We interpret universal quantification as an unbounded conjunctive probability, which is true if it is vacuously satisfied ($n = 0$) (Paris, 2010).

Let $\bigvee_p(a_0 : T_0, a_1 : T_1, \ldots)$ be the disjunctive probability of judgements $a_0 : T_0, a_1 : T_1, \ldots$. It is computed by $\bigvee_p(a_0 : T_0, \ldots, a_n : T_n) = \bigvee_p(a_0 : T_0, \ldots, a_{n-1} : T_{n-1}) + p(a_n : T_n) - \bigwedge_p(a_0 : T_0, \ldots, a_{n-1} : T_{n-1})p(a_n : T_n \mid a_0 : T_0, \ldots, a_{n-1} : T_{n-1})$. If $n = 0$, $\bigvee_p(a_0 : T_0, \ldots, a_n : T_n) = 0$.

We take existential quantification to be an unbounded disjunctive probability, which is false if it lacks a single non-nil probability instance ($n = 0$).

Conditional Conjunctive Probabilities are computed by $\bigwedge_p(a_0 : T_0, \ldots, a_n : T_n \mid a : T) = \bigwedge_p(a_0 : T_0, \ldots, a_{n-1} : T_{n-1} \mid a : T)p(a_n : T_n \mid a_0 : T_0, \ldots, a_{n-1} : T_{n-1}, a : T))$. If $n = 0$, $\bigwedge_p(a_0 : T_0, \ldots, a_n : T_n \mid a : T) = 1$.

Function Types give, for any types T_1 and T_2, the type $(T_1 \to T_2)$. This is the type of total functions with domain the set of all objects of type T_1 and range included in objects of type T_2. The probability that a function f is of type $(T_1 \to T_2)$ is the probability that everything in its domain is of type T_1 and that everything in its range is of type T_2, and furthermore that everything not in its domain which has some probability of being of type T_1 is *not* in fact of type T_1. $p(f : (T_1 \to T_2)) = \bigwedge_{p,\, a \in \mathrm{dom}(f)}(a : T_1, f(a) : T_2)(1 - \bigvee_{p,\, a \notin \mathrm{dom}(f)}(a : T_1))$

Suppose that T_1 is the type of event where there is a flash of lightning and T_2 is the type of event where there is a clap of thunder. Suppose that f maps lightning events to thunder events, and that it has as its domain all events which have been judged to have probability greater than 0 of being lightning events. Let us consider that all the putative lightning events were clear examples of lightning (i.e. judged with probability 1 to be of type T_1) and are furthermore associated by f with clear events of thunder (i.e. judged with probability 1 to be of type T_2). Suppose there were four such pairs of events. Then the probability of f being of type $(T_1 \to T_2)$ is $(1 \times 1)^4$, that is, 1.

Suppose, alternatively, that for one of the four events f associates the lightning event with a silent event, that is, one whose probability of being of T_2 is 0. Then the probability of f being of type $(T_1 \to T_2)$ is $(1 \times 1)^3 \times (1 \times 0) = 0$. One clear counterexample is sufficient to show that the function is definitely not of the type.

In cases where the probabilities of the antecedent and the consequent type judgements are higher than 0, the probability of the entire judgement on the existence of a functional type f will decline in proportion to the size of $\mathrm{dom}(f)$. Assume, for example that there are k elements $a \in \mathrm{dom}(f)$, where for each such a $p(a : T_1) = p(f(a) : T_2) \geq .5$. Every a_i that is added to $\mathrm{dom}(f)$ will reduce the value of $p(f : (T_1 \to T_2))$, even if it yields higher values for $p(a : T_1)$ and $p(f(a) : T_2)$. This is due to the fact that we are treating the probability of $p(f : (T_1 \to T_2))$ as the likelihood of there being a function that is satisfied by all objects in its domain. The larger the domain, the less probable that all elements in it fulfill the functional relation.

We are, then, interpreting a functional type judgement of this kind as a universally quantified assertion over the pairing of objects in $\mathrm{dom}(f)$ and $\mathrm{range}(f)$. The probability of such an assertion is given by the conjunction of assertions corresponding to the co-occurrence of each element a in f's domain as an instance of T_1 with $f(a)$ as an instance of T_2. This probability is the product of the probabilities of these individual assertions.

This seems reasonable, but it only deals with functions whose domain is all objects which have been judged to have some probability, however low, of being of type T_1. Intuitively, functions which leave out some of the objects with lower likelihood of being of type T_1 should also have a probability of being of type $(T_1 \to T_2)$. This factor in the probability is represented by the second element of the product in the formula.

Negation $\neg T$, of type T, is the function type $(T \rightarrow \bot)$, where $\bot$ is a necessarily empty type and $p(\bot) = 0$. It follows from our rules for function types that $p(f : \neg T) = 1$ if $\mathrm{dom}(f) = \emptyset$, that is T is empty, and 0 otherwise.

We also assign probabilities to judgements concerning the (non-)emptiness of a type, $p(T)$. we pass over the details of how we compute the probabilities of such judgements, but we note that our account of negation entails that $p(T \vee \neg T) = 1$, and (ii) $p(\neg\neg T) = p(T)$. Therefore, we sustain classical Boolean negation and disjunction, in contrast to Martin-Löf's (1984) intuitionistic type theory.

Dependent Types are functions from objects to types. Given appropriate arguments as functions they will return a type. Therefore, the account of probabilities associated with functions above applies to dependent types.

Record Types A record in a type system associated with a set of labels is a set of ordered pairs (*fields*) whose first member is a label and whose second member is an object of some type (possibly a record). Records are required to be functional on labels (each label in a record can only occur once in the record's left projection).

A dependent record type is a set of fields (ordered pairs) consisting of a label ℓ followed by T as above. The set of record types is defined by:

1. $[]$, that is the empty set or *Rec*, is a record type. $r : Rec$ just in case r is a record.

2. If T_1 is a record type, ℓ is a label not occurring in T_1, and T_2 is a type, then $T_1 \cup \{\langle \ell, T_2 \rangle\}$ is a record type. $r : T_1 \cup \{\langle \ell, T_2 \rangle\}$ just in case $r : T_1$, $r.\ell$ is defined (ℓ occurs as a label in r) and $r.\ell : T_2$.

3. If T is a record type, ℓ is a label not occuring in T, $\mathcal{T}$ is a dependent type requiring n arguments, and $\langle \pi_1, \ldots, \pi_n \rangle$ is an n-place sequence of paths in T,[4] then $T \cup \{\langle \ell, \langle \mathcal{T}, \langle \pi_1, \ldots, \pi_n \rangle \rangle \rangle\}$ is a record type. $r : T \cup \{\langle \ell, \langle \mathcal{T}, \langle \pi_1, \ldots, \pi_n \rangle \rangle \rangle\}$ just in case $r : T$, $r.\ell$ is defined and $r.\ell : \mathcal{T}(r.\pi_1, \ldots, r.\pi_n)$.

The probability that an object r is of a record type T is given by the following clauses:

1. $p(r : Rec) = 1$ if r is a record, 0 otherwise

2. $p(r : T_1 \cup \{\langle \ell, T_2 \rangle\}) = \bigwedge_p (r : T_1, r.\ell : T_2)$

3. If $\mathcal{T} : (T_1 \rightarrow (\ldots \rightarrow (T_n \rightarrow Type)\ldots))$, then $p(r : T \cup \{\langle \ell, \langle \mathcal{T}, \langle \pi_1, \ldots, \pi_n \rangle \rangle \rangle\}) = \bigwedge_p (r : T, r.\ell : \mathcal{T}(r.\pi_1, \ldots, r.\pi_n) \mid r.\pi_1 : T_1, \ldots, r.\pi_n : T_n)$

[4] In the full version of TTR we also allow absolute paths which point to particular records, but we will not include them here.

3 Compositional Semantics

Montague (1974) determines the denotation of a complex expression by applying a function to an intensional argument (as in $[\![\text{NP}]\!]([\![{}^\wedge\text{VP}]\!])$). We employ a variant of this general strategy by applying a probabilistic evaluation function $[\![\cdot]\!]_p$ to a categorical (non-probabilistic) semantic value. For semantic categories that are interpreted as functions, $[\![\cdot]\!]_p$ yields functions from categorical values to probabilities. For sentences it produces probability values.

The probabilistic evaluation function $[\![\cdot]\!]_p$ produces a probabilistic interpretation based on a classical compositional semantics. For sentences it will return the probability that the sentence is true. For categories that are interpreted as functions it will return functions from (categorical) interpretations to probabilities. We are not proposing strict compositionality in terms of probabilities. Probabilities are like truth-values (or rather, truth-values are the limit cases of probabilities).

We would not expect to be able to compute the probability associated with a complex constituent on the basis of the probabilities associated with its immediate constituents, any more than we would expect to be able to compute a categorical interpretation entirely in terms of truth-functions and extensions. However, the simultaneous computation of categorical and probabilistic interpretations provides us with a compositional semantic system that is closely related to the simultaneous computation of intensions and extensions in classical Montague semantics.

The following definition of $[\![\cdot]\!]_p$ for a fragment of English is specified on the basis of our probabilistic type system and a non-probabilistic interpretation function $[\![\cdot]\!]$, which we do not give in this version of the paper. (It's definition is given by removing the probability p from the definition below.)

$$[\![[_S \text{ S}_1 \text{ and S}_2]]\!]_p = \text{p}(\begin{bmatrix} \text{e}_1 : [\![\text{S}_1]\!] \\ \text{e}_2 : [\![\text{S}_2]\!] \end{bmatrix})$$

$$[\![[_S \text{ S}_1 \text{ or S}_2]]\!]_p = \text{p}(\begin{bmatrix} \text{e} : [\![\text{S}_1]\!] \vee [\![\text{S}_2]\!] \end{bmatrix})$$

$$[\![[_S \text{ Neg S}]]\!]_p = [\![\text{Neg}]\!]_p([\![\text{S}]\!])$$

$$[\![[_S \text{ NP VP}]]\!]_p = [\![\text{NP}]\!]_p([\![\text{VP}]\!])$$

$$[\![[_{NP} \text{ Det N}]]\!]_p = [\![\text{Det}]\!]_p([\![\text{N}]\!])$$

$$[\![[_{NP} \text{ N}_{prop}]]\!]_p = [\![\text{N}_{prop}]\!]_p$$

$$[\![[_{VP} \text{ V}_t \text{ NP}]]\!]_p = [\![\text{V}_t]\!]_p([\![\text{NP}]\!])$$

$$[\![[_{VP} \text{ V}_i]]\!]_p = [\![\text{V}_i]\!]_p$$

$$[\![[_{Neg} \text{ "it's not true that"}]]\!]_p = \lambda T{:}RecType(\text{p}(\begin{bmatrix} \text{e} : \neg T \end{bmatrix}))$$

$$[\![[_{Det} \text{ "some"}]]\!]_p = \lambda Q{:}Ppty(\lambda P{:}Ppty(\text{p}(\begin{bmatrix} \text{e} : \text{some}(Q, P) \end{bmatrix})))$$

$$[\![[_{Det} \text{ "every"}]]\!]_p = \lambda Q{:}Ppty(\lambda P{:}Ppty(\text{p}(\begin{bmatrix} \text{e} : \text{every}(Q, P) \end{bmatrix})))$$

$$[\![[_{Det} \text{ "most"}]]\!]_p = \lambda Q{:}Ppty(\lambda P{:}Ppty(\text{p}(\begin{bmatrix} \text{e} : \text{most}(Q, P) \end{bmatrix})))$$

$\llbracket\, [_{\text{N}}\ \text{“boy”}]\, \rrbracket_p = \lambda r{:}\left[\text{x:}\mathit{Ind}\right](\text{p}(\left[\text{e:boy}(r.\text{x})\right]))$

$\llbracket\, [_{\text{N}}\ \text{“girl”}]\, \rrbracket_p = \lambda r{:}\left[\text{x:}\mathit{Ind}\right](\text{p}(\left[\text{e:girl}(r.\text{x})\right]))$

$\llbracket\, [_{\text{Adj}}\ \text{“green”}]\, \rrbracket_p =$
$\quad \lambda P{:}\mathit{Ppty}(\lambda r{:}\left[\text{x:}\mathit{Ind}\right](\text{p}((\left[\text{e:green}(r.\text{x},P)\right])))))$

$\llbracket\, [_{\text{Adj}}\ \text{“imaginary”}]\, \rrbracket_p =$
$\quad \lambda P{:}\mathit{Ppty}(\lambda r{:}\left[\text{x:}\mathit{Ind}\right](\text{p}((\left[\text{e:imaginary}(r.\text{x},P)\right])))))$[5]

$\llbracket\, [_{\text{N}_{prop}}\ \text{“Kim”}]\, \rrbracket_p = \lambda P{:}\mathit{Ppty}(\text{p}(P(\left[\text{x=kim}\right])))$

$\llbracket\, [_{\text{N}_{prop}}\ \text{“Sandy”}]\, \rrbracket_p = \lambda P{:}\mathit{Ppty}(\text{p}(P(\left[\text{x=sandy}\right])))$

$\llbracket\, [_{\text{V}_t}\ \text{“knows”}]\, \rrbracket_p =$
$\quad \lambda \mathcal{P}{:}\mathit{Quant}(\lambda r_1{:}\left[\text{x:}\mathit{Ind}\right](\text{p}(\mathcal{P}(\lambda r_2{:}(\left[\text{e:know}(r_1.\text{x},r_2.\text{x})\right])))))$

$\llbracket\, [_{\text{V}_t}\ \text{“sees”}]\, \rrbracket_p =$
$\quad \lambda \mathcal{P}{:}\mathit{Quant}(\lambda r_1{:}\left[\text{x:}\mathit{Ind}\right](\text{p}(\mathcal{P}(\lambda r_2{:}(\left[\text{e:see}(r_1.\text{x},r_2.\text{x})\right])))))$

$\llbracket\, [_{\text{V}_i}\ \text{“smiles”}]\, \rrbracket_p = \lambda r{:}\left[\text{x:}\mathit{Ind}\right](\text{p}(\left[\text{e:smile}(r.\text{x})\right]))$

$\llbracket\, [_{\text{V}_i}\ \text{“laughs”}]\, \rrbracket_p = \lambda r{:}\left[\text{x:}\mathit{Ind}\right](\text{p}(\left[\text{e:laugh}(r.\text{x})\right]))$

A probability distribution d for this fragment, based on a set of situations $\mathcal{S}$, is such that:

$p_d(a : \mathit{Ind}) = 1$ if a is kim or sandy[6]

$p_d(s : T) \in [0, 1]$ if $s \in \mathcal{S}$ and T is a ptype

$p_d(s : T) = 0$ if $s \notin \mathcal{S}$ and T is a ptype[7]

$p_d(a : [^{\tau} P]) = p_d(P(\left[\text{x}{=}a\right]))$

$p_d(\text{some}(P, Q)) = p_d([^{\tau} P] \wedge [^{\tau} Q])$

$p_d(\text{every}(P, Q)) = p_d([^{\tau} P] \rightarrow [^{\tau} Q])$

$p_d(\text{most}(P, Q)) = \min(1, \frac{p_d([^{\tau} P] \wedge [^{\tau} Q]}{\theta_{most}\ p_d([^{\tau} P])})$

The probability that an event e is of the type in which the relation *some* holds of the properties P and Q is the probability that e is of the conjunctive type $P \wedge Q$. The probability that e is of the *every* type for P and Q is the likelihood that it instantiates the functional type $P \rightarrow Q$. As we have defined the probabilities associated with functional types in terms of universal quantification (an unbounded conjunction of the pairings between the elements of the domain P of the function and its range Q), this definition sustains the desired reading of *every*. The likelihood that e is of the type *most* for P and Q is the likelihood that e is of type $P \wedge Q$, factored by the product of the contextually determined parameter θ_{most} and the likelihood that e is of type P, where this fraction is less than 1, and 1 otherwise.

Consider a simple example.

$\llbracket\, [_{\text{S}}\ [_{\text{NP}}\ [_{\text{N}_{prop}}\ \text{Kim}]]\ [_{\text{VP}}\ [_{\text{V}_i}\ \text{smiles}]]]\, \rrbracket_p =$
$\lambda P{:}\mathit{Ppty}(\text{p}(P(\left[\text{x=kim}\right])))(\lambda r{:}\left[\text{x:}\mathit{Ind}\right](\left[\text{e:smile}(r.\text{x})\right])) =$
$p(\lambda r{:}\left[\text{x:}\mathit{Ind}\right](\left[\text{e:smile}(r.\text{x})\right])(\left[\text{x=kim}\right])) =$
$p(\left[\text{e:smile(kim)}\right])$

[5]Notice that we characterize adjectival modifiers as relations between records of individuals and properties. We can then invoke subtyping to capture the distinction between intersective and non-intersective modifier relations.

[6]This seems an intuitive assumption, though not a necessary one.

[7]Again this seems an intuitive, though not a necessary assumption.

Suppose that $p_d(s_1\text{:smile(kim)}) = .7$, $p_d(s_2\text{:smile(kim)}) = .3$, $p_d(s_3\text{:smile(kim)}) = .4$, and there are no other situations s_i such that $p_d(s_i\text{:smile(kim)}) > 0$. Furthermore, let us assume that these probabilities are independent of each other, that is, $p_d(s_3\text{:smile(kim)}) = p_d(s_3\text{:smile(kim)} \mid s_1\text{:smile(kim)}, s_2\text{:smile(kim)})$ and so on. Then

$p_d(\text{smile(kim)}) =$

$\bigvee^{p}{}_{d}(s_1 : \text{smile(kim)}, s_2 : \text{smile(kim)}, s_3 : \text{smile(kim)}) =$

$\bigvee^{p}{}_{d}(s_1 : \text{smile(kim)}, s_2 : \text{smile(kim)}) + .4 - .4\bigvee^{p}{}_{d}(s_1 :$

$\text{smile(kim)}, s_2 : \text{smile(kim)}) =$

$(.7 + .3 - .7 \times .3) + .4 - .4(.7 + .3 - .7 \times .3) =$

$.874$

This means that $p_d(\left[\text{e:smile(kim)}\right]) = .874$. Hence $\llbracket\, [_{\text{S}}\ [_{\text{NP}}\ [_{\text{N}_{prop}}\ \text{Kim}]]\ [_{\text{VP}}\ [_{\text{V}_i}\ \text{smiles}]]]\, \rrbracket_{p_d} = .874$ (where $\llbracket\ \alpha\ \rrbracket_{p_d}$ is the result of computing $\llbracket\ \alpha\ \rrbracket_p$ with respect to the probability distribution d).

Just as for categorical semantics, we can construct type theoretic objects corresponding to probabilistic judgements. We call these *probabilistic Austinian propositions*. These are records of type

$$\begin{bmatrix} \text{sit} & : & \mathit{Sit} \\ \text{sit-type} & : & \mathit{Type} \\ \text{prob} & : & [0,1] \end{bmatrix}$$

where [0,1] is used to represent the type of real numbers between 0 and 1. They assert that the probability that a situation s is of type $Type$ is the value of $prob$.

The definition of $\llbracket \cdot \rrbracket_p$ specifies a compositional procedure for generating an Austinian proposition (record) of this type from the meanings of the syntactic constituents of a sentence.

4 An Outline of Semantic Learning

We outline a schematic theory of semantic learning on which agents acquire classifiers that form the basis for our probabilistic type system. For simplicity and ease of presentation we take these to be Naive Bayes classifiers, which an agent acquires from observation. In future developments of this theory we will seek to extend the approach to Bayesian networks (Pearl, 1990).

We assume that agents keep records of observed situations and their types, modelled as probabilistic Austinian propositions. For example, an observation of a man running might yield the following Austinian proposition for some a:*Ind*, s_1:man(a), s_2:run(a):

$$\begin{bmatrix} \text{sit} & = & \begin{bmatrix} \text{ref} & = & a \\ \text{c}_{\text{man}} & = & s_1 \\ \text{c}_{\text{run}} & = & s_2 \end{bmatrix} \\ \text{sit-type} & = & \begin{bmatrix} \text{ref} & : & \textit{Ind} \\ \text{c}_{\text{man}} & : & \text{man(ref)} \\ \text{c}_{\text{run}} & : & \text{run(ref)} \end{bmatrix} \\ \text{prob} & = & 0.7 \end{bmatrix}$$

An agent, A, makes judgements based on a finite string of probabilistic Austinian propositions, $\mathfrak{J}$, corresponding to prior judgements held in memory. For a type, T, $\mathfrak{J}_T$ represents that set of Austinian propositions j such that j.sit-type $\sqsubseteq T$. If T is a type and $\mathfrak{J}$ a finite string of probabilistic Austinian propositions, then $||\ T\ ||_{\mathfrak{J}}$ represents the sum of all probabilities associated with T in $\mathfrak{J}$ ($\sum_{j \in \mathfrak{J}_T} j.prob$). $\mathcal{P}(\mathfrak{J})$ is the sum of all probabilities in $\mathfrak{J}$ ($\sum_{j \in \mathfrak{J}} j.prob$).

We use $\text{prior}_{\mathfrak{J}}(T)$ to represent the prior probability that anything is of type T given $\mathfrak{J}$, that is $\frac{||T||_{\mathfrak{J}}}{\mathcal{P}(\mathfrak{J})}$ if $\mathcal{P}(\mathfrak{J}) > 0$, and 0 otherwise.

$p_{A,\mathfrak{J}}(s : T)$ denotes the probability that agent A assigns with respect to prior judgements $\mathfrak{J}$ to s being of type T. Similarly, $p_{A,\mathfrak{J}}(s : T_1 \mid s : T_2)$ is the probability that agent A assigns with respect to prior judgements $\mathfrak{J}$ to s being of type T_1, given that A judges s to be of type T_2.

When an agent A encounters a new situation s and considers whether it is of type T, he/she uses probabilistic reasoning to determine the value of $p_{A,\mathfrak{J}}(s : T)$. A uses conditional probabilities to calculate this value, where A computes these conditional probabilities with the equation $p_{A,\mathfrak{J}}(s : T_1 \mid s : T_2) = \frac{||T_1 \wedge T_2||_{\mathfrak{J}}}{||T_2||_{\mathfrak{J}}}$, if $||\ T_2\ ||_{\mathfrak{J}} \neq 0$. Otherwise, $p_{A,\mathfrak{J}}(s : T_1 \mid s : T_2) = 0$.

This is our type theoretic variant of the standard Bayesian formula for conditional probabilities: $p(A \mid B) = \frac{|A\&B|}{|B|}$. But instead of counting categorical instances, we sum the probabilities of judgements. This is because our "training data" is not limited to categorical observations. Instead it consists of probabilistic observational judgements that situations are of particular types.[8]

Assume that we have the following types:

$\text{T}_{\text{man}} = \begin{bmatrix} \text{ref} & : & \textit{Ind} \\ \text{c}_{\text{man}} & : & \text{man(ref)} \end{bmatrix}$ and

$\text{T}_{\text{run}} = \begin{bmatrix} \text{ref} & : & \textit{Ind} \\ \text{c}_{\text{run}} & : & \text{run(ref)} \end{bmatrix}$

[8] As a reviewer observes, by using an observer's previous judgements for the probability of an event being of a particular type, as the prior for the rule that computes the probability of a new event being of that type, we have, in effect, compressed information that properly belongs in a Bayesian network into our specification of a naive Bayesian classifier. This is a simplification that we adopt here for ease of exposition. In future work, we will characterise classifier learning through full Bayesian networks.

Assume also that $\mathfrak{J}_{T_{\text{man}} \wedge T_{\text{run}}}$ has three members, corresponding to judgements by A that a man was running in three observed situations s_1, s_3, and s_4, and that these Austinian propositions have the probabilities 0.6, 0.6. and 0.5 respectively.

Take $\mathfrak{J}_{T_{\text{man}}}$ to have five members corresponding to judgements by A that there was a man in $s_1, \ldots, s_5$, and that the Austinian propositions assigning T_{man} to $s_1, \ldots, s_5$ all have probability 0.7. Given these assumptions, the conditional probability that A will assign on the basis of $\mathfrak{J}$ to someone runs, given that he is a man is $p_{A,\mathfrak{J}}(r : \text{T}_{\text{run}} \mid r : \text{T}_{\text{man}}) = \frac{||T_{\text{man}} \wedge T_{\text{run}}||_{\mathfrak{J}}}{||T_{\text{man}}||_{\mathfrak{J}}} = \frac{0.6+0.6+0.5}{0.7+0.7+0.7+0.7+0.7} = .486$

We use conditional probabilities to construct a Naive Bayes classifier. A classifies a new situation s based on the prior judgements $\mathfrak{J}$, and whatever evidence A can acquire about s. This evidence has the form $p_{A,\mathfrak{J}}(s : T_{e_1}), \ldots, p_{A,\mathfrak{J}}(s : T_{e_n})$, where $T_{e_1}, \ldots, T_{e_n}$ are the *evidence types*. The Naive Bayes classifier assumes that the evidence is independent, in that the probability of each piece of evidence is independent of every other piece of evidence.

We first formulate Bayes' rule of conditional probability. This rule defines the conditional probability of a conclusion $r : T_c$, given evidence $r : T_{e_1}, r : T_{e_2}, \ldots, r : T_{e_n}$, in terms of conditional probabilities of the form $p(s_i : T_{e_i} \mid s_i : T_c)$, $1 \leq i \leq n$, and *priors* for conclusion and evidence:

$$p_{A,\mathfrak{J}}(r : T_c \mid r : T_{e_1}, \ldots, r : T_{e_n}) = \text{prior}_{\mathfrak{J}}(T_c) \frac{\frac{||T_{e_1} \wedge T_c||_{\mathfrak{J}}}{||T_c||_{\mathfrak{J}}} \cdots \frac{||T_{e_n} \wedge T_c||_{\mathfrak{J}}}{||T_c||_{\mathfrak{J}}}}{\text{prior}_{\mathfrak{J}}(T_{e_1}) \ldots \text{prior}_{\mathfrak{J}}(T_{e_n})}$$

The conditional probabilities are computed from observations as indicated above. The rule of conditional probability allows the combination of several pieces of evidence, without requiring previous observation of a situation involving all the evidence types.

We formulate a Naive Bayes classifier as a function from evidence types $T_{e_1}, T_{e_2}, \ldots, T_{e_n}$ (i.e. from a record of type $T_{e_1} \wedge T_{e_2} \wedge \ldots \wedge T_{e_n}$) to conclusion types $T_{c_1}, T_{c_2}, \ldots, T_{c_m}$. The conclusion is a disjunction of one or more $T \in \{T_{c_1}, T_{c_2}, \ldots, T_{c_m}\}$, where m ranges over all possible non-disjunctive conclusions distinguished by the classifier. This function is specified as follows.

$$\kappa : (T_{e_1} \wedge \ldots \wedge T_{e_n}) \to (T_{c_1} \vee \ldots \vee T_{c_m}) \text{ such that } \kappa(r) = (\bigvee \underset{T \in \langle T_{c_1}, \ldots, T_{c_m} \rangle}{\text{argmax}} p_{A,\mathfrak{J}}(r : T \mid r : T_{e_1}, \ldots, r : T_{e_n})$$

The classifier returns the type T which maximises the conditional probability of $r : T$ given the evidence provided by r. The argmax operator here takes a sequence of arguments and a function and yields a sequence containing the arguments which maximise the function (if there are more than one).

The classifier will output a disjunction in case both possibilities have the same probability. The $\bigvee$ operator takes a sequence and returns the disjunction of all elements of the sequence.

In addition to computing the conclusion which receives the highest probability given the evidence, we also want the *posterior* probability of the judgement above, i.e. the probability of the judgement in light of the evidence. We obtain the non-normalised probabilities ($p^{\text{nn}}_{A,\mathfrak{J}}$) of the different possible conclusions by factoring in the probabilities of the evidence:

$p^{\text{nn}}_{A,\mathfrak{J}}(r : \kappa(r)) =$
$\sum_{T \in \bigvee^{-1}\kappa(r)} p_{A,\mathfrak{J}}(r : T \mid r : T_{e_1}, \ldots, r : T_{e_n}) p_{A,\mathfrak{J}}(r : T_{e_1}) \ldots p_{A,\mathfrak{J}}(r : T_{e_n})$

where $\bigvee^{-1}$ is the inverse of $\bigvee$, i.e. a function that takes a disjunction and returns the set of disjuncts.

We then take the probability of $r : \kappa(r)$ and normalise over the sum of the probabilities of all the possible conclusions. This gives us the normalised probability of the judgement resulting from classification $p(r : \kappa(r)) = \frac{p^{\text{nn}}_{A,\mathfrak{J}}(r:\kappa(r))}{\sum_{1 \leq i \leq m} p^{\text{nn}}_{A,\mathfrak{J}}(r:T_{c_i})}$.

However, since the probabilities of the evidence are identical for all possible conclusions, we can ignore them and instead compute the normalised probability with the following equation (where m ranges over all possible non-disjunctive conclusions distinguished by the classifier, as above).

$$p_{A,\mathfrak{J}}(r : \kappa(r)) = \frac{\sum_{T \in \bigvee^{-1}\kappa(r)} p_{A,\mathfrak{J}}(r:T \mid r:T_{e_1}, \ldots, r:T_{e_n})}{\sum_{1 \leq i \leq m} p_{A,\mathfrak{J}}(r:T_{c_i} \mid r:T_{e_1}, \ldots, r:T_{e_n})}$$

The result of classification can be represented as an Austinian proposition

$$\begin{bmatrix} \text{sit} & = & s \\ \text{sit-type} & = & \kappa(s) \\ \text{prob} & = & p_{A,\mathfrak{J}}(s : \kappa(s)) \end{bmatrix}$$

which A adds to $\mathfrak{J}$ as a result of observing and classifying s, and is thus made available for subsequent probabilistic reasoning.

5 Conclusions and Future Work

We have presented a probabilistic version of a rich type theory with records, relying heavily on classical equations for types formed with meet, join, and negation. This has permitted us to sustain classical equivalences and Boolean negation for complex types within an intensional type theory. We have replaced the truth of a type judgement with the probability of it being the case, and we have applied this approach to judgements that a situation if of type T.

Our probabilistic formulation of a rich type theory with records provides the basis for a compositional semantics in which functions apply to categorical semantic objects in order to return either functions from categorical interpretations to probabilistic judgements, or, for sentences, to probabilistic Austinian propositions. One of the interesting ways in which this framework differs from classical model theoretic semantics is that the basic types and type judgements at the foundation of the type system correspond to perceptual judgements concerning objects and events in the world, rather than to entities in a model and set theoretic constructions defined on them.

We have offered a schematic view of semantic learning. On this account observations of situations in the world support the acquisition of naive Bayesian classifiers from which the basic probabilistic types of our type theoretical semantics are extracted. Our type theory is, then, the interface between observation-based learning of classifiers for objects and the situations in which they figure on one hand, and the computation of complex semantic values for the expressions of a natural language from these simple probabilistic types and type judgements on the other. Therefore our general model of interpretation achieves a highly integrated bottom-up treatment of linguistic meaning and perceptually-based cognition that situates meaning in learning how to make observational judgements concerning the likelihood of situations obtaining in the world.

The types of our semantic theory are intensional. They constitute ways of classifying situations, and they cannot be reduced to set of situations. The theory achieves fine-grained intensionality through a rich and articulated type system, where the foundation of this system is anchored in perceptual observation.

The meanings of expressions are acquired on the basis of speakers' experience in the application of classifiers to objects and events that they encounter. Meanings are dynamic and updated in light of subsequent experience.

Probability is distributed over alternative situation types. Possible worlds, construed as maximal consistent sets of propositions (ultrafilters in a proof theoretic lattice of propositions) play no role in this framework.

Bayesian reasoning from observation provides the incremental basis for learning and refining predicative types. These types feed the combinatorial semantic procedures for interpreting the sentences of a natural language.

In future work we will explore implementations of our learning theory in order to study the viability of our probabilistic type theory as an interface between perceptual judgement and compositional semantics. We hope to show that, in addition to its cognitive and theoretical interest, our proposed framework will yield results in robotic language learning, and dialogue modelling.

Acknowledgments

We are grateful to two anonymous reviewers for very helpful comments on an earlier draft of this paper. We also thank Alex Clark, Jekaterina Denissova, Raquel Fernández, Jonathan Ginzburg, Noah Goodman, Dan Lassiter, Michiel van Lambalgen, Poppy Mankowitz, Aarne Ranta, and Peter Sutton for useful discussion of ideas presented in this paper. Shalom Lappin's participation in the research reported here was funded by grant ES/J022969/1 from the Economic and Social Research Council of the UK, and a grant from the Wenner-Gren Foundations. We also gratefully acknowledge the support of Vetenskapsrådet, project 2009-1569, Semantic analysis of interaction and coordination in dialogue (SAICD); the Department of Philosophy, Linguistics, and Theory of Science; and the Centre for Language Technology at the University of Gothenburg.

References

Jon Barwise and John Perry. 1983. *Situations and Attitudes*. Bradford Books. MIT Press, Cambridge, Mass.

I. Beltagy, C. Chau, G. Boleda, D. Garrette, K. Erk, and R. Mooney. 2013. Montague meets markov: Deep semantics with probabilistic logical form. In *Second Joint Conference on Lexical and Computational Semantics, Vol. 1*, pages 11–21. Association of Computational Linguistics, Atlanta, GA.

R. Carnap. 1947. *Meaning and Necessity*. University of Chicago Press, Chicago.

A. Clark and S. Lappin. 2011. *Linguistic Nativism and the Poverty of the Stimulus*. Wiley-Blackwell, Chichester, West Sussex, and Malden, MA.

Robin Cooper. 2012. Type theory and semantics in flux. In Ruth Kempson, Nicholas Asher, and Tim Fernando, editors, *Handbook of the Philosophy of Science*, volume 14: Philosophy of Linguistics. Elsevier BV, 271–323. General editors: Dov M. Gabbay, Paul Thagard and John Woods.

C. Fox and S. Lappin. 2010. Expressiveness and complexity in underspecified semantics. *Linguistic Analysis, Festschrift for Joachim Lambek*, 36:385–417.

J. Halpern. 2003. *Reasoning About Uncertainty*. MIT Press, Cambridge MA.

H. Kamp and U. Reyle. 1993. *From Discourse to Logic: Introduction to Modeltheoretic Semantics of Natural Language, Formal Logic and Discourse Representation Theory*. Kluwer, Dordrecht.

A.N. Kolmogorov. 1950. *Foundations of Probability*. Chelsea Publishing, New York.

Per Martin-Löf. 1984. *Intuitionistic Type Theory*. Bibliopolis, Naples.

Richard Montague. 1974. *Formal Philosophy: Selected Papers of Richard Montague*. Yale University Press, New Haven. ed. and with an introduction by Richmond H. Thomason.

C. Papadimitriou. 1995. *Computational Complexity*. Addison-Wesley Publishing Co., Readin, MA.

J. Paris. 2010. Pure inductive logic. Winter School in Logic, Guangzhou, China.

J. Pearl. 1990. Bayesian decision methods. In G. Shafer and J. Pearl, editors, *Readings in Uncertain Reasoning*, pages 345–352. Morgan Kaufmann.

Probabilistic Type Theory for Incremental Dialogue Processing

Julian Hough and Matthew Purver
Cognitive Science Research Group
School of Electronic Engineering and Computer Science
Queen Mary University of London
{j.hough,m.purver}@qmul.ac.uk

Abstract

We present an adaptation of recent work on probabilistic Type Theory with Records (Cooper et al., 2014) for the purposes of modelling the incremental semantic processing of dialogue participants. After presenting the formalism and dialogue framework, we show how probabilistic TTR type judgements can be integrated into the inference system of an incremental dialogue system, and discuss how this could be used to guide parsing and dialogue management decisions.

1 Introduction

While classical type theory has been the predominant mathematical framework in natural language semantics for many years (Montague, 1974, inter alia), it is only recently that probabilistic type theory has been discussed for this purpose. Similarly, type-theoretic representations have been used within dialogue models (Ginzburg, 2012); and probabilistic modelling is common in dialogue systems (Williams and Young, 2007, inter alia), but combinations of the two remain scarce. Here, we attempt to make this connection, taking (Cooper et al., 2014)'s probabilistic Type Theory with Records (TTR) as our principal point of departure, with the aim of modelling incremental inference in dialogue.

To our knowledge there has been no practical integration of probabilistic type-theoretic inference into a dialogue system so far; here we discuss computationally efficient methods for implementation in an extant incremental dialogue system. This paper demonstrates their efficacy in simple referential communication domains, but we argue the methods could be extended to larger domains and additionally used for on-line learning in future work.

2 Previous Work

Type Theory with Records (TTR) (Betarte and Tasistro, 1998; Cooper, 2005) is a rich type theory which has become widely used in dialogue models, including information state models for a variety of phenomena such as clarification requests (Ginzburg, 2012; Cooper, 2012) and non-sentential fragments (Fernández, 2006). It has also been shown to be useful for incremental semantic parsing (Purver et al., 2011), incremental generation (Hough and Purver, 2012), and recently for grammar induction (Eshghi et al., 2013).

While the technical details will be given in section 3, the central judgement in type theory $s : T$ (that a given object s is of type T) is extended in TTR so that s can be a (potentially complex) *record* and T can be a *record type* – e.g. s could represent a dialogue gameboard state and T could be a dialogue gameboard state type (Ginzburg, 2012; Cooper, 2012). As TTR is highly flexible with a rich type system, variants have been considered with types corresponding to real-number-valued perceptual judgements used in conjunction with linguistic context, such as visual perceptual information (Larsson, 2011; Dobnik et al., 2012), demonstrating its potential for embodied learning systems. The possibility of integration of perceptron learning (Larsson, 2011) and naive Bayes classifiers (Cooper et al., 2014) into TTR show how linguistic processing and probabilistic conceptual inference can be treated in a uniform way within the same representation system.

Probabilistic TTR as described by Cooper et al. (2014) replaces the categorical $s : T$ judgement with the real number valued $p(s : T) = v$ where $v \in [0,1]$. The authors show how standard probability theoretic and Bayesian equations can be applied to TTR judgements and how an agent might learn from experience in a simple classification game. The agent is presented with instances of a situation and it learns with each round by updating its set of probabilistic type judgements to best predict the type of object in focus — in this case updating the probability judgement that something is an apple given its observed colour and shape $p(s : T_{apple} \mid s : T_{Shp}, s : T_{Col})$ where $Shp \in \{shp1, shp2\}$ and $Col \in \{col1, col2\}$. From a cognitive modelling perspective, these judgements can be viewed as probabilistic perceptual information derived from learning. We use similar methods in our toy domain, but show how prior judgements could be constructed efficiently, and how classifications can be made without exhaustive iteration through individual type classifiers.

There has also been significant experimental work on simple referential communication games in psycholinguistics, computational and formal modelling. In terms of production and generation, Levelt (1989) discusses speaker strategies for generating referring expressions in a simple object naming game. He showed how speakers use informationally redundant features of the objects, violating Grice's Maxim of Quantity. In natural language generation (NLG), referring expression generation (REG) has been widely studied (see (Krahmer and Van Deemter, 2012) for a comprehensive survey). The incremental algorithm (IA) (Dale and Reiter, 1995) is an iterative feature selection procedure for descriptions of objects based on computing the distractor set of referents that each adjective in a referring expression could cause to be inferred. More recently Frank and Goodman (2012) present a Bayesian model of optimising referring expressions based on surprisal, the information-theoretic measure of how much descriptions reduce uncertainty about their intended referent, a measure which they claim correlates strongly to human judgements.

The element of the referring expression domain we discuss here is incremental processing. There is evidence from (Brennan and Schober, 2001)'s experiments that people reason at an incredibly time-critical level from linguistic information. They demonstrated *self-repair* can speed up semantic processing (or at least object reference) in such games, where an incorrect object being partly vocalized and then repaired in the instructions (e.g. "the yell-, uh, purple square") yields quicker response times from the onset of the target ("purple") than in the case of the fluent instructions ("the purple square"). This example will be addressed in section 5. First we will set out the framework in which we want to model such processing.

3 Probabilistic TTR in an incremental dialogue framework

In TTR (Cooper, 2005; Cooper, 2012), the principal logical form of interest is the *record type* ('RT' from here), consisting of sequences of *fields* of the form $[\, l : T \,]$ containing a label l and a type T.[1] RTs can be witnessed (i.e. judged as inhabited) by *records* of that type, where a record is a set of label-value pairs $[\, l = v \,]$. The central type judgement in TTR that a record s is of (record) type R, i.e. $s : R$, can be made from the component type judgements of individual fields; e.g. the one-field record $[\, l = v \,]$ is of type $[\, l : T \,]$ just in case v is of type T. This is generalisable to records and RTs with multiple fields: a record s is of RT R if s includes fields with labels matching those occurring in the fields of R, such that all fields in R are matched, and all matched fields in s must have a value belonging to the type of the corresponding field in R. Thus it is possible for s to have more fields than R and for $s : R$ to still hold, but not vice-versa: $s : R$ cannot hold if R has more fields than s.

$$R_1 : \left[\begin{array}{lcl} l_1 & : & T_1 \\ l_2 & : & T_2 \\ l_3 & : & T_3(l_1) \end{array}\right] \quad R_2 : \left[\begin{array}{lcl} l_1 & : & T_1 \\ l_2 & : & T_{2'} \end{array}\right] \quad R_3 : []$$

Figure 1: Example TTR record types

Fields can have values representing predicate types (*ptypes*), such as T_3 in Figure 1, and consequently fields can be *dependent* on fields preceding them (i.e. higher) in the RT, e.g. l_1 is bound in the predicate type field l_3, so l_3 depends on l_1.

Subtypes, meets and joins A relation between RTs we wish to explore is $\sqsubseteq$ ('is a subtype of'), which can be defined for RTs in terms of fields as simply: $R_1 \sqsubseteq R_2$ if for all fields $[\, l : T_2 \,]$ in R_2, R_1 contains $[\, l : T_1 \,]$ where $T_1 \sqsubseteq T_2$. In Figure 1, both $R_1 \sqsubseteq R_3$ and $R_2 \sqsubseteq R_3$; and $R_1 \sqsubseteq R_2$ iff $T_2 \sqsubseteq T_{2'}$. The transitive nature of this relation (if $R_1 \sqsubseteq R_2$ and $R_2 \sqsubseteq R_3$ then $R_1 \sqsubseteq R_3$) can be used effectively for type-theoretic inference.

[1] We only introduce the elements of TTR relevant to the phenomena discussed below. See (Cooper, 2012) for a detailed formal description.

We also assume the existence of *manifest* (singleton) types, e.g. T_a, the type of which only a is a member. Here, we write manifest RT fields such as $[\, l : T_a \,]$ where $T_a \sqsubseteq T$ using the syntactic sugar $[\, l_{=a} : T \,]$. The subtype relation effectively allows progressive instantiation of fields (as addition of fields to R leads to R' where $R' \sqsubseteq R$), which is practically useful for an incremental dialogue system as we will explain.

We can also define *meet* and *join* types of two or more RTs. The representation of the meet type of two RTs R_1 and R_2 is the result of a merge operation (Larsson, 2010), which in simple terms here can be seen as union of fields. A meet type is also equivalent to the extraction of a maximal common subtype, an operation we will call $MaxSub(R_i..R_n)$:[2]

$$\text{if } R_1 = \begin{bmatrix} l_1 : T_1 \\ l_2 : T_2 \end{bmatrix} \text{and } R_2 = \begin{bmatrix} l_2 : T_2 \\ l_3 : T_3 \end{bmatrix}$$
$$R_1 \wedge R_2 = \begin{bmatrix} l_1 : T_1 \\ l_2 : T_2 \\ l_3 : T_3 \end{bmatrix} = MaxSub(R_1, R_2)$$

R_1 and R_2 here are common *supertypes* of the resulting $R_1 \wedge R_2$. On the other hand, the join of two RTs R_1 and R_2, the type $R_1 \vee R_2$ cannot be represented by field intersection. It is defined in terms of type checking, in that $s : R_1 \vee R_2$ iff $s : R_1$ or $s : R_2$. It follows that if $R_1 \sqsubseteq R_2$ then $s : R_1 \wedge R_2$ iff $s : R_1$, and $s : R_1 \vee R_2$ iff $s : R_2$.

While technically the maximally common supertype of R_1 and R_2 is the join type $R_1 \vee R_2$, here we introduce the maximally common *simple* (non disjunctive) supertype of two RTs R_1 and R_2 as field intersection:

$$\text{if } R_1 = \begin{bmatrix} l_1 : T_1 \\ l_2 : T_2 \end{bmatrix} \text{and } R_2 = \begin{bmatrix} l_2 : T_2 \\ l_3 : T_3 \end{bmatrix}$$
$$MaxSuper(R_1, R_2) = \begin{bmatrix} l_2 : T_2 \end{bmatrix}$$

We will explore the usefulness of this new operation in terms of RT lattices in sec. 4.

3.1 Probabilistic TTR

We follow Cooper et al. (2014)'s recent extension of TTR to include probabilistic type judgements of the form $p(s : R) = v$ where $v \in [0,1]$, i.e. the real valued judgement that a record s is of RT R. Here we use probabilistic TTR to model a common psycholinguistic experimental set up in section 5. We repeat some of Cooper et al.'s calculations here for exposition, but demonstrate efficient graphical methods for generating and incrementally retrieving probabilities in section 4.

Cooper et al. (2014) define the probability of the meet and join types of two RTs as follows:

$$\begin{aligned} p(s : R_1 \wedge R_2) &= p(s : R_1) p(s : R_2 \mid s : R_1) \\ p(s : R_1 \vee R_2) &= p(s : R_1) + p(s : R_2) - p(s : R_1 \wedge R_2) \end{aligned} \tag{1}$$

It is practically useful, as we will describe below, that the join probability can be computed in terms of the meet. Also, there are equivalences between meets, joins and subtypes in terms of type judgements as described above, in that assuming if $R_1 \sqsubseteq R_2$ then $p(s : R_2 \mid s : R_1) = 1$, we have:

$$\begin{aligned} &\text{if } R_1 \sqsubseteq R_2 \\ p(s : R_1 \wedge R_2) &= p(s : R_1) \\ p(s : R_1 \vee R_2) &= p(s : R_2) \\ p(s : R_1) &\le p(s : R_2) \end{aligned} \tag{2}$$

The conditional probability of a record being of type R_2 given it is of type R_1 is:

$$p(s : R_2 \mid s : R_1) = \frac{p(s : R_1 \wedge s : R_2)}{p(s : R_1)} \tag{3}$$

We return to an explanation for these classical probability equations holding within probabilistic TTR in section 4.

Learning and storing probabilistic judgements When dealing with referring expression games, or indeed any language game, we need a way of storing perceptual experience. In probabilistic TTR this can be achieved by positing a judgement set J in which an agent stores probabilistic type judgements.[3] We refer to the sum of the value of probabilistic judgements that a situation has been judged to be of type R_i within J as $\|R_i\|_J$ and the sum of all probabilistic judgements in J simply as $P(J)$; thus the prior probability that anything is of type R_i under the set of judgements J is $\frac{\|R_i\|_J}{P(J)}$. The conditional probability $p(s : R_1 \mid s : R_2)$ under J can be reformulated in terms of these sets of judgements:

$$p_J(s : R_1 \mid s : R_2) = \begin{cases} \frac{\|R_1 \wedge R_2\|_J}{\|R_2\|_J} & \text{iff } \|R_2\|_J \neq 0 \\ 0 & \text{otherwise} \end{cases} \tag{4}$$

[2]Here we concern ourselves with simple examples that avoid label-type clashes between two RTs (i.e. where R_1 contains $l_1 : T1$ and R_2 contains $l_1 : T2$); in these cases the operations are more complex than field concatenation/sharing.

[3](Cooper et al., 2014) characterise a type judgement as an Austinian proposition that a situation is of a given type with a given probability, encoded in a TTR record.

where the sample spaces $||R_1 \wedge R_2||_J$ and $||R_2||_J$ constitute the observations of the agent so far. J can have new judgements added to it during learning. We return to this after introducing the incremental semantics needed to interface therewith.

3.2 DS-TTR and the DyLan dialogue system

In order to permit type-theoretic inference in a dialogue system, we need to provide suitable TTR representations for utterances and the current pragmatic situation from a parser, dialogue manager and generator as instantaneously and accurately as possible. For this purpose we use an incremental framework DS-TTR (Eshghi et al., 2013; Purver et al., 2011) which integrates TTR representations with the inherently incremental grammar formalism Dynamic Syntax (DS) (Kempson et al., 2001).

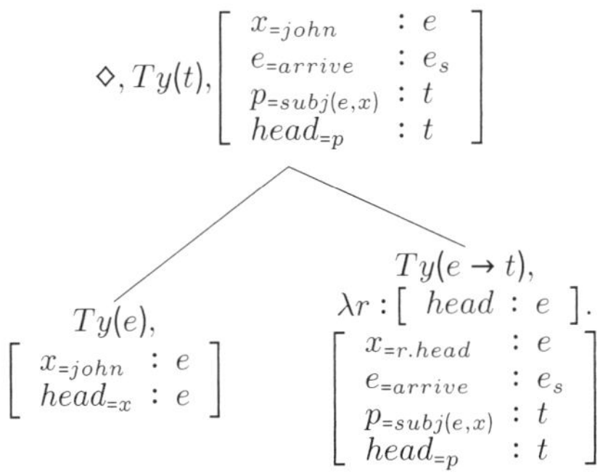

Figure 2: DS-TTR tree

DS produces an incrementally specified, partial logical tree as words are parsed/generated; following Purver et al. (2011), DS tree nodes are decorated not with simple atomic formulae but with RTs, and corresponding lambda abstracts representing functions of type $RT \rightarrow RT$ (e.g. $\lambda r : [\, l_1 : T_1\,].[\, l_{2=r.l_1} : T_1\,]$ where $r.l_1$ is a *path* expression referring to the label l_1 in r) – see Figure 2. Using the idea of manifestness of fields as mentioned above, we have a natural representation for underspecification of leaf node content, e.g. $[\, x : e\,]$ is unmanifest whereas $[\, x_{=john} : e\,]$[4] is manifest and the latter is a subtype of the former. Functional application can apply incrementally, allowing a RT at the root node to be compiled for any partial tree, which is incrementally further specified as parsing proceeds (Hough and Purver, 2012). Within a given parse path, due to DS-TTR's monotonicity, each maximal RT of the tree's root node is a subtype of the parser's previous maximal output.

Following (Eshghi et al., 2013), DS-TTR tree nodes include a field $head$ in all RTs which corresponds to the DS tree node type. We also assume a neo-Davidsonian representation of predicates, with fields corresponding to an event term and to each semantic role; this allows all available semantic information to be specified incrementally in a strict subtyping relation (e.g. providing the $subj()$ field when subject but not object has been parsed) – see Figure 2.

We implement DS-TTR parsing and generation mechanisms in the `DyLan` dialogue system[5] within Jindigo (Skantze and Hjalmarsson, 2010), a Java-based implementation of the incremental unit (IU) framework of (Schlangen and Skantze, 2009). In this framework, each module has input and output IUs which can be `added` as edges between vertices in module buffer graphs, and become `committed` should the appropriate conditions be fulfilled, a notion which becomes important in light of hypothesis change and repair situations. Dependency relations between different graphs within and between modules can be specified by *groundedIn* links (see (Schlangen and Skantze, 2009) for details).

The `DyLan` interpreter module (Purver et al., 2011) uses Sato (2011)'s insight that the context of DS parsing can be characterized in terms of a Directed Acyclic Graph (DAG) with trees for nodes and DS actions for edges. The module's state is characterized by three linked graphs as shown in Figure 3:

- *input:* a time-linear word graph posted by the ASR module, consisting of word hypothesis edge IUs between vertices W_n
- *processing:* the internal DS parsing DAG, which adds parse state edge IUs between vertices S_n *groundedIn* the corresponding word hypothesis edge IU
- *output:* a concept graph consisting of domain concept IUs (RTs) as edges between vertices C_n, *groundedIn* the corresponding path in the DS parsing DAG

Here, our interest is principally in the parser output, to support incremental inference; a DS-TTR generator is also included which uses RTs as goal concepts (Hough and Purver, 2012) and uses the

[4]This is syntactic sugar for $[\, x : e_{john}\,]$ and the = sign is not the same semantically as that in a record.

[5]Available from http://dylan.sourceforge.net/

same parse graph as the interpreter to allow self-monitoring and compound contributions, but we omit the details here.

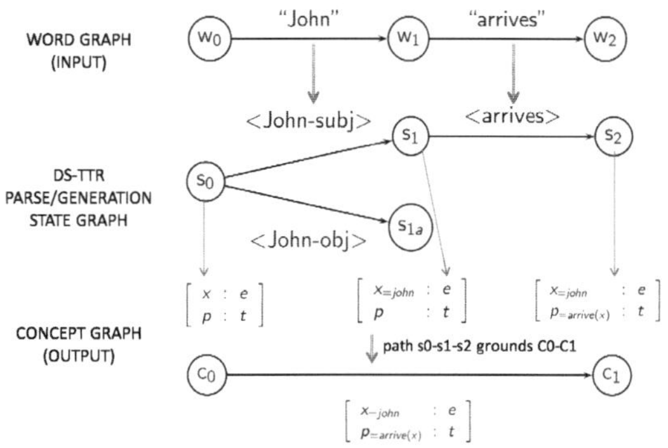

Figure 3: Normal incremental parsing in Dylan

4 Order theoretic and graphical methods for probabilistic TTR

RT lattices to encode domain knowledge To support efficient inference in DyLan, we represent dialogue domain concepts via partially ordered sets (*posets*) of RT judgements, following similar insights used in inducing DS-TTR actions (Eshghi et al., 2013). A poset has several advantages over an unordered list of un-decomposed record types: the possibility of incremental type-checking; increased speed of type-checking, particularly for pairs of/multiple type judgements; immediate use of type judgements to guide system decisions; inference from negation; and the inclusion of learning within a domain. We leave the final challenge for future work, but discuss the others here.

We can construct a poset of type judgements for any single RT by decomposing it into its constituent supertype judgements in a *record type lattice*. Representationally, as per set-theoretic lattices, this can be visualised as a Hasse diagram such as Figure 4, however here the ordering arrows show $\sqsubseteq$ ('subtype of') relations from descendant to ancestor nodes.

To characterize an RT lattice G ordered by $\sqsubseteq$, we adapt Knuth (2005)'s description of lattices in line with standard order theory: for a pair of RT elements R_x and R_y, their lower bound is the set of all $R_z \in G$ such that $R_z \sqsubseteq R_x$ and $R_z \sqsubseteq R_y$. In the event that a unique greatest lower bound exists, this is their meet, which in G happily corresponds to the TTR meet type $R_x \wedge R_y$. Dually, if their unique least upper bound exists, this is their

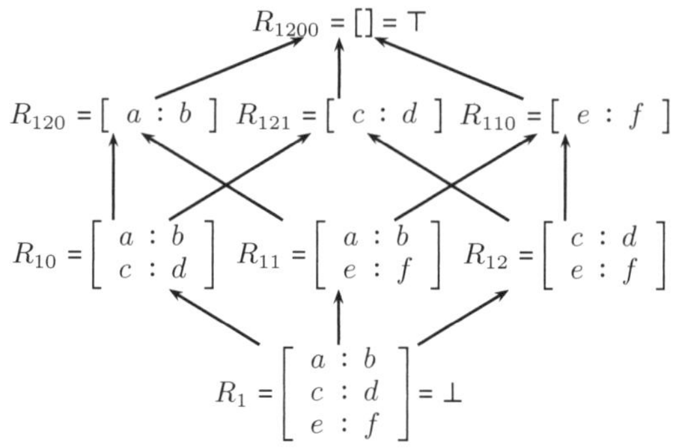

Figure 4: Record Type lattice ordered by the subtype relation

join and in TTR terms is $MaxSuper(R_x, R_y)$ but not necessarily their join type $R_x \vee R_y$ as here we concern ourselves with simple RTs. One element *covers* another if it is a direct successor to it in the subtype ordering relation hierarchy. G has a greatest element ($\top$) and least element ($\bot$), with the *atoms* being the elements that cover $\bot$; in Figure 4 if R_1 is viewed as $\bot$, the atoms are $R_{\{10,11,12\}}$. An RT element R_x has a *complement* if there is a unique element $\neg R_x$ such that $MaxSuper(R_x, \neg R_x) = \top$ and $R_x \wedge \neg R_x = \bot$ (the lattice in Figure 4 is *complemented* as this holds for every element).

Graphically, the join of two elements can be found by following the connecting edges upward until they first converge on a single RT, giving us $MaxSuper(R_{10}, R_{12}) = R_{121}$ in Figure 4, and the meet can be found by following the lines downward until they connect to give their meet type, i.e. $R_{10} \wedge R_{12} = R_1$.

If we consider R_1 to be a domain concept in a dialogue system, we can see how its RT lattice G can be used for incremental inference. As incrementally specified RTs become available from the interpreter they are matched to those in G to determine how far down towards the final domain concept R_1 our current state allows us to be. Different sequences of words/utterances lead to different paths. However, any practical dialogue system must entertain more than one possible domain concept as an outcome; G must therefore contain multiple possible final concepts, constituting its atoms, each with several possible dialogue move sequences, which correspond to possible downward paths – e.g. see the structure of Figure 5. Our aim here is to associate each RT in G with a probabilistic judgement.

Initial lattice construction We define a simple bottom-up procedure in Algorithm 1 to build a RT lattice G of all possible simple domain RTs and their prior probabilistic judgements, initialised by the disjunction of possible final state judgements (the priors),[6] along with the absurdity $\bot$, stipulated a priori as the least element with probability 0 and the meet type of the atomic priors. The algorithm recursively removes one field from the RT being processed at a time (except fields referenced in a remaining dependent *ptype* field), then orders the new supertype RT in G appropriately.

Each node in G contains its RT R_i and a sum of probability judgements $\{||R_k||_J + .. + ||R_n||_J\}$ corresponding to the probabilities of the priors it stands in a supertype relation to. These sums are propagated up from child to parent node as it is constructed. It terminates when all simple maximal supertypes[7] have been processed, leaving the maximally common supertype as $\top$ (possibly the empty type [ ]), associated with the entire probability mass $P(J)$, which constitutes the denominator to all judgements- given this, only the numerator of equation $\frac{||R_i||_J}{P(J)}$ needs to be stored at each node.

Algorithm 1 Probabilistic TTR record type lattice construction algorithm

```
INPUT: priors                          ▷ use the initial prior judgements for G's atoms
OUTPUT: G
G = newGraph(priors)                   ▷ P(J) set to equal sum of prior probs
agenda = priors                        ▷ Initialise agenda
while not agenda is empty do
    RT = agenda.pop()
    for field ∈ RT do
        if field ∈ RT.paths then       ▷ Do not remove bound fields
            continue
        superRT = RT - field
        if superRT ∈ G then            ▷ not new? order w.r.t. RT and inherit RT's priors
            G.order(RT.address,G.getNode(superRT),⊑)
        else                           ▷ new?
            superNode = G.newNode(superRT)    ▷ create new node w. empty priors
            for node ∈ G do            ▷ order superNode w.r.t. other nodes in G
                if superRT.fields ⊂ node.fields then
                    G.order(node,superNode,⊑)  ▷ superNode inherits node's priors
            agenda.append(superRT)     ▷ add to agenda for further supertyping
```

Direct inference from the lattice To explain how our approach models incremental inference, we assume Brennan and Schober (2001)'s experimental referring game domain described in section 2: three distinct domain situation RTs R_1, R_2 and R_3 correspond to a purple square, a yellow square and a yellow circle, respectively.

The RT lattice G constructed initially upon observation of the game (by instructor or instructee) shown in Figure 5 uses a uniform distribution for the three disjunctive final situations. Each node shows an RT R_i on the left and the derivation of its prior probability $p_J(R_i)$ that any game situation record will be of type R_i on the right, purely in terms of the relevant priors and the global denominator $P(J)$.

G can be searched to make inferences in light of partial information from an ongoing utterance. We model inference as predicting the likelihood of relevant type judgements $R_y \in G$ of a situation s, given the judgement $s : R_x$ we have so far. To do this we use conditional probability judgements following Knuth's work on distributive lattices, using the $\sqsubseteq$ relation to give a choice function:

$$p_J(s : R_y \mid s : R_x) = \begin{cases} 1 & \text{if } R_x \sqsubseteq R_y \\ 0 & \text{if } R_x \wedge R_y = \bot \\ p & \text{otherwise, where } 0 \le p \le 1 \end{cases} \quad (5)$$

The third case is the degree of inclusion of R_y in R_x, and can be calculated using the conditional probability calculation (4) in sec. 3. For negative RTs, a lattice generated from Algorithm 1 will be distributive but not guaranteed to be complemented, however we can still derive $p_J(s : R_y \mid s : \neg R_x)$ by obtaining $p_J(s : R_y)$ in G modulo the probability mass of R_x and that of its subtypes:

$$p_J(s : R_y \mid s : \neg R_x) = \begin{cases} 0 & \text{if } R_y \sqsubseteq R_x \\ \frac{p_J(s:R_y) - p_J(s:R_x \wedge R_y)}{p_J(s:\top) - p_J(s:R_x)} & \text{otherwise} \end{cases} \quad (6)$$

The subtype relations and atomic, join and meet types' probabilities required for (1) - (6) can be calculated efficiently through graphical search algorithms by characterising G as a DAG: the reverse direction of the subtype ordering edges can be viewed as reachability edges, making $\top$ the source and $\bot$ the sink. With this characterisation, if R_x is reachable from R_y then $R_x \sqsubseteq R_y$.

In DAG terms, the probability of the meet of two RTs R_x and R_y can be found at their highest common descendant node – e.g. $p_J(R_4 \wedge R_5)$ in Figure 5 can be found as $\frac{1}{3}$ directly at R_1. Note if R_x is reachable from R_y, i.e. $R_x \sqsubseteq R_y$, then due to the equivalences listed in (2), $p_J(R_x \wedge R_y)$ can be found directly at R_x. If the meet of two nodes is $\bot$ (e.g. R_4 and R_3 in Figure 5), then their meet probability is 0 as $p_J(\bot)$=0.

While the lattice does not have direct access to the join types of its elements, a join type probability $p_J(R_x \vee R_y)$ can be calculated in terms of $p_J(R_x \wedge R_y)$ by the join equation in (1), which holds for all probabilistic distributive lat-

[6]Although the priors' disjunctive probability sums to 1 after G is constructed, i.e. in Figure 5 $\frac{||R_1||_J + ||R_2||_J + ||R_3||_J}{P(J)} = 1$, the real values initially assigned to them need not sum to unity, as they form the atoms of G (see (Knuth, 2005)).

[7]Note that it does not generate the join types but maximal common supertypes defined by field intersection.

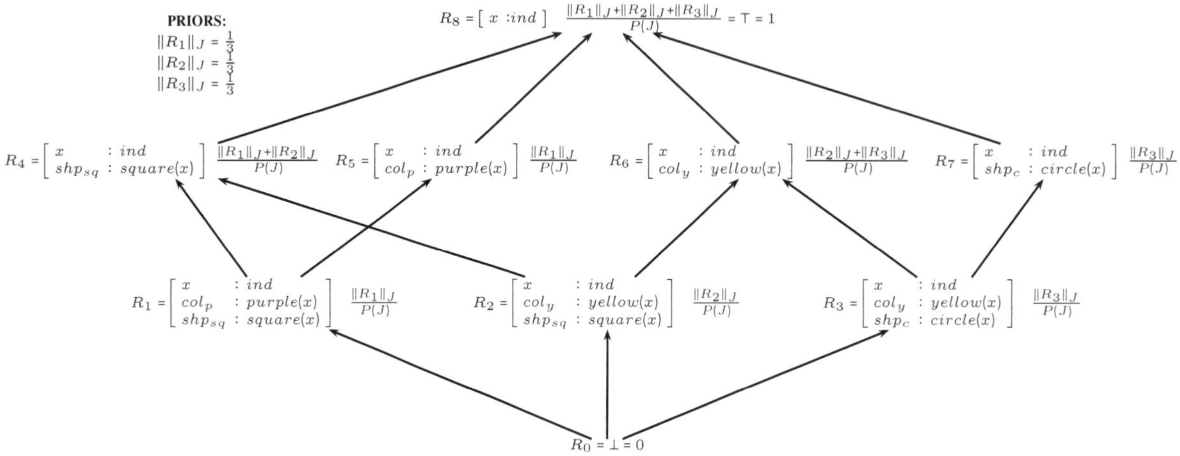

Figure 5: Record type lattice with initial uniform prior probablities

tices (Knuth, 2005).[8] As regards efficiency, worst case complexity for finding the meet probability at the common descendant of R_x and R_y is a linear $O(m+n)$ where m and n are the number of edges in the downward (possibly forked) paths $R_x \to \bot$ and $R_y \to \bot$.[9]

5 Simulating incremental inference and self-repair processing

Interpretation in DyLan and its interface to the RT lattice G follows evidence that dialogue agents parse self-repairs efficiently and that repaired dialogue content (reparanda) is given special status but not removed from the discourse context. To model Brennan and Schober (2001)'s findings of disfluent spoken instructions speeding up object recognition (see section 2), we demonstrate a self-repair parse in Figure 6 for "The yell-, uh, purple square" in the simple game of predicting the final situation from $\{R_1, R_2, R_3\}$ continuously given the type judgements made so far. We describe the stages T1-T4 in terms of the current word being processed- see Figure 6:

At **T1:'the'** the interpreter will not yield a subtype checkable in G so we can only condition on R_8 ($\top$), giving us $p_J(s : R_i \mid s : R_8) = \frac{1}{3}$ for $i \in \{1,2,3\}$, equivalent to the priors. At **T2: 'yell-'**, the best partial word hypothesis is now "yellow";[10] the interpreter therefore outputs an RT which matches the type judgement $s : R_6$ (i.e. that the object is a yellow object). Taking this judgement as the conditioning evidence using function (5) we get $p_J(s : R_1 \mid s : R_6) = 0$ and using (4) we get $p_J(s : R_2 \mid s : R_6) = 0.5$ and $p_J(s : R_3 \mid s : R_6) = 0.5$ (see the schematic probability distribution at stage T2 in Figure 6 for the three objects). The meet type probabilities required for the conditional probabilities can be found graphically as described above.

At **T3:'uh purple'**, low probability in the interpreter output causes a self-repair to be recognised, enforcing backtracking on the parse graph which informally operates as follows (see Hough and Purver (2012)) :

> **Self-repair:**
> IF from parsing word W the edge SE_n is insufficiently likely to be constructed from vertex S_n OR IF there is no sufficiently likely judgement $p(s : R_x)$ for $R_x \in G$
> THEN parse word W from vertex S_{n-1}. IF successful add a new edge to the top path, without removing any committed edges beginning at S_{n-1}; ELSE set $n = n-1$ and repeat.

This algorithm is consistent with a local model for self-repair backtracking found in corpora (Shriberg and Stolcke, 1998; Hough and Purver, 2013). As regards inference in G, upon detection of a self-repair that revokes $s : R_6$, the type judgement $s : \neg R_6$, i.e. that this is not a yellow object,

[8] The search for the meet probability is generalisable to conjunctive types by searching for the conjuncts' highest common descendant. The join probability is generalisable to the disjunctive probability of multiple types, used, albeit programatically, in Algorithm 1 for calculating a node's probability from its child nodes.

[9] While we do not give details here, simple graphical search algorithms for conjunctive and disjunctive multiple types are linear in the number of conjuncts and disjuncts, saving considerable time in comparison to the algebraic calculations of the sum and product rules for distributive lattices.

[10] In practice, ASR modules yielding partial results are less reliable than their non-incremental counterparts, but progress is being made here (Schlangen and Skantze, 2009).

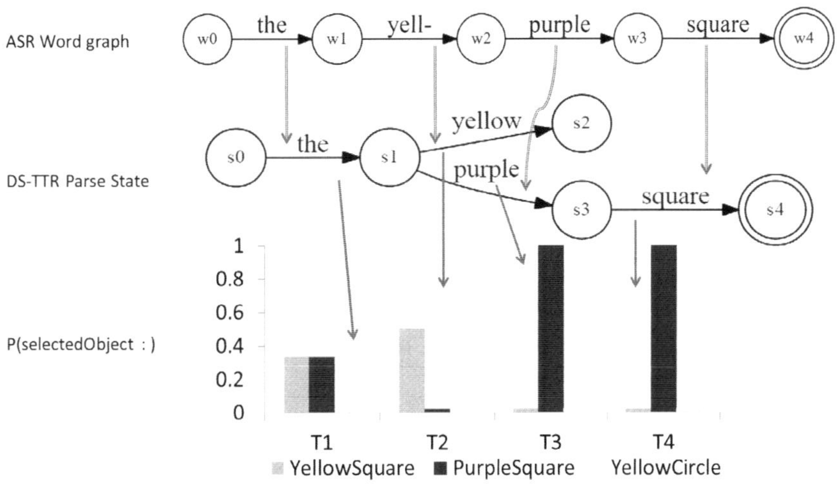

Figure 6: Incremental DS-TTR self-repair parsing. Inter-graph *groundedIn* links go top to bottom.

is immediately available as conditioning evidence. Using (6) our distribution of RT judgements now shifts: $p_J(s : R_1 \mid s : \neg R_6) = 1$, $p_J(s : R_2 \mid s : \neg R_6) = 0$ and $p_J(s : R_3 \mid s : \neg R_6) = 0$ before "purple" has been parsed – thus providing a probabilistic explanation for increased subsequent processing speed. Finally at **T4: 'square'** given $p_J(s : R_1 \mid s : R_1) = 1$ and $R_1 \wedge R_2 = R_1 \wedge R_3 = \bot$, the distribution remains unchanged.

The system's processing models how listeners reason about the revocation itself rather than predicting the outcome through positive evidence alone, in line with (Brennan and Schober, 2001)'s results.

6 Extensions

Dialogue and self-repair in the wild To move towards domain-generality, generating the lattice of all possible dialogue situations for interesting domains is computationally intractable. We intend instead to consider incrementally occurring *issues* that can be modelled as questions (Larsson, 2002). Given one or more issues manifest in the dialogue at any time, it is plausible to generate small lattices dynamically to estimate possible answers, and also assign a real-valued relevance measure to questions that can be asked to resolve the issues. We are exploring how this could be implemented using the inquiry calculus (Knuth, 2005), which defines information theoretic relevance in terms of a probabilistic question lattice, and furthermore how this could be used to model the cause of self-repair as a time critical trade-off between relevance and accuracy.

Learning in a dialogue While not our focus here, lattice G's probabilities can be updated through observations after its initial construction. If a reference game is played over several rounds, the choice of referring expression can change based on mutually salient functions from words to situations- see e.g. (DeVault and Stone, 2009). Our currently frequentist approach to learning is: given an observation of an existing RT R_i is made with probability v, then $||R_i||_J$, the overall denominator $P(J)$, and the nodes in the upward path from R_i to $\top$ are incremented by v. The approach could be converted to Bayesian update learning by using the prior probabilities in G for calculating v before it is added. Furthermore, observations can be added to G that include novel RTs: due to the DAG structure of G, their subtype ordering and probability effects can be integrated efficiently.

7 Conclusion

We have discussed efficient methods for constructing probabilistic TTR domain concept lattices ordered by the subtype relation and their use in incremental dialogue frameworks, demonstrating their efficacy for realistic self-repair processing. We wish to explore inclusion of join types, the scalability of RT lattices to other domains and their learning capacity in future work.

Acknowledgements

We thank the two TTNLS reviewers for their comments. Purver is supported in part by the European Community's Seventh Framework Programme under grant agreement no 611733 (ConCreTe).

References

G. Betarte and A. Tasistro. 1998. Extension of Martin-Löf type theory with record types and subtyping. In G. Sambin and J. Smith, editors, *25 Years of Constructive Type Theory*. Oxford University Press.

S. Brennan and M. Schober. 2001. How listeners compensate for disfluencies in spontaneous speech. *Journal of Memory and Language*, 44(2):274–296.

R. Cooper, S. Dobnik, S. Lappin, and S. Larsson. 2014. A probabilistic rich type theory for semantic interpretation. In *Proceedings of the EACL Workshop on Type Theory and Natural Language Semantics (TTNLS)*.

R. Cooper. 2005. Records and record types in semantic theory. *Journal of Logic and Computation*, 15(2):99–112.

R. Cooper. 2012. Type theory and semantics in flux. In R. Kempson, N. Asher, and T. Fernando, editors, *Handbook of the Philosophy of Science*, volume 14: Philosophy of Linguistics, pages 271–323. North Holland.

R. Dale and E. Reiter. 1995. Computational interpretations of the gricean maxims in the generation of referring expressions. *Cognitive Science*, 19(2):233–263.

D. DeVault and M. Stone. 2009. Learning to interpret utterances using dialogue history. In *Proceedings of the 12th Conference of the European Chapter of the Association for Computational Linguistics (EACL)*.

S. Dobnik, R. Cooper, and S. Larsson. 2012. Modelling language, action, and perception in type theory with records. In *Proceedings of the 7th International Workshop on Constraint Solving and Language Processing (CSLP12)*.

A. Eshghi, J. Hough, and M. Purver. 2013. Incremental grammar induction from child-directed dialogue utterances. In *Proceedings of the 4th Annual Workshop on Cognitive Modeling and Computational Linguistics (CMCL)*.

R. Fernández. 2006. *Non-Sentential Utterances in Dialogue: Classification, Resolution and Use*. Ph.D. thesis, King's College London, University of London.

M. C. Frank and N. D. Goodman. 2012. Predicting pragmatic reasoning in language games. *Science*, 336(6084):998–998.

J. Ginzburg. 2012. *The Interactive Stance: Meaning for Conversation*. Oxford University Press.

J. Hough and M. Purver. 2012. Processing self-repairs in an incremental type-theoretic dialogue system. In *Proceedings of the 16th SemDial Workshop on the Semantics and Pragmatics of Dialogue (SeineDial)*.

J. Hough and M. Purver. 2013. Modelling expectation in the self-repair processing of annotat-, um, listeners. In *Proceedings of the 17th SemDial Workshop on the Semantics and Pragmatics of Dialogue (DialDam)*.

R. Kempson, W. Meyer-Viol, and D. Gabbay. 2001. *Dynamic Syntax: The Flow of Language Understanding*. Blackwell.

K. H. Knuth. 2005. Lattice duality: The origin of probability and entropy. *Neurocomputing*, 67:245–274.

E. Krahmer and K. Van Deemter. 2012. Computational generation of referring expressions: A survey. *Computational Linguistics*, 38(1):173–218.

S. Larsson. 2002. *Issue-based Dialogue Management*. Ph.D. thesis, Göteborg University. Also published as Gothenburg Monographs in Linguistics 21.

S. Larsson. 2010. Accommodating innovative meaning in dialogue. *Proc. of Londial, SemDial Workshop*, pages 83–90.

S. Larsson. 2011. The TTR perceptron: Dynamic perceptual meanings and semantic coordination. In *Proceedings of the 15th Workshop on the Semantics and Pragmatics of Dialogue (SemDial 2011 - Los Angelogue)*.

W. Levelt. 1989. *Speaking: From Intention to Articulation*. MIT Press.

R. Montague. 1974. *Formal Philosophy: Selected Papers of Richard Montague*. Yale University Press.

M. Purver, A. Eshghi, and J. Hough. 2011. Incremental semantic construction in a dialogue system. In J. Bos and S. Pulman, editors, *Proceedings of the 9th International Conference on Computational Semantics*.

Y. Sato. 2011. Local ambiguity, search strategies and parsing in Dynamic Syntax. In E. Gregoromichelaki, R. Kempson, and C. Howes, editors, *The Dynamics of Lexical Interfaces*. CSLI Publications.

D. Schlangen and G. Skantze. 2009. A general, abstract model of incremental dialogue processing. In *Proceedings of the 12th Conference of the European Chapter of the ACL (EACL 2009)*.

E. Shriberg and A. Stolcke. 1998. How far do speakers back up in repairs? A quantitative model. In *Proceedings of the International Conference on Spoken Language Processing*.

G. Skantze and A. Hjalmarsson. 2010. Towards incremental speech generation in dialogue systems. In *Proceedings of the SIGDIAL 2010 Conference*.

J. Williams and S. Young. 2007. Scaling POMDPs for spoken dialog management. *IEEE Transactions on Audio, Speech, and Language Processing*, 15(7):2116–2129.

Propositions, Questions, and Adjectives: a rich type theoretic approach

Jonathan Ginzburg
CLILLAC-ARP
& Laboratoire d'Excellence (LabEx)–Empirical Foundations of Linguistics
Université Paris-Diderot, Sorbonne Paris-Cité
yonatan.ginzburg@univ-paris-diderot.fr

Robin Cooper
University of Gothenburg
cooper@ling.gu.se

Tim Fernando
Trinity College, Dublin
Tim.Fernando@cs.tcd.ie

Abstract

We consider how to develop types corresponding to propositions and questions. Starting with the conception of *Propositions as Types*, we consider two empirical challenges for this doctrine. The first relates to the putative need for a single type encompassing questions and propositions in order to deal with Boolean operations. The second relates to adjectival modification of question and propositional entities. We partly defuse the Boolean challenge by showing that the data actually argue against a single type covering questions and propositions. We show that by analyzing both propositions and questions as records within Type Theory with Records (TTR), we can define Boolean operations over these distinct semantic types. We account for the adjectival challenge by embedding the record types defined to deal with Boolean operations within a theory of semantic frames formulated within TTR.

1 Introduction

Propositions as types has long been viewed as a *sine qua non* of many a type theoretic approach to semantics (see e.g., the seminal work of (Ranta, 1994)). Although this has lead to a variety of very elegant formal accounts, one can question its appropriateness as a type for NL propositions—the denotata of declaratives and of nouns such as 'claim' and the objects of assertion. One immediate issue concerns semantic selection—how to specify the semantic types of predicates such as 'believe' and 'assert' so that they will not select for e.g., the type of biscuits or the type of natural numbers, given their inappropriateness as objects of belief or assertion. However, one resolves this issue, we point to two other significant challenges:

1. Recently there have been a number of proposals that questions and propositions are of a single ontological category (see (Nelken and Francez, 2002; Nelken and Shan, 2006)) and most influentially work in Inquisitive Semantics (IS) (Groenendijk and Roelofsen, 2009). A significant argument for this is examples like (1), where propositions and questions can apparently be combined by boolean connectives.

   (1) If Kim is not available, who should we ask to give the talk?

   In Inquisitive Semantics, such data are handled by postulating a common type for questions and propositions as sets of sets of worlds. It is not *a priori* clear how *propositions as types* can account for such cases.

2. Adjectives pose a challenge to all existing theories of questions and propositions, possible worlds based (e.g., (Karttunen, 1977; Groenendijk and Stokhof, 1997; Groenendijk and Roelofsen, 2009), or type theoretic, as in Type Theory with Records (TTR, (Cooper, 2012; Ginzburg, 2012)). There is nothing in the semantic entity associated with a polar question as in (2), be it a two cell partition (as in partition semantics) or a constant function from records into propositions (as in Ginzburg 2012) that will allow it to distinguish *difficult* from *easy* questions. Similarly, since the denotation of a question is not conceived as an event, this denotation is not appropriate for the adjective *quick*:

   (2) A: I have a quick question: is every number above 2 the sum of two primes?

   B: That's a difficult question.

And yet, these two distinct classes of adjectives can simultaneously apply to a question together with 'resolved', a target of all existing theories of questions, as in (3), calling for a unified notion of question:

(3) The quick question you just posed is difficult and for the moment unresolved.

'Difficult' and 'silly' apply to both propositional and question entities, suggesting the need for a unified meaning for the adjective and a means of specifying its selection so that it can modify both questions and propositions:

(4) a. *silly claim* (a claim silly to assert)
b. *silly question* (a question silly to ask);
c. *difficult claim* (a claim difficult to prove)

In this paper we partly defuse the Boolean challenge by showing that the data actually argue against a single type covering questions and propositions. We show that by analyzing both propositions and questions as records within TTR, we can define Boolean operations over these distinct semantic types. We then propose to deal with the adjectival challenge by embedding the types initially defined within a theory of semantic frames (Fillmore, 1985; Pustejovsky, 1995) formulated within TTR.

2 Questions and Propositions: a unified semantic type?

Although there has been a recent trend to assume a commonality of type for questions and propositions, both Hamblin and Karttunen gave arguments for distinguishing questions as an ontological category from propositions—(Hamblin, 1958) pointing out that interrogatives lack truth values; to which one can add their incompatibility with a wider scoping alethic modality:

(5) a. It's true/false who came yesterday
b. # Necessarily, who will leave tomorrow?

Whereas (Karttunen, 1977) pointed to the existence of predicates that select interrogatives, but not for declaratives and vice versa:

(6) a. Bo asked/investigated/wondered/# believed /# claimed who came yesterday.
b. Bo # asked/# investigated/# wondered/ believed /claimed that Mary came yesterday.

We argue that although speech acts involving questions and propositions can be combined by boolean connectives they are not closed under boolean operations. Furthermore, we argue that the propositions and questions *qua* semantic objects cannot be combined by boolean operations at all. This, together with the examples above, strongly suggests that questions and propositions are distinct types of semantic objects.

We use embedding under attitude verbs as a test for propositions and questions as semantic objects. Here we do not find mixed boolean combinations of questions and propositions. Thus, for example, *wonder* selects for an embedded question and *believe* for an embedded proposition but a mixed conjunction does not work with either, showing that it is neither a question nor a proposition:

(7) The manager *wonders/*believes that several people left and what rooms we need to clean.

The verb *know* is compatible with both interrogative and declarative complements, though(Vendler, 1972; Ginzburg and Sag, 2000) argue that such predicates do not take questions or propositions as genuine arguments (i.e. not purely referentially), but involve *coercions* which leads to a predication of a *fact*. The well formedness of these coercion processes require that sentences involving decl/int conjunctions such as (8) can only be understood where the verb is distributed over the two conjuncts: "knows that John's smart and knows what qualifications he has":

(8) The manager knows that John's smart and what qualifications he has.

Compare (9a,b)—in the second mixed case there is only a reading which entails that it is surprising the conference was held at the usual time whereas arguably in the first sentence only the conjunction but not the individual conjuncts need be surprising.

(9) a. It's surprising that the conference was held at the usual time and so few people registered.

b. It's surprising that the conference was held at the usual time and how few people registered.

Embedded conditional questions are impossible although, of course, embedded questions containing conditionals are fine:

(10) *The manager wonders if Hollande left, whether we need to clean the west wing.

a. The manager wonders whether, if Hollande left, we need to clean the west wing.

Why, then, do apparent mixed boolean combinations appear in root sentences? Our answer is that natural language connectives, in addition to their function as logical connectives combining propositions, can be used to combine speech acts into another single speech act. This, however, can only be expressed in root sentences and speech acts are not closed under operations corresponding to boolean connectives. For example in (11a), where a query follows an assertion is fine whereas the combination of an assertion with a preceding query is not, as in (11b):

(11) a. John's very smart but does he have any qualifications?

b. *Does John have any qualifications and/but he's smart

This is puzzling because a discourse corresponding to a string of the same separate speech acts works well:

(12) Does John have any qualifications? (no answer) But he's smart.

Similarly, while we can apparently conditionalize a query with a proposition, we cannot conditionalize an assertion with a question, nor can we conditionalize a query with a question:

(13) a. If Hollande left, do we need to clean the west wing? ("If Hollande left, I ask you whether we need to clean the west wing"),

b. *If whether Hollande left/did Hollande leave, we need to clean the west wing?

c. *If who left, do we need to clean the west wing?

However we treat these facts, it seems clear that it would be dangerous to collapse questions and propositions into the same type of semantic object and allow general application of semantic boolean operators. This would seem to force you into a situation where you have to predict acceptability of these sentences purely on the basis of a theory of syntax, although semantically/pragmatically they would have made perfect sense. It seems to us that distinguishing between questions and propositions and combinations of speech acts offers a more explanatory approach.

3 Austinian Types for Propositions and Questions

3.1 TTR as synthesizing Constructive Type Theory and Situation Semantics

The system we sketch is formulated in TTR (Cooper, 2012). TTR is a framework that draws its inspirations from two quite distinct sources. One source is Constructive Type Theory, whence the repertory of type constructors, and in particular records and record types, and the notion of witnessing conditions. The second source is situation semantics (Barwise and Perry, 1983; Barwise, 1989) which TTR follows in viewing *semantics as ontology construction*. This is what underlies the emphasis on specifying structures in a model theoretic way, introducing structured objects for explicating properties, propositions, questions etc. It also takes from situation semantics an emphasis on *partiality* as a key feature of information processing. This aspect is exemplified in a key assumption of TTR—the witnessing relation between records and record types: the basic relationship between the two is that a record r is of type RT if each value in r assigned to a given label l_i satisfies the typing constraints imposed by RT on l_i:

(14) record witnessing

The record: $\begin{bmatrix} l_1 & = & a_1 \\ l_2 & = & a_2 \\ \ldots & & \\ l_n & = & a_n \end{bmatrix}$ is of type:

$$\begin{bmatrix} l_1 & : & T_1 \\ l_2 & : & T_2(l_1) \\ \ldots & & \\ l_n & : & T_n(l_1, l_2, \ldots, l_{n-1}) \end{bmatrix}$$

iff $a_1 : T_1, a_2 : T_2(a_1), \ldots, a_n : T_n(a_1, a_2, \ldots, a_{n-1})$

This allows for cases where there are fields in the record with labels not mentioned in the record type. This is important when e.g., records are used to model contexts and record types model rules about context change—we do not want to have to predict in advance all information that could be in a context when writing such rules. (15) illustrates this: the record (15a) is of the type (15b), though the former has also a field for FACTS; (15b) constitutes the preconditions for a greeting, where FACTS—the contextual presuppositions—has no role to play.

(15) a. $\begin{bmatrix} \text{spkr} & = & \text{A} \\ \text{addr} & = & \text{B} \\ \text{utt-time} & = & \text{t1} \\ \text{c1} & = & \text{p1} \\ \text{Moves} & = & \langle\rangle \\ \text{qud} & = & \{\} \\ \text{facts} & = & \text{cg1} \end{bmatrix}$

b. $\begin{bmatrix} \text{spkr : IND} \\ \text{addr : IND} \\ \text{utt-time : TIME} \\ \text{c1 : addressing(spkr,addr,utt-time)} \\ \text{Moves} = \langle\rangle\text{: list(LocProp)} \\ \text{qud} = \{\}\text{: set(Question)} \end{bmatrix}$

3.2 Propositions

Our starting point is the situation semantics notion of an Austinian proposition (Barwise and Etchemendy, 1987). (Ginzburg, 2012) introduces Austinian propositions as records of the form:

(16) $\begin{bmatrix} \text{sit} & = & s \\ \text{sit-type} & = & T \end{bmatrix}$

This gives us a type theoretic object corresponding to a judgement. The type of Austinian propositions is the record type (17a),where the type *RecType*† is a basic type which denotes the type of (*non-dependent*) record types closed under meet, join and negation.[1] Truth conditions for Austinian propositions are defined in (17b):

(17) a. *AustProp* $=_{def}$ $\begin{bmatrix} \text{sit} & : & \textit{Rec} \\ \text{sit-type} & : & \textit{RecType}^\dagger \end{bmatrix}$

b. A proposition $p = \begin{bmatrix} \text{sit} & = & s_0 \\ \text{sit-type} & = & ST_0 \end{bmatrix}$ is true iff $s_0 : ST_0$

We introduce negative types by the clause in (18a). Motivated in part by data concerning negative perception complements ((Barwise and Perry, 1983; Cooper, 1998), we can characterize witnesses for negative types by (18b).

(18) a. If T is a type then $\neg T$ is a type

b. $a : \neg T$ iff there is some T' such that $a : T'$ and T' precludes T. We assume the existence of a binary, irreflexive and symmetric relation of *preclusion* which satisfies also the following specification:
T' *precludes* T iff either (i) $T = \neg T'$ or, (ii) T, T' are non-negative and there is no a such that $a : T$ and $a : T'$ for any models assigning witnesses to basic types and p(red)types

(19a) and (19b) follow from these two definitions:

(19) a. $a : \neg\neg T$ iff $a : T$

b. $a : T \vee \neg T$ is *not* necessary (a may not be of type T and there may not be any type which precludes T either).

Thus this negation is a hybrid of classical and intuitionistic negation in that (19a) normally holds for classical negation but not intuitionistic whereas (19b), that is failure of the law of the excluded middle, normally holds for intuitionistic negation but not classical negation.

The type of negative (positive) Austinian propositions can be defined as (20a,b), respctively:

(20) a. $\begin{bmatrix} \text{sit} & : & \textit{Rec} \\ \text{sit-type} & : & \textit{RecType}^{\neg\dagger} \end{bmatrix}$

b. $\begin{bmatrix} \text{sit} & : & \textit{Rec} \\ \text{sit-type} & : & \textit{RecType} \end{bmatrix}$

[1] When we say 'the type of record types', this should be understood in a relative, not absolute way. That is, this means the type of record types up to some level of stratification, otherwise foundational problems such as russellian paradoxes can potentially ensue. See (Cooper, 2012) for discussion and a more careful development.

If p:*Prop* and p.sit-type is $T_1 \wedge T_2$ ($T_1 \vee T_2$) we say that p is the conjunction (disjunction) of $\begin{bmatrix} \text{sit} & = & p.\text{sit} \\ \text{sit-type} & = & T_1 \end{bmatrix}$ and $\begin{bmatrix} \text{sit} & = & p.\text{sit} \\ \text{sit-type} & = & T_2 \end{bmatrix}$.

3.3 Questions

Extensive motivation for the view of questions as propositional abstracts has been provided in (Ginzburg, 1995; Ginzburg and Sag, 2000)—TTR contributes to this by providing an improved notion of simultaneous, restricted abstraction: A (basic, non-compound) question is a function from records into propositions. In particular, a polar question is a 0-ary propositional abstract, which in TTR makes it a constant function from the universe of all records into propositions. We propose a refinement of this view which we believe maintains the essential insights of the propositional function approach, motivated in part by the need to enable conjunction and disjunction to be defined for questions.

We introduce a notion of *Austinian questions* defined as records containing a record and a function into record types, the latter associated with the label 'abstr(act)'. The role of *wh*-words on this view is to specify the domains of these functions; in the case of polar questions there is no restriction, hence the function component of such a question is a constant function. (21) exemplifies this for a unary 'who' question and a polar question:

(21) a. *Who* = $\begin{bmatrix} \text{x}_1 : \textit{Ind} \\ \text{c1} : \text{person}(\text{x}_1) \end{bmatrix}$; *Whether* = *Rec*;

b. 'Who runs' $\mapsto$ $\begin{bmatrix} \text{sit} = r_1 \\ \text{abstr} = \lambda r{:}\textit{Who}(\begin{bmatrix} \text{c} : \text{run}(r.x_1) \end{bmatrix}) \end{bmatrix}$;

c. 'Whether Bo runs' $\mapsto$ $\begin{bmatrix} \text{sit} = r_1 \\ \text{abstr} = \lambda r{:}\textit{Whether}(\begin{bmatrix} \text{c} : \text{run(b)} \end{bmatrix}) \end{bmatrix}$

We characterize the type AustQuestion within TTR by means of the parametric type given in (22); the parametric component of the type characterizes the range of abstracts that build up questions:

(22) *AustQuestion*(T) $=_{def}$ $\begin{bmatrix} \text{sit} & : & \textit{Rec} \\ \text{abstr} & : & (T \rightarrow \textit{RecType}) \end{bmatrix}$

Given this, we define the following relation between a situation and a function, which is the basis for defining key coherence answerhood notions such as resolvedness and aboutness (weak partial answerhood (Ginzburg and Sag, 2000)) and question dependence (cf. erotetic implication,(Wiśniewski, 2001)):

(23) s *resolves* q, where q is $\lambda r : (T_1)T_2$, (in symbols $s?q$) iff **either**
(i) for some $a : T_1$ $s : q(a)$,
or
(ii) $a : T_1$ implies $s : \neg q(a)$

Austinian questions can be conjoined and disjoined though not negated. The definition for conj/disj-unction, from which it follows that q_1 and (or) q_2 is resolved iff q_1 is resolved and (or) q_2 is resolved, is as follows:

(24) $\begin{bmatrix} \text{sit} & = & s \\ \text{abstr} & = & \lambda r : T_1\ (T_2) \end{bmatrix} \wedge\ (\vee)$ $\begin{bmatrix} \text{sit} & = & s \\ \text{abstr} & = & \lambda r : T_3\ (T_4) \end{bmatrix} =$ $\begin{bmatrix} \text{sit = s} \\ \text{abstr} = \lambda r{:}\begin{bmatrix} \text{left:}T_1 \\ \text{right:}T_3 \end{bmatrix} \\ (q_1(r.\text{left}) \wedge (\vee) q_2(r.\text{right})) \end{bmatrix}$

Following (Cooper and Ginzburg, 2012)) we argue that "negative questions" involve questions relating to negative propositions rather than negations of positive questions. As Cooper and Ginzburg show, such negative questions are crucially distinct from the corresponding positive question. Since we have a clear way of distinguishing negative and positive propositions, we do not conflate positive and negative polar questions.

4 Connectives in dialogue

We assume a gameboard dialogue semantics (Ginzburg, 2012) which keeps track of questions under discussion (QUD). One of the central conversational rules in KoS is QSPEC, a conversational rule that licenses either speaker to follow up q, the maximal element in QUD with assertions and queries whose QUD update Depends on

q. These in turn become MaxQUD. Consequently, QSPEC seems to be able to handle the commonest case of successive questions, as in (25).

(25)

a. Ann: Anyway, talking of over the road, where is she? Is she home?
Betty: No. She's in the Cottage.

b. Arthur: How old is she? Forty?
Evelyn: Forty one!

Nonetheless, not all cases of successive questions do involve a second question which is a subquestion of the first, as exemplified in (26):

(26) On the substantive front, we now have preliminary answers to two key questions: What did the agency do wrong? And who ordered it to target conservative groups? Notwithstanding Miller's resignation, which the President himself announced on Tuesday evening, the answers appear to be: not nearly as much as recent headlines suggest; and, nobody in the Obama Administration. (The New Yorker, May 16, 2013)

In contrast to cases covered by QSPEC, these cases are strange if the second question is posed by the addressee of the first question—one gets the feeling that the original question was ignored:

(27) A: What did the agency do wrong? B: Who ordered it to target conservative groups?

(Ginzburg, 2012) postulates an additional conversational rule that allows a speaker to follow up an initial question with a non-influencing question, where the initial question remains QUD-maximal. We believes this basic treatment allows one to explain how the mixed cases involving conjunctions of assertions and queries can be captured. *and,but* and *or* can be used as *discourse particles* which express a relationship between a speech act and the one preceding it:

- *and* can indicate that the following question is Independent of MaxQUD.
- *but* indicates that the following question is not independent, but unexpected given MaxQUD:
  - *John's smart* (no response) *But what qualifications does he have?*
  - *John's smart* might be offered as an enthymematic argument (Breitholtz, 2011; Breitholtz and Cooper, 2011) to a conclusion, e.g. "we should hire John". *but* indicates that the answer to the question might present an enthymematic argument against this conclusion.
- *or* can indicate that $q1$ addresses the same ultimate issue as MaxQUD, so retain both as MaxQUD; sufficient to address one issue since it will resolve both simultaneously:

(28) a. Would you like coffee and biscuits or would you like some fruit or a piece of bread and jam or what do you fancy?

b. are you gonna stay on another day or what are you doing?

c. David Foster Wallace is overrated or which novel by him refutes this view?

5 Abstract Entities and Adjectives

How to deal with adjectival modification of propositional and question entities, exemplified in (3,4) above? The extended notion of question required can be explicated within Cooper 2012's theory of semantic frames, inspired by (Fillmore, 1985; Pustejovsky, 1995). Neither Ty2 (Groenendijk and Stokhof, 1997) nor inquisitive semantics in propositional or first order formulation support the development of such an ontology. Cooper formulates a frame as a *record type* (RT). In (29) we exemplify a possible frame for question. Here, the $illoc$ role represents a question's role in discourse, whereas the telic role describes the goal of the process associated with resolving a question — finding a resolving answer. The frame represents a 'default' view of a question, which various in effect non-subsective adjectives can modify (e.g., 'unspoken question' negates the existence of an associated utterance, while 'open question' negates the end point of the resolution event).[2]

[2]Here $Resolve$ maps an austinian proposition and an austinian question to a predicate type. In a more detailed account one would add an additional argument for an information state, given the arguments that this notion is agent–relative (Ginzburg, 1995) and much subsequent literature.

(29) Question $=_{def}$

$$\begin{bmatrix} \text{T : Type} \\ \text{external : AustQuestion(T),} \\ \text{illoc : } \begin{bmatrix} \text{u : Event} \\ \text{A : Ind} \\ \text{c2 : Ask(A,external,u)} \end{bmatrix} \\ \text{telic : } \begin{bmatrix} \text{p : AustProp} \\ \text{c1 : Resolve(p,external)} \end{bmatrix} \end{bmatrix}$$

A type-driven compositional analysis is formulated with adjectives as record type modifiers (functions from RTs to RTs) that pick out frame elements of the appropriate type (for a related view cf. Asher & Luo 2012). For example, *difficult question* has the record type in (30):

(30)
$$\begin{bmatrix} \text{T : Type} \\ \text{external : AustQuestion} \\ \text{telic : } \begin{bmatrix} \text{p : AustProp} \\ \text{c1 : difficult(Resolve(p,external))} \end{bmatrix} \end{bmatrix}$$

Records and record types come with a well-known notion of subtyping, often construed syntactically (see e.g., (Betarte and Tasistro, 1998)). However, given our ontological perspective on semantics, we take a semantic perspective on subtyping (see e.g. (Frisch et al., 2008) for a detailed exposition of such an approach.), wherein $T \sqsubset T'$ iff $\{s|s : T\} \subset \{s|s : T'\}$. Given this, a record of the type (29) above can be viewed as also having type:

(31)
$$\begin{bmatrix} \text{T : Type} \\ \textit{external} \text{ : AustQuestion(T)} \end{bmatrix}$$

This forms the basis of our account of how an adjective such as *difficult* applies simultaneously to *question* and to *path*. *Difficult* is specified as in (32)— a function from record types subsumed by the record type given in the domain whose output involves a modification of the restriction field of the telic role. This yields (32b) when combined with *question* and (32c) when combined with *path*:[3]

(32) a. f : (RT $\sqsubset$
$$\begin{bmatrix} \text{external : Type} \\ \text{P : Type} \\ \text{telic : } \begin{bmatrix} \text{c1 : P} \end{bmatrix} \end{bmatrix}\text{)RT[P} \rightsquigarrow \text{difficult(P)]}$$

b.
$$\begin{bmatrix} \text{T : Type} \\ \text{external : AustQuestion(T)} \\ \text{telic : } \begin{bmatrix} \text{p : AustProp} \\ \text{c1 : difficult(Resolve(p,external))} \end{bmatrix} \end{bmatrix}$$

c.
$$\begin{bmatrix} \text{external : PhysTrajectory} \\ \text{telic : } \begin{bmatrix} \text{a : Ind} \\ \text{c1 : difficult(Cross(a,external))} \end{bmatrix} \end{bmatrix}$$

[3]Here $difficult$ maps any type P into the predicate type $difficult(P)$. One probably needs to narrow this specification somewhat.

Turning to propositions, we postulate (33) as a type for proposition. This allows us, for instance, to specify the adjective *silly* as modifying along the *illoc* dimension, thereby capturing *silly claim* (a claim silly to assert) and *silly question* (a question silly to ask); given the specification of the telic dimension and our lexical entry for *difficult*, *difficult claim* is correctly predicted to mean 'a claim difficult to prove'.

(33) Proposition $=_{def}$

$$\begin{bmatrix} \text{external : AustProp,} \\ \text{illoc : } \begin{bmatrix} \text{u : Event} \\ \text{A : Ind} \\ \text{c2 : Assert(A,external,u)} \end{bmatrix} \\ \text{telic : } \begin{bmatrix} \text{f : Fact} \\ \text{c1 : Prove(f,external)} \end{bmatrix} \end{bmatrix}$$

Subject matter adjectives such as *political, personal, moral, philosophical* as in (34) lead us to another intrinsic advantage for rich type theories such as TTR over possible worlds based type theories, relating to the types *AustQuestion/Prop*.

(34) a. A: Are you involved with Demi Lovato?
B: That's a personal question.

b. A: One shouldn't eat meat. B: That's a moral claim.

Subject matter adjectives target the *external* role of a question/proposition. This can be explicated on the basis of the predicate types which constitute the sit-type (abstr type) field in propositions (questions). Given the coarse granularity of possible worlds, it to unclear how to do so in ontologies based on sets of possible worlds.

Acknowledgments

Earlier versions of portions of this work were presented at the workshop *Conference on Logic,*

Questions and Inquiry (LoQI) in Paris and at a course on TTR given in June 2013 in Gothenburg. We thanks audiences on those occasions, as well as two anonymous referees for very stimulating comments. This work is supported by the French Investissements d'Avenir–Labex EFL program (ANR-10-LABX-0083).

References

Jon Barwise and John Etchemendy. 1987. *The Liar*. Oxford University Press, New York.

Jon Barwise and John Perry. 1983. *Situations and Attitudes*. Bradford Books. MIT Press, Cambridge.

Jon Barwise. 1989. *The Situation in Logic*. CSLI Lecture Notes. CSLI Publications, Stanford.

Gustavo Betarte and Alvaro Tasistro. 1998. Martin-löf's type theory with record types and subtyping. In G. Sambin and J. Smith, editors, *25 Years of Constructive Type Theory*. Oxford University Press.

Ellen Breitholtz and Robin Cooper. 2011. Enthymemes as rhetorical resources. In Ron Artstein, Mark Core, David DeVault, Kallirroi Georgila, Elsi Kaiser, and Amanda Stent, editors, *SemDial 2011 (Los Angelogue): Proceedings of the 15th Workshop on the Semantics and Pragmatics of Dialogue*.

Ellen Breitholtz. 2011. Enthymemes under Discussion: Towards a micro-rhetorical approach to dialogue modelling. In *Proceedings of SPR-11 ILCLI International Workshop on Semantics, Pragmatics, and Rhetoric Donostia, 9-11 November 2011*.

R. Cooper and J. Ginzburg. 2012. Negative inquisitiveness and alternatives-based negation. In Maria Aloni, Vadim Kimmelman, Floris Roelofsen, GalitW. Sassoon, Katrin Schulz, and Matthijs Westera, editors, *Logic, Language and Meaning*, volume 7218 of *Lecture Notes in Computer Science*, pages 32–41. Springer Berlin Heidelberg.

Robin Cooper. 1998. Austinian propositions, davidsonian events and perception complements. In Jonathan Ginzburg, Zurab Khasidashvili, Jean Jacques Levy, Carl Vogel, and Enric Vallduvi, editors, *The Tbilisi Symposium on Logic, Language, and Computation: Selected Papers*, Foundations of Logic, Language, and Information, pages 19–34. CSLI Publications, Stanford.

Robin Cooper. 2012. Type theory and semantics in flux. In Ruth Kempson, Nicholas Asher, and Tim Fernando, editors, *Handbook of the Philosophy of Science*, volume 14: Philosophy of Linguistics. Elsevier, Amsterdam.

C.J. Fillmore. 1985. Frames and the semantics of understanding. *Quaderni di semantica*, 6(2):222–254.

Alain Frisch, Giuseppe Castagna, and Véronique Benzaken. 2008. Semantic subtyping: Dealing set-theoretically with function, union, intersection, and negation types. *Journal of the ACM (JACM)*, 55(4):19.

Jonathan Ginzburg and Ivan A. Sag. 2000. *Interrogative Investigations: the form, meaning and use of English Interrogatives*. Number 123 in CSLI Lecture Notes. CSLI Publications, Stanford: California.

Jonathan Ginzburg. 1995. Resolving questions, i. *Linguistics and Philosophy*, 18:459–527.

Jonathan Ginzburg. 2012. *The Interactive Stance: Meaning for Conversation*. Oxford University Press, Oxford.

J. Groenendijk and F. Roelofsen. 2009. Inquisitive semantics and pragmatics. In *Meaning, Content, and Argument: Proceedings of the ILCLI International Workshop on Semantics, Pragmatics, and Rhetoric. www. illc. uva. nl/inquisitive-semantics*.

Jeroen Groenendijk and Martin Stokhof. 1997. Questions. In Johan van Benthem and Alice ter Meulen, editors, *Handbook of Logic and Linguistics*. North Holland, Amsterdam.

C. L. Hamblin. 1958. Questions. *Australian Journal of Philosophy*, 36:159–168.

Lauri Karttunen. 1977. Syntax and semantics of questions. *Linguistics and Philosophy*, 1:3–44.

Rani Nelken and Nissim Francez. 2002. Bilattices and the semantics of natural language questions. *Linguistics and Philosophy*, 25:37–64.

Rani Nelken and Chung-Chieh Shan. 2006. A modal interpretation of the logic of interrogation. *Journal of Logic, Language, and Information*, 15:251–271.

James Pustejovsky. 1995. *The Generative Lexicon*. MIT Press, Cambridge.

Aarne Ranta. 1994. *Type Theoretical Grammar*. Oxford University Press, Oxford.

Zeno Vendler. 1972. *Res Cogitans*. Cornell University Press, Ithaca.

Andrzej Wiśniewski. 2001. Questions and inferences. *Logique et Analyse*, 173:5–43.

Author Index